Chicago Collection

Chicago Lincoln Statue, Lincoln Square

178

The Civil War Round Table:
Fifty Years of Scholarship and Fellowship

Round Table founder Ralph G. Newman in the Abraham Lincoln Book Shop at 18 East Chestnut Street, Chicago

The Civil War Round Table

Fifty Years of Scholarship and Fellowship

Barbara Hughett

The Civil War Round Table, Chicago, Illinois

Published by The Civil War Round Table, 357 West Chicago Avenue,
Chicago, Illinois 60610, (312) 944-3085

Library of Congress Catalog Card Number 90-84288

Hughett, Barbara
The Civil War Round Table: Fifty Years of Scholarship
and Fellowship (First Edition)
Includes index

For all members of The Civil War Round Table,
past, present, and future

Contents

The War We Remember

An Introductory Note by Ralph G. Newman

MORE THAN TWENTY YEARS AGO Bruce Catton pointed out that the Civil War did not divide our country; it came because we were already divided. In the 125 years since the great conflict, it has given us, North and South, a common memory. In some mystical way, it unites us.

No matter what name we call it, Civil War, War Between the States, the Brothers' War, or the War of Northern Aggression, it remains the greatest collective experience of the American people. When William Tecumseh Sherman said "War is Hell," this is the war he was speaking about. Yet, despite its more than 600,000 deaths, it occupies a special place in our hearts and in our memories. We study the events and the men and women of this period in our past with mingled emotions. Though we may have different reasons for our remembrances, we all agree that in its colorful personalities, its stirring events, its incredible drama, and in the remarkable literature it has inspired, nothing else has a grip on our emotions to match these four years of bloodshed and death, pageantry and color, hope and despair.

Carl Sandburg once wrote that it was a war about a verb. Before 1861, we would say, "The United States *are*." After 1865, it became "The United States *is*." Americans from all sections of our country share the pride in the heroism and magnificent leadership of the men who wore the blue and the gray. They are no longer northern and southern heroes, but our heroes. It has created a vast literature which numbers an average of more than a book or pamphlet published every day since April 12, 1861, when the Confederate guns fired on Fort Sumter.

The Civil War Round Table came into existence because a few men (and now also women) wanted to share their enthusiasm and interest in this special period in our history with others who were like-minded. They soon learned that there were many who shared their enthusiasm and love for this unique time in our national past. They learned that an individual who has an interest in the Civil War need never be lonesome. Almost every community, every city and town, has one or more individuals within its borders who have a lively curiosity about the years of this entirely American war. One need only to inquire at a newspaper, library, or book shop to be directed to a person or persons who would drop everything they were doing to join you in a journey to the 1860s.

The Civil War Round Table has provided the perfect vehicle for those who want to travel back to the days of Abraham Lincoln and Robert E. Lee. Those of us who were present at the beginning rejoice and take pride in the scholarship, fellowship, and good life enjoyed by all during the past fifty years. For us "veterans" it has been a wonderful adventure.

Foreword

B ORN IN A BOOK SHOP, The Civil War Round Table in Chicago has never escaped its origins. Men who bought, collected, and read books avidly seized an opportunity to come together to discuss the Civil War. No doubt that small group functioned better as a genuine round table than the larger audiences of later years. After a half-century, however, The Round Table maintains headquarters in the book shop and still retains its enthusiasm and intellectual vigor.

Nor, indeed, has The Round Table escaped the impact of the bookseller who organized and sustained the group. Ralph G. Newman, a fount of bright ideas, promoter *par excellence*, a man who could have amassed an enormous fortune in any business except books, assembled The Round Table, provided a clubhouse and office, recruited members and located speakers, and gave other founders little responsibility beyond attendance. Newman also set his stamp on The Round Table through his sense of humor. He encouraged members to take the war seriously, but not each other; camaraderie fostered the pursuit of knowledge. For years, there was little distinction between regular and sustaining customers of the Abraham Lincoln Book Shop and members of The Round Table. Physical as well as intellectual hunger drove early members from the shop to the Bismarck Hotel; had Newman served dinner, The Round Table concept might have been abandoned as a wasteful extravagance and a foolish excursion from the pleasures of a well-stocked book shop.

Superficially, membership was open to all men with an interest in the Civil War. In reality, potential members could learn about the existence of The Round Table in only one place and thus had to enter the shop with a serious intention of buying a book. Members of many prestigious and expensive clubs would have failed such an initiation test.

Although Newman was virtually omnipresent through the founding years, he rarely starred as speaker. The Round Table first provided a forum for members, then gradually expanded with invitations to outside experts and scholars.

Had The Round Table been established solely for the magnification of member egos, it might long since have perished. Gradually, members assumed the management Newman had once provided The Round Table, and the group acquired self-perpetuating maturity.

Over the years, The Round Table has functioned as a cultural institution, bringing to Chicago renowned Civil War scholars as speakers and encouraging scholarship among its members. Listing merely publications of the two surviving founders, Newman and Elmer Gertz, would fill pages, and yet constitute only a beginning. Scholars across the country have taken advantage of opportunities to speak to The Round Table to test ideas, expand research, interact with an audience, and answer critics. For one young member, E.B. (Pete) Long, the group offered encouragement, stimulation, and opportunity equal to or surpassing that available through years of graduate school.

Chicago origins have given the original Round Table another distinctive characteristic. While similar groups attract a preponderance of lost cause sympathizers and lovers of war, the Chicago heritage incorporates a healthy respect for the most distinguished citizen of Illinois. Absorbing the function of a local Lincoln group, The Round Table expanded its mandate and membership to include more than military affairs and to consider the Civil War's complex meanings with greater sophistication.

When The Round Table began, professorial experts viewed the Civil War itself with disgust. At the University of Illinois, J.G. Randall proclaimed the war "needless," and at The University of Chicago, Avery Craven added "repressible."

> [T]he net results of a war which blackened the years from 1861 to 1865 must be couched in terms of the triumph of industry over agriculture; of centralization over local democracy; of one section over another; of the Republican party, representing bourgeois acquisitiveness, over its Democratic rival, representing an older agrarian ideal. . . . Industrial capitalism, with the banners of righteousness, patriotism, and progress over its head and with all critics hushed in disgrace and defeat, went on to its fullness and perhaps its ruin. Men today are looking back regretfully toward a Constitution which might have protected rights, an agrarian way of life which might have fostered a rich American culture and a sane economic order, a decentralized government wherein individuals and localities might have realized a more satisfactory democracy. We are back where we started. We have begun to realize what it costs a people to permit emotion to rule and to allow pious men to lead them into "irrepressible conflicts."

In this spirit, biographers exalted Stephen A. Douglas and Andrew Johnson at the expense of Lincoln and Ulysses S. Grant. Once called "revisionist," the views of Randall and Craven have since been completely revised by a new generation of scholars. Round Table members have held front-row seats for an exhilarating battle of ideas that can never reach its Appomattox. Interest is sustained through an understanding that the Civil War, a central event in American history, remains a kaleidoscope of changing interpretations with continuing implications for the present and future.

From the start, The Round Table opened its rolls to all men who wanted to join and since 1977 has admitted women—a step a few others have yet to take. With such an open process of self-selection, members have represented a wide variety of occupations and professions, a diversity of abilities and beliefs, yet have come together in surprising harmony to pursue a common goal of increasing knowledge of the Civil War for themselves and others. Membership has attained a level of relative stability as younger people take the places of those lost to time. As an intellectual success, the story of The Round Table deserves preservation. Drawing on the records and memories of longtime members, Barbara Hughett has created both an affectionate chronicle and an institutional history.

Round Table success stems partly from an admirable modesty of financial goals. Dues and meals remain affordable; similar groups have been enmeshed in frantic efforts to buy battlefields, build monuments, or endow libraries, but The Round Table usually leaves benefactions to its members individually. With relatively little need for fundraising, The Round Table is not for sale. Interest in the Civil War drives its members and elects its officers. The tangible measure of its achievements lies in the scores of flourishing Round Tables elsewhere, all modeled in varying degrees on that of Chicago, to say nothing of the shelves of books written by, written for, and made marketable by Round Table members. Few anticipated more public interest in the Civil War at the 125th anniversary commemorations than at the centennial, yet this surprising reality owes much to those who maintained constant encouragement to scholars and public alike.

Achieving a half-century of continuous endeavor represents a proud milestone for any voluntary organization. Surely nobody present at the first meeting could have predicted this. At the half-century mark, however, predicting its centennial seems entirely reasonable.

John Y. Simon
The Ulysses S. Grant Association
Southern Illinois University
Carbondale, Illinois

Preface

THIS IS A HISTORY of The Civil War Round Table at the time of its fiftieth anniversary. It was more than fifty years ago that a young bookseller in Chicago conceived an idea to begin a Civil War discussion group. Others over the years may have had a similar idea. However, this young man was a person of action, and he acted to make his concept a reality. Ralph Geoffrey Newman from childhood had been intrigued with the life of Abraham Lincoln and the period of the American Civil War. The people of this age were not merely characters on the pages of books to him. They were alive and they spoke to him of their experiences. He believed we could learn and be enriched by what they had to say to us and by the legacy they left us. Pervading all of this was his feeling that the study of history is fun.

When he shared his idea with some of his customers, most of them many years his senior, they were enthusiastic and wanted to be part of it. These sixteen men who first met for four years at lunch and then founded The Civil War Round Table had no intention of beginning a worldwide movement which would be thriving a half-century later. They were just doing something they loved to do: studying an era they cared about, an era they believed held lessons which could benefit those in the present. And they were having fun doing it. Newman's idea was such a good one that it caught on, endured, and has been copied many times over. Ralph Newman, by the sheer force of his winning personality and his passionate caring for what he pursued, thus became the "Pied Piper" of popular interest in Civil War study.

Since it was the first, the group in Chicago is known as *The* Civil War Round Table. Its birth and success have inspired the formation of over 150 Civil War Round Tables now meeting regularly in this country and around the globe. American Civil War Round Tables can be found in such diverse locations as England, Belgium, Germany, Norway, and Australia.

The Round Table in Chicago, which has grown to

include some 350 members, has continued and added to the rich traditions begun in 1940. It meets the second Friday of each month, from September through June, for dinner and an address by a leading scholar of the Civil War period. Additionally, it sponsors an annual battlefield tour, occasional assemblies and other special events, and contributes funds for the preservation of our Civil War battlefields. Membership ranges from people of modest means to millionaires. The only requirement for membership in The Civil War Round Table is a genuine interest in the Civil War and its era.

The heart of the story of The Civil War Round Table centers on its people and the spirit and fellowship which has developed and grown throughout the past half-century. It is my privilege to attempt to convey this story. I began work on this project in the spring of 1989 at the request of the chairman of The Round Table's History Committee, David Richert. It has been a most enjoyable and rewarding journey.

I have spent countless hours with archival materials—newspaper and magazine articles, books, newsletters, personal correspondence, and various records—most of which had been gathered and organized by the co-chairman of The Round Table's Archives Committee, Jerry Warshaw. I taped twenty-one interviews with Round Table members and had numerous additional conversations with members and friends of The Round Table.

Because I am a Round Table member and editor of the newsletter, the history I have written is one from an "insider's" point-of-view. Though The Civil War Round Table holds a very special place in my heart, I have tried to be objective. I have written the history chronologically, from The Round Table's germination in the 1930s and birth in 1940 to the eve of its fiftieth anniversary. I tell about the nature and purpose of the organization, the events it has sponsored, its influence on Civil War scholarship, and the people who shaped it and continue to shape it. This is a personal and anecdotal history, which has relied heavily on the reminiscences of Round Table members. In addition to providing a factual history, my intention has been to convey some of the spirit and joy of The Civil War Round Table.

So many people have helped me in accomplishing this work, there is not room to thank everyone in these pages. However, I must name a few. First of all, I want to thank David Richert for giving me this opportunity and for providing invaluable advice and assistance over the past sixteen months. Without Jerry Warshaw's gathering of archival materials, this history could not have been written. Ralph Newman has generously given of his time and his knowledge, and has made his records readily available to me. His calling me one afternoon in July to tell me that he'd been reading my drafts and felt that I'd "caught the spirit of The Round Table" provided one of the most gratifying experiences in my memory. John Y. Simon's support, encouragement, and recommendations have been of enormous significance. His belief in me and my ability sustained me through some of the more difficult phases in accomplishing this work. I want to thank each person I interviewed, whether in a taped session or in a personal or telephone conversation. Everyone was extremely helpful.

I must thank my reviewers, who read each and every word of this book in its various forms and stages and offered very useful suggestions. Their contributions cannot be overestimated. To assure a balanced assessment from different viewpoints, six are Round Table members and four are not associated with The Civil War Round Table. My reviewers from the membership of The Round Table were: Mary Munsell Abroe, C. Robert Douglas, Ralph G. Newman, David R. Richert, Roy L. Sanford, and John Y. Simon. Those from outside Round Table membership were: Marianne Bankert, Rachael Cunningham, Everett A. Johnson, and Jay Wilcoxen.

There are a few more thank-yous. Betsey and Brooks Davis searched their files and found information and photographs that were needed. Bob Douglas, Marshall Krolick, Ralph Newman, and Bill Sullivan cheerfully accepted numerous fact-finding and fact-checking telephone calls and never failed to provide answers to my questions. Ted Birndorf prepared the appendices, including the listing of every speaker and topic for 492 meetings of The Civil War Round Table. Mary Abroe and Joyce Warshaw carefully proofread the final manuscript. David Richert and Jerry Warshaw collected the photographs to use in the book and Dave, with his expert editor's talent, arranged their placement. Donna Cook (Richert) very generously gave of her time and talent to design the book jacket. Stanley Kowalski ably assisted with the typesetting.

I want to express my gratitude for someone without whom this book might not have become a reality—Muriel Underwood, the designer and typographer. The span of time we had to complete the book, in order to have it ready in time for The Round Table's fiftieth anniversary celebration, was extremely limited. She spent many hours, often at night and over weekends, to assure that the work was done well and on time. Her knowledge and expertise are deeply appreciated.

Finally, I thank all of my friends, who did not abandon me in the midst of my sometimes frenzied pace to finish the book in time to meet the deadline; they gave me, with their love, understanding, and support, the strength and inspiration I needed to complete the work on this volume. The study of the years 1861 through 1865 is even more meaningful and important to me now than it was when I began this adventure. It has been a very life-affirming experience.

Barbara Hughett
August 1990

Chapter 1 ☆ *In the Beginning*

"OUT TO LUNCH. Shove money under door." So read the sign which began appearing once a week at noon on the door of Ralph G. Newman's book shop at 155 West Madison Street in downtown Chicago. The year was 1936. America would be involved in a world war in a few years, but discussion of another era's war was the impetus for the sign on the door. Newman and several of his regular customers were down at the Tiffin Tea Room above the Stop and Shop specialty grocery on Washington Street, enjoying lunch and some lively discussion about the American Civil War. (No one ever shoved money under the door as the sign suggested.)

After being in the book business for a short time, Newman had decided to specialize in books on Abraham Lincoln and the Civil War era. This specialization reflected his own interests and those of a number of his customers, including Carl Sandburg and Lloyd Lewis. (His shop would become the Abraham Lincoln Book Shop. But, from 1933 when the twenty-two-year old bought an existing store—with borrowed money and a great deal of faith—until 1940, Newman's business was known as The Home of Books.)

The bulk of his customers were, of course, Civil War buffs. Sometimes, when a shipment of books came in, he would invite a few of them to join him for dinner. After dinner they would return to the shop to help him unpack. "It was diabolical," Newman recalls. "They would enjoy unpacking the books and, as they were doing so, they would be selling them to one another."[1] Before the evening was over, half the stock would be stacked up and reserved and the rest would be placed on the shelves by the eager workforce.

The Tiffin Room lunches were growing. Members began having dinners at one another's homes. They are remembered as lovely evenings filled with stimulating Civil War discussions. In late 1940, it was decided to meet once a month in a public place. A dinner would be followed by a presentation on a Civil War topic.

The *Chicago Tribune* sent a reporter and a photographer to the Bismarck Hotel on the evening of December 3, 1940. They had gotten word that sixteen veterans of the Civil War would be meeting there. What they found instead was a group of sixteen men interested in the study of the American Civil War who were gathering for the very first meeting of The Civil War Round Table. The *Tribune's* representatives went away disappointed, but not the founders of The Round Table! They enjoyed dinner and then heard one of their own, Percival G. Hart, speak on "Stonewall Jackson's Valley Campaign, *with Maps.*"[2]

That evening happened to be Hart's birthday. Another founder, Newton C. Farr, set the stage for the tradition of a friendly irreverence for speakers at subsequent Round Table gatherings. He tied a blue and gray ribbon around a beautifully polished apple. However, before presenting it to Hart, he took a big bite out of it. Speakers in subsequent years, however, have been, and continue to be, presented with more dignified mementos in honor of their appearances before The Round Table.[3]

Alexander J. Isaacs, another of the founders, coined the name "The Civil War Round Table" for the group. A resident of Hyde Park near the University of Chicago, he was familiar with the popular radio program of the time, "The University of Chicago Round Table." Founding member Vernon Hanson obtained the services of Chicago calligrapher Raymond J. DaBoll to design a logo for the new organization—the now familiar drum with a crossed saber and rifle, with the lettering "The Civil War Round Table."

The group's structure was very loose in those beginning days, with a member presiding at each meeting and another presenting a paper. One member, usually Vernon Hanson, collected the dinner fees. No constitution was drafted. No by-laws were adopted.

A formal slate of officers would not be elected for five years. However, Ralph Newman served as ex-officio secretary of the group. He arranged for speakers and meeting places and prepared monthly meeting notices on double postal cards for reservation returns. In other words, he did most of the work of The Round Table during those first years.

Who were these sixteen men who founded the first Civil War Round Table? Some were pillars of the community, such as stockbroker David H. Annan and real estate executive Newton C. Farr; others were up-and-coming young men just starting out on life's adventure, like Newman and lawyer Elmer Gertz. The next chapter will provide a brief biography of each of them.

Chapter 2 ☆ *The Founders*

W E BEGIN THE BIOGRAPHICAL SKETCHES with those of the two living founders of The Civil War Round Table and continue with the other fourteen founders.

Without **Ralph Geoffrey Newman,** The Civil War Round Table might never have come into being and certainly would not have flourished as it has. He is the true "father" of The Round Table. Throughout the past fifty years, he has contributed more to The Round Table than any other individual. His contributions continue as The Round Table enters its second half-century. It was Ralph Newman's vision—and his incredible energy and spirit to back up the vision with action—that gave The Round Table its life and ensured its longevity.

Ralph Geoffrey Newman

So much can be said about Ralph Newman! He has done so much for the field of Lincoln and Civil War scholarship. A full-length biography could be written about him. What we will do here is just "scratch the surface," and attempt to convey the essence of the man. Allan Nevins called him "a great national resource."[1] Historian Frank E. Vandiver, former president of three universities (Rice, Northern Texas, and Texas A & M) has said that, "If ever there was an entrepreneur of the Civil War, it has to be Ralph Newman. . . . I'm not sure the Civil War would be the popular subject it is today were it not for Ralph. He gave it, through The Round Table and his wide network of friends, a kind of currency I'm not sure anyone else could have given it. . . . It's difficult to find anyone who is literally larger than life, but I think Ralph may be one of those rarities . . . and he is also a warm human being, with a thoroughly winning personality. "[2]

Born on November 3, 1911 in Chicago, Newman was a champion sprinter and baseball player at Crane Tech High School. He attended Northwestern University for a year, but dropped out when he was offered the opportunity to play minor league baseball for the Arizona State League and later the Western Association. In 1931 and 1932, he played for teams in Tucson and Wichita. His budding career came to a halt when he was injured while trying to steal second base.

Newman's fascination with the Lincoln story began at an early age. As a young boy, during a visit to his grandfather's home, he found a Lincoln biography (Wayne Whipple's 1909 *The Story-Life of Lincoln*) on a bookshelf with his mother's name inscribed on the front. Intrigued, he picked up the book and subsequently read it. He was hooked. The world of Lincoln and Civil War scholarship was to benefit tremendously from the repercussions of that simple act.

After returning to Chicago in 1933, Newman borrowed the money to buy an existing used book store. Located near the offices of the *Chicago Daily News*, the store was a natural attraction for writers and editors from the newspaper. Asked why he decided to deal in Lincoln and Civil War books, he replied: "I had begun to think that the life of an antiquarian bookseller was strange. People stay up all night thinking of books to ask for that you haven't got. And then when you get them, an occult rule takes over and says that no one will ask for them again. This being a world of specialization where a lawyer will only handle divorces and a doctor will only remove your left tonsil, I thought, 'why don't I specialize?' Since my interests were Lincoln and Civil War and American History, specializing in this area appealed to me very much. I asked the opinions of Carl Sandburg, Lloyd Lewis, and those other fellows from the *Daily News*. They all thought it was a sensational idea. They didn't know what the probability for my success would be; but it would be convenient for them, because those were the books they wanted. So, over the next year, I borrowed, bartered, traded, swapped, sold our old stock, and converted the establishment into what became the Abraham Lincoln Book Shop."[3]

Ralph Newman's Abraham Lincoln Book Shop was more than just a book shop—it was a gathering place of warm hospitality where companions met to share their interest in the events of mid-nineteenth century America. The sixteen founders met at Ralph Newman's book shop. It was, in earlier days, at its various locations, a gathering place—a sort of club house for Round Tablers. It continues to be the official address of The Civil War Round Table, though Newman sold the business to Daniel R. Weinberg in January 1984.

Newman has done a great deal to help others in the Civil War field. Fellow founder Elmer Gertz, reminiscing about those early days, said that "Ralph was notable for his never-ending kindnesses to people."[4] He has served as a mentor to many. Barbara Long Pleiter, widow of historian, researcher, and author E.B. (Pete) Long, spoke of her years of association with Ralph: "He was such a help to so many people. He was—and still is—an idea person; he would get these ideas and then find someone to carry them out, which would give that person an experience, and perhaps a liveli-hood. . . . He did that with us. . . . I owe Ralph a great deal because he was the one who took Pete under his wing and saw to it that he had work in the Civil War field."[5] John Y. Simon, professor of history at Southern Illinois University and editor of the Ulysses S. Grant papers, spent the summers of his undergraduate years employed as a stock clerk at the Abra-ham Lincoln Book Shop and claims to have learned more working for Ralph Newman at his book shop than he did in graduate school.[6] Considering that he did all his graduate work at Harvard University, that's quite a compliment to Mr. Newman. People who have worked with and for Newman speak positively of that experience. Margaret April, Newman's administrative assistant for thirty-eight years, observed: "Through all the years, we've never had one problem. That's a lot to say, but it's true."[7]

Mark E. Neely, Jr., director of the Louis A. Warren Lin-coln Library and Museum, described Ralph Newman: "A man of irrepressible energy with a fertile and inventive mind, Mr. Newman has headed, shaped, aided, rescued, or advised dozens of important historical institutions and organizations." Dr. Neely added that Newman "has been at the hub of the great wheel of Lincoln interest for five decades."[8]

We will list but a few of the man's accomplishments and honors. Ralph Newman's civic and public contributions in-clude fourteen years as president of the board of directors of the Chicago Public Library; he led the work to restore the Cultural Center of the Main Library. He has been honored as a laureate of the Lincoln Academy of Illinois and serves as a member of its board of regents. He has served as president of the Illinois State Historical Society, the Adult Education Council of Greater Chicago, the Urban Libraries Council, the Stephen A. Douglas Association, and the Illinois Association for the Advancement of History. He served in the United States Navy from 1944-1945. He was chairman of the Chicago Civil War Centennial Commission, the Illinois Commission of the New York World's Fair, the Illinois Sesquicentennial Commission, and the Board of Trustees of Ford's Theater Society. Currently, he serves on the library division of the U.S. Information Agency, is chairman of the board of directors of the Stephen A. Douglas Association, and serves as a trustee of Lincoln College and Lincoln Memorial University. He is a member of the board of directors of the Abraham Lincoln Association, president of The Ulysses S. Grant Association, and vice president of the United States Capitol Historical Society.

His literary works include *The American Iliad* (1947),

Lincoln For The Ages (1960), *The Civil War Digest* (1960), and *Abraham Lincoln's Last Full Measure of Devotion* (1981). In a number of writings, he collaborated with fellow Round Table members Otto Eisenschiml and E.B. (Pete) Long.

Today he leads an extremely active life as a rare manuscripts dealer and appraiser and bookseller. His business dealings take him all over the world. He maintains two suites of offices in the John Hancock Center in Chicago, in addition to owning the book store and gift and food concessions at Lincoln's New Salem State Park.

He is the friend of many of the great and near-great individuals in the world. He is perhaps the country's foremost appraiser of presidential and other historical papers. Recently, he purchased for a client a copy of the first printing of the Declaration of Independence for a record $1.6 million.

Newman was a close friend of the last surviving Lincoln descendant, Robert Todd Lincoln Beckwith. He was present in 1976 when James Hickey made the very exciting discovery of the "MTL Insanity File" and Robert Lincoln's letter books in a double-locked closet in a bedroom at Hildene, Robert Todd Lincoln's home in Manchester, Vermont.

Newman served as secretary of The Round Table from 1940-1945, making all the arrangements for speakers and meeting places. He was the tenth president of The Round Table (1954-1955). Newman has been the meeting speaker on eight occasions and served as a member of a panel or assembly seven times. The Round Table honored him with their Nevins-Freeman Award in 1975. It was through Newman's leadership that The Round Table awarded graduate fellowships in Civil War history, established a Civil War Research Center, and created the Nevins-Freeman Award. It was Ralph Newman who spearheaded the effort to allow women to become members of The Round Table. Year after year, he would bring the issue up at Executive Committee meetings. Year after the year, the matter was voted down. In 1977, The Round Table had finally caught up with Ralph Newman's foresight and women were admitted as members.

A brilliant and eloquent lecturer, he has spoken at cultural and educational institutions and meetings throughout the country. He wrote a weekly column for the *Chicago Tribune*, ("Do You Remember?") which was a popular feature for over ten years, and during the Civil War Centennial, wrote a syndicated column, "The Civil War Scrap Book."

The Civil War Round Table and the American historical community owe a great debt to Ralph Geoffrey Newman. At a ceremony in Washington, D.C. several years ago where tribute was paid to Newman, the late David C. Mearns of The Library of Congress referred to him as an "Acknowledged authority ... preceptor of the past for the enlightenment of the future."[9]

Elmer Gertz is a Chicago lawyer, educator, writer, and civic leader. Born on September 14, 1906 on the southeast side of Chicago, he is The Round Table's other living founder.

As a boy, Gertz loved to write stories and poetry. He remembers being chastised by an elementary school teacher when she caught him writing instead of paying attention to her presentation in class. Following his mother's death when he was ten years of age, Gertz's father placed his six children in orphanages for a few years until he could make arrangements for their care at home. (Gertz is quick to point out that his father paid for the boarding of his children and maintained close and warm contact with them throughout this period.)[10]

While in the orphanage, one of the caretakers who admired young Elmer's poetry took him to meet his friend Carl Sandburg, who was at that time the movie critic for the *Chicago Daily News*. This began a lifelong friendship between Gertz and Sandburg. Elmer Gertz's interest in Lincoln and the Civil War began at an early age. When he was fourteen, he was one of the winners in a Lincoln essay contest sponsored by the Hearst newspapers. He was rewarded with a silver Lincoln medal and the thrill of seeing his essay printed in the newspaper.[11]

Elmer Gertz

He received a bachelor's degree in economics and a law degree from the University of Chicago. As a lawyer, he has participated in some celebrated cases, such as the freeing of Nathan Leopold, the setting aside of the death sentence of Jack Ruby, and many censorship cases, including those involving Henry Miller's *Tropic of Cancer*. *Gertz v. Robert Welch, Inc.* was a landmark libel case, the results of which caused the Supreme Court to modify the law in that basic area. He has not been reluctant to tackle difficult cases and causes. Carl Sandburg said of him, "Elmer Gertz fears no dragons."[12]

Currently an adjunct professor of law at John Marshall Law School, he has also taught at the University of Chicago, Northwestern University, the Jewish Peoples Institute, Roosevelt University, and the University of Wisconsin. He was a delegate to the 1969 Illinois Constitutional Convention.

Throughout his career, Gertz has been absorbed in all aspects of human relations, particularly in the field of housing. He was a founder and president of the Public Housing Association, legislative chairman of Mayor Kelly's Emergency Housing Committee, chairman of the veterans' housing committee, and counsel for various building projects and cooperative housing groups. He has received mail addressed to "Mr. Housing."

Gertz has received numerous honors for his work, including two awards from the Chicago Council Against Racial and Religious Discrimination and several awards from the Illinois division of the American Civil Liberties Union. He has served as president of the Adult Education Council of Chicago, the Decalogue Society of Lawyers, and the America Jewish Congress. A founder of the George Bernard Shaw Society, he has written and spoken on Shaw and related subjects.

Gertz has made a special study of Lincoln as a lawyer and has contributed material about Clarence Darrow to *Encyclopaedia Britannica*. He was a friend of former President Harry S. Truman (who helped to found the Kansas City Civil War Round Table) and is a fellow of the Truman Library. He currently serves as president of the Blind Service Association.

Gertz is the author of several books, including *A Handful of Clients* (1965) about some of his more memorable law cases, and his memoirs, *To Life* (1974). He and his wife went on extended world journeys in 1984, 1985, and 1986. Each time, he wrote a series of articles on his travels for the *Chicago Sun-Times*.

Elmer Gertz was the eighth president of The Round Table (1952-53). Highlights of his tenure were the first battlefield tour to Gettysburg in June 1952, William H. Townsend's moving oration on "Cassius Marcellus Clay" in October 1952, and the third battlefield tour to Richmond, during which Round Table members were the guests at the home of Douglas Southall Freeman. He has spoken to The Round Table four times and has been a participant in a Round Table panel discussion or symposium on six occasions. He was the speaker at the second meeting of The Civil War Round Table on January 17, 1941. His topic was "Wilbur F. Storey and the *Chicago Times* in the Civil War."

David H. Annan, a native Chicagoan, graduated from the University of Chicago in 1919. Following service in the United States Navy, he served as American Vice Consul in Kobe, Japan from 1920-1921. A highly successful stockbroker, he accumulated over $1 million before the market crashed in 1929. He sold his holdings before the crash, emerging in a very healthy financial state. Annan then returned to Japan to join the staff of the American Embassy in Tokyo and lived there throughout the Depression years. During World War II, he was an assistant to the Secretary of the Navy.

Married and divorced four times, he parted amicably with each wife, none of whom requested alimony as each was financially secure. He was a member of the board of trustees of Lincoln College and Lincoln Memorial University. He made numerous donations throughout his life, including an indoor track to the University of Chicago; a gym and swimming pool to Lincoln Memorial University; and a swimming pool to Lincoln College. David Annan was once described by Ralph Newman as "the most generous Scotsman I have ever known."[13]

Annan built a sizeable Civil War collection which he donated to the Chicago Historical Society before moving to West Palm Beach, Florida, where he spent his last years. He died, at the age of ninety-five, in 1982.

Monroe F. Cockrell, a graduate of Virginia Military Academy, was a vice president of Continental Illinois Bank. He was the host of one of the dinners which preceded the formal organization of The Civil War Round Table.

Cockrell was a stern man who paid attention to minute details. He was liked by some, disliked by many others because he was a nitpicker who often made a big fuss about some very minor inaccuracy. He was the author of a few pamphlets dealing with special phases of the Civil War. Cockrell became the first president of The Civil War Round Table in 1945. (As stated earlier, until the 1945-1946 term, The Round Table did not elect a formal slate of officers.) He spoke before The Round Table on two occasions. His topic on October 30, 1941 was "General Nathan Bedford Forrest." On September 30, 1949, he spoke on "The Siege of Vicksburg by Land and Water."

Otto Eisenschiml is considered by most who remember him as perhaps the most colorful and certainly the most controversial of The Round Table founders. Born and educated in Austria, where he graduated from Vienna's Polytechnical Institute, he was a chemist by profession. As a boy, his interest in American history had been aroused by stories his father told him about the American Civil War. His father, who had become an American citizen, served as an officer in an Illinois regiment and fought in the Battle of Shiloh before returning to Austria to marry.

After coming to America in 1901, Eisenschiml first worked in a boiler factory in Pittsburgh and then in a linseed oil plant in Chicago. His ambition and brilliance soon led him to become a consultant for businessmen with chemical problems. One of the problems he solved by inventing a process by which a new and greatly improved window envelope could

Otto Eisenschiml

be produced. He formed his own company, Scientific Oil Compounding Company, a distributor of materials for paints, varnishes, and fungicides.

His success in applying his chemical knowledge to business enabled him to spend more time on his avocation: Civil War history. He wrote a number of books on the subject, including *The Story of Shiloh* (1946), *The Celebrated Case of Fitz-John Porter* (1950), and, with Ralph G. Newman, *The American Iliad* (1947).

But his most controversial writing was done on the assassination of Abraham Lincoln. His 1937 *Why Was Lincoln Murdered?* asked questions about the murder of Lincoln and set forth theories that there was possible involvement in the assassination plot by some well-known Radical Republicans.

In this same vein, he wrote *In the Shadow of Lincoln's Death* (1940) and *The Case of A.L., Aged 56* (1943). Though on the Lincoln assassination he was quick to point out that the title of his initial book posed a question rather than making a statement of fact, the historical community found his theories dubious. He answered his critics in a paper he delivered in February 1940 at the William L. Clements Library at the University of Michigan. The Library published the paper, "Reviewers Reviewed," the same year in book form.[14]

"O.E."—as he liked to be called—seemed to thrive on controversy. The question and answer period following the presentation of a paper at Round Table meetings was enlivened by his penetrating and persistent questions. He enjoyed stirring up a debate on any subject. Ralph G. Newman and E.B. Long said in an article in the Winter 1963 *Lincoln Herald*, shortly after Eisenschiml's death, that he "saw life as a question mark composed of a multitude of smaller question marks."

For a few years, from the late 1930s through the early 1940s, there was an organization in Chicago known as The Lincoln Group. This organization held regular meetings and lauded and worshipped, rather than studied, the life of the sixteenth president. When *Why Was Lincoln Murdered?* appeared, Eisenschiml was dropped from its rolls. Several future Round Table founders resigned their memberships in protest—not necessarily because they agreed with Eisenschiml's theories, but because they felt that people should never be barred from a historical organization because its leadership disagreed with their opinions.

It was around this time that The Round Table founders began having the informal dinner discussion groups in the homes of various members. Eisenschiml was one of the first hosts to the group, at his apartment in the fashionable Belden-Stratford Hotel overlooking Lincoln Park and Lake Michigan.

"O.E." was a man of eccentricities. He is remembered as

having never worn an overcoat—even in Chicago's always gusty and frequently below-zero winters. Elmer Gertz observed that he "seemed to ignore the snow and the other inclemencies of nature and man."[15] He was an absolute stickler for punctuality with his employees and insisted that they all gather for lunch in the company cafeteria at 12:00 noon sharp each workday. Yet, he was benevolent in providing employee benefits in an age when this was not mandatory.

In a message to "O.E." in a booklet that was prepared for him on the occasion of his eightieth birthday in 1960, Ralph Newman said: "We have never entirely agreed and have thoroughly enjoyed our differences. We have, however, always agreed that history is not dull but that it unfortunately at times, filters through the hands of dull people who, utilizing a rare perverse genius, can make Paul Revere's ride sound like a routine ride on the subway. You have proven that history, chemistry and life itself can be exciting, challenging, rewarding and just sheer fun."[16] In that same publication Carl Sandburg said of Eisenschiml: "He is one of the rare and fine exhibits of assured genius now going in Chicago."[17] Although Eisenschiml never agreed to serve as Round Table president, he was a meeting speaker six times and was part of a panel discussion or symposium on four occasions.

Eisenschiml died on December 7, 1963. He was eighty-three. His father's stories of the Battle of Shiloh had left an enduring impression. At his request, Otto Eisenschiml's ashes were scattered over the monument of the 55th Illinois, his father's old regiment, on the battlefield at Shiloh.

Round Table member Lloyd Miller at the 55th Illinois Monument during the 1969 battlefield tour to Shiloh.

Fred C.Evers

Fred C. Evers is remembered as a good, kind, and gentle man who loved books and music. He was a fine cellist. Although he held no degree, a fellow founder remembers Evers as "better read than most of us."[18] He accumulated a large library, specializing in Lincoln and the Civil War, Illinois and Chicago history, and English and American essays, though his wide range of interests included books on many other subjects.

He was president of Acme Printing and Sample Company which made fabric sample books for clothing and upholstery houses. At one time, he made sample books for a wallpaper and fabric project created by Frank Lloyd Wright.

Newton C. Farr was one of the wealthiest men in Chicago and owned some of its choicest land, including at one time the site on Michigan Avenue where Bloomingdale's department store now stands. His father was a pioneer realtor in the city and "Newt" succeeded him as president of Farr & Company, later to become Farr, Chinnock & Sampson. He graduated from Cornell University in 1909 with a degree in civil engineering. He was a life-long bachelor, in spite of the fact that he caught Betsey Davis' bridal bouquet in 1964.[19]

He served as president of the YMCA of Metropolitan Chicago; president of the board of trustees of the Greater North Michigan Avenue Association; president of the Illinois State Historical Society; president of the National Association of Real Estate Boards; president of the board of trustees of Lincoln Memorial University; and trustee of Illinois Institute of Technology. He made liberal contributions to the institutions and associations in which he participated.

Newton Farr was The Round Table's second president (1946-1947). He was a meeting speaker twice. His topics were "The Secession Movement and Some of Its Fathers" on May 28, 1941, and "Reconstruction After the Civil War" on April 25, 1946.

Farr tried to walk home from his office during Chicago's blizzard of January 1967. He gave up and spent the night at the University Club. But after this harsh exposure to the elements, he became ill and never recovered. He died the following November, a month-and-a-half before what would have been his eightieth birthday.

Newton C. Farr

Seymour J. Frank was a brilliant and strong-willed attorney who was interested in the economic aspects of the Civil War. He wrote articles which were published in historical journals. A noted Civil War scholar called one of his efforts

("The Conspiracy To Implicate The Confederate Leaders in
Lincoln's Assassination" which appeared in *The Mississippi
Valley Historical Review* in March 1954) "one of the finest pieces
ever written."[20]

In addition to Civil War literature, he had a great interest
in the better English and American historical novels. He was
the seventh president of The Round Table (1951-1952). The
first Round Table battlefield tour took place during his presidency.[21]

Twice Frank was the featured speaker at a Round Table
meeting. He spoke on "A Civil War Illusion: Northern Pros-
perity" on November 27, 1945. His topic on September 20,
1951 was "We'll Hang Jeff Davis from a Sour Apple Tree."

Seymour J. Frank

Vernon Hanson, at the time of The Round Table's founding, was secretary of the Audit Bureau of Circulation, which
certifies the circulation of newspapers and periodicals. Their
findings determine advertising rates. As noted in Chapter 1,
it was Hanson who asked Raymond J. DaBoll to design The
Round Table's insignia.

A book collector with a wide range of interests, he amassed
a fine collection of Henry Fielding and American illustrators
and typographers, as well as Civil War and Lincolniana and
some choice works of Americana. He was a gentle, quiet-
spoken man for whom all Round Tablers had great affection.

Percival G. Hart, a realtor and investment broker, was—as
mentioned earlier—the speaker at the first meeting of The
Civil War Round Table on December 3, 1940. "The scholarly
and interesting manner of that first talk," Ralph Newman
observed, "set a high standard for future Round Table addresses."[22]

A graduate of Yale University, during his student years
he and Stephen Vincent Benet were co-editors of the *Yale
Literary Magazine.* A World War I aviator, he served in the
romantic Lafayette Esquadrille. After the United States entered
the war, he became a member of the 135th Aero Squadron and
later wrote the history of the squadron. During World War II
he was a colonel in charge of procurement at the converted
Ford Motor Company plant in Dearborn, Michigan.

When he moved to Los Angeles to become manager of
procurement for Hughes Aircraft Company, he became a
member of the Civil War Round Table there while still maintaining his membership in the Chicago group. On November
4, 1960, he returned to Chicago to give the address for The
Round Table's Twentieth Anniversary meeting. He spoke on

Percival G. Hart

"The Battle of Chancellorsville." A member of the "old school," he sent a letter of resignation to The Civil War Round Table in Chicago upon learning of the vote to admit women as members in 1977.[23]

Walter S. Holden, a lawyer who became a judge, was the only founder who was a contemporary of Abraham Lincoln—although for a very short time. He was born in 1865, about a month before Lincoln was assassinated. In his youth, he lived on the near west side of Chicago, not far from where Mary Lincoln and her son Tad lived from June of 1866 until August of 1867 and where Tad attended Ogden School. This connection inspired the young Holden to develop an interest in Lincoln and he began his fine Lincoln collection at an early age.

Those who remember Walter Holden do so with fondness. A fellow founder recalls one incident in particular: "At one Round Table meeting, when an over-enthusiastic member suggested we print the remarks of the speaker, Walter moved that we not publish the address because the inaccuracies in the speech would prove to be a later source of embarrassment to the speaker. This set the tone for the irreverance Round Table members often exhibited toward their speakers if they were not too careful with facts."[24]

Although Walter Holden never served as Round Table president, he did address the group once—in May of 1943. His topic was "Abraham Lincoln, Man of Inner Conflict." At the time of The Round Table's founding, he lived in a Frank Lloyd Wright house in Oak Park, Illinois.

Alexander J. Isaacs

Alexander J. Isaacs is remembered as a friendly, intelligent, and good man who never quite found his niche in life. As mentioned earlier, it was he who gave The Civil War Round Table its name. A graduate of Harvard University, he was a lawyer who didn't take to lawyering. He has been described as "a lawyer who knew the law who was often thwarted by a lawyer who knew the judge."[25]

He drifted into the book business where he enjoyed a modest success. His father was a well-known physician and his brother-in-law was drama critic at the *Chicago Sun-Times*. Isaacs was a knowledgeable student of the Civil War era.

Henry J. Lackey, a retired Chicago businessman when The Round Table was founded, was an enthusiastic student of the Civil War who had a fine Lincoln collection. His proudest possession was a copy of a very rare campaign biography of Abraham Lincoln written by John Locke Scripps and published in 1860 by the *Chicago Press and Tribune.*

Lackey holds the distinction of being the only founder (or anyone else) to die at a meeting of The Civil War Round Table. Described as "a wonderful old man who loved The Round Table," he attended a Round Table meeting on March 21, 1943 when historian Paul M. Angle spoke on "B.H. Grierson: Cavalryman." At the close of the meeting, he told his dinner companions: "This has been a wonderful evening, one of the best evenings I've ever had." At that point, he keeled over, dead from an apparent heart attack. Physicians in attendance that evening were unable to revive him. But, he died happy. Angle later remarked that he had never before had that effect on anyone.[26]

Walter W.L. Meyer was a judge of the Probate Court. He has been described as "a big, jolly chap with a very bright mind."[27] He had a winter home in Brownsville, Texas, but always attended Round Table meetings when he was in Chicago.

He developed an interest in Lincoln and the Civil War at an early age. His keen mind prompted him to take a special interest in some of the more controversial incidents in the Lincoln and Civil War stories. Meyer was a great storyteller and entertained the members from his vast repertoire before and after Round Table meetings.

C(harles). Norton Owen, a wholesaler of children's clothing, was a keen student of the Lincoln-Civil War story. He was also an accomplished violinist and owned a Stradivarius violin.

He had an expert's knowledge of Lincoln and Civil War manuscripts and acquired many fine items at very low prices by his careful and discerning study of dealers' catalogues. His manuscripts were sold at the Parke-Bernet Gallery after his death.

James Rosenthal, a lawyer, was a partner in the firm of Rosenthal, Hamil and Wormser, which dated back to the time of Abraham Lincoln. Known as "Jimmy" to his friends, Rosenthal is remembered as an individual with a delightful

C.N. Owen

sense of humor. When asked if he knew Abraham Lincoln, he would smile and his eyes would twinkle as he replied: "No, but my children went to school with him."[28]

A Lincoln collector, he specialized in pictorial material—
paintings, photographs, engravings, etchings, prints, and the
like—of our sixteenth president. His collection was given to
the Chicago Historical Society.

Chapter 3 ☆ *The First Decade*

T HE SECOND MEETING of The Civil War Round Table convened on January 17, 1941, again at the Bismarck, with founding member Elmer Gertz speaking on "Wilbur F. Storey and the *Chicago Times* in the Civil War." The group continued to meet each month through May. New names appeared on the meeting attendance lists maintained by secretary Newman. The largest attendance was twenty- two at the April meeting. When meetings resumed in October, attendance was thirty-one, and from then on, more than thirty.[1]

For six of the nine meetings held from December 1940 through December 1941, a founding member delivered the address. (See Appendix A for a complete list of meeting speakers and topics.) Meeting places for this first decade, other than the Bismarck, included the Brevoort, LaSalle, Pearson, and Maryland hotels, and the University Club.

The first Round Table symposium was held in April 1942. The topic was "George Brinton McClellan." The participants were Otto Eisenschiml and Percival G. Hart, with Elmer Gertz serving as moderator. *Chicago Tribune* cartoonist—and Round Table member—Joseph Parrish prepared the maps.

In October 1942 Round Table members traveled to Harrogate, Tennessee for the dedication of the Civil War Library at Lincoln Memorial University. Newton C. Farr was at the time a member of the board of trustees of the University. The ceremonies took place over the weekend of October 17-18.

Present at the dedication was Captain Harry S. Howard, son of Union General Oliver Otis Howard, one of the founders of the University. Captain Howard spoke on the subject "Reminiscences of My Father: Soldier and a Christian with Courage." Roy P. Basler, later to serve as editor of *The Collected Works of Abraham Lincoln* (9 vols., 1953-1955), led a discussion on "Who Wrote the Bixby Letter?" (Dr. Basler concluded that the masterpiece of prose was definitely the work of Mr.

Stanley F. Horn (right) with (from right) Elmer Gordon, Ralph Newman, Ollie Felton and Seymour Frank

Lincoln.) An address was given by Round Table member Stanley F. Horn, author of *The Army of Tennessee* (1941), on Confederate General Hood's invasion of Tennessee in 1864, after the fall of Atlanta.[2]

Carl Sandburg substituted for a speaker who couldn't get into the city because of a snowstorm in February of 1944. Sandburg was drafted when he happened to walk into Ralph Newman's Abraham Lincoln Book Shop shortly after it had been learned that Robert Kincaid, then president of Lincoln Memorial University, was snowbound in Tennessee. Enroute to the meeting, with Sandburg as a passenger, Newman's car broke down. The renowned writer of prose and poetry got out and helped push the vehicle until it started to function properly. That evening he took Dr. Kincaid's place in a panel discussion on the "Lincoln the Lover" articles, which had appeared in the *Atlantic Monthly* magazine, and *The Diary of a Public Man*.[3] Other participants were Seymour J. Frank, Elmer Gertz, John M. Hamer, and Ralph G. Newman. One member recalls it as one of the best Round Table evenings he'd attended.[4]

Formal organization of the group became necessary in the spring of 1944 when secretary and meeting planner Ralph Newman enlisted in the United States Navy. A constitution and by-laws were drawn up and regularly constituted officers with a one-year tenure were elected, with the terms of office to run from the fall of 1945 until the spring of 1946. Monroe Cockrell was chosen as the first president. (See

"Sailor" Ralph G. Newman in 1944

Appendix B for a list of presidents of The Civil War Round Table.)

Newman was given a farewell dinner by fellow Round Tablers and presented with a watch. "I'll write you from Tokyo Bay," he remarked.[5] Round Table member John Valentine bought half-interest in the book shop and kept it going during Newman's absence. (During the winter of 1944-1945, the book shop had moved to 16 North Michigan Avenue, where it occupied the entire second floor.) As it turned out, Newman spent all of his two-year stint in the armed forces stationed at the Great Lakes Naval Base near Chicago, which made it quite convenient for him to keep in touch with Round Table and book shop activities.

One of the great events of that first decade was the opening of the Robert Todd Lincoln papers in the Library of Congress. Lincoln had given his father's papers to the Library with the stipulation that they not be opened until twenty-one years after his death (which came on July 26, 1926, six days before what would have been his eighty-third birthday). No one, except President Lincoln's secretaries John G. Nicolay and John Hay (to whom he gave exclusive access to the papers for use in the preparation of their biography of his father),[6] and perhaps a few other intimates of Robert Lincoln, had viewed the papers all those years.

The historical community was filled with excitement when the day for the opening finally arrived on July 26, 1947. Thirty-seven Round Table members were present for the event. Among them were the authors of more than 250 books on Lincoln and the Civil War. Later, a special Round Table meeting was held at the home of *Chicago Tribune* Washington bureau chief (and Round Table member) Walter Trohan. Ralph Newman recalls the thrill, on the eve of the opening of the papers, of being seated between Ulysses S. Grant 3rd, grandson of General Grant, and Robert Todd Lincoln Beckwith, great-grandson of Abraham Lincoln.[7]

A November 19, 1947 *St. Louis Dispatch* article by Al Weisman about The Round Table lists membership at 140. In the article Weisman describes the atmosphere he found at a 1947 Round Table meeting: "... The visitor ... would sense immediately that this is no ordinary service club or lodge in session and no gathering of the usual American jolly good fellow. The atmosphere of the meeting is spectacularly informal. Coats and vests are tossed over the backs of chairs, books and briefcases are lying about, smoke swirls about from cigars and cigarettes. Members wander about the room, holding earnest whispered conversations on some point the speaker is making. But they listen to everything he says. One man normally retires to a lonely corner ... and he seems to be

*Robert Todd Lincoln
Beckwith with Laura
Douglas (daughter of
member C. Robert Douglas)
on the 1966 battlefield tour
to Washington, D.C.*

lost in reveries until the speaker has finished. At that point, he leaps to his feet to say, 'I question the accuracy of your statement that . . .' His phrase is a favorite with Round Table members and another is 'Upon what do you base your statement that . . .'"

Referring further to the sometimes brutal question and answer sessions following an address, Wiseman wrote: "The Round Table members know their history and every man present is an expert on some battle or period of the war and can make it rough on any speaker who gets a little loose with his facts. One guest who had heard about the 'sniping' he was likely to receive devoted his entire speech to a sharp criticism of books and pamphlets on the Civil War written by members of The Round Table, thus beating them to the punch, so to speak. However, the debate that followed was one of the most heated in the memory of the members. . . ."

Frank Vandiver attests to the brutality of those early question and answer sessions. A prodigy in the field of history, Vandiver wrote his first scholarly article at the age of sixteen. He holds the record as the youngest person to ever address a Round Table meeting. He was twenty-two. In December 1947, he appeared before the group to speak on "Josiah Gorgas" about whom he later wrote a book, *Ploughshares Into Swords* (1952).

That evening remains vivid in Dr. Vandiver's memory. He recalls: ". . . I had really worked on this talk. I was scared of the whole organization. I'd heard all these great stories about the critical audience . . . and I had not done a lot of public speaking. I really worked on this speech bravely.

"I remember saying somewhere in the speech that during the siege of Atlanta, the [Confederate] reserve ammunition train had gotten stuck on the spur of a railroad track and that something like 100 cars of ammunition and a locomotive had gone up. . . . This was just an aside; I hadn't really meant to say it. At the end of my talk, during the question and answer period, a man got up and said something like this: 'I have spent the last twenty years studying the blowing up of that reserve ammunition train. It was not 100 cars, it was 128 cars; it was not one locomotive, it was three locomotives and their numbers were __, __, and __.' Well, I got smaller and smaller, and I decided that everything I'd heard about The Round Table audience was an underestimation of the horror that it represented. It was absolutely terrible. But, I'll tell you one thing—I never used that line again!"[8]

The Round Table celebrated the publication of member Don Russell's *Lincoln Raises An Army* (1948) in June of that year. On October 22, David C. Mearns, of the Library of Congress, spoke on "The Robert Todd Lincoln Papers." A special guest that evening was John W. Barringer, president of the Missouri Pacific Railroad.

On March 7, 1948, the Abraham Lincoln Book Shop moved from 16 North Michigan Avenue to 18 East Chestnut Street, where it was to remain for forty-two years. The moving day was memorable—and unique—because the many volumes of Lincoln and Civil War books were toted to the new location not by professional movers, but by members of The Civil War Round Table in a procession of cars. According to member Al Meyer, this was done "because we felt that ordinary moving people shouldn't be handling the important Civil War historical materials that Ralph had in the book shop."[9] Elmer Gertz remembers: "We had a real procession going from Michigan Avenue to 18 East Chestnut." He added, "I think I was one of the martyrs of the move. I was injured in an automobile in connection with the moving."[10] Al Meyer memorialized the occasion by arranging to have a drawing made of himself lugging a heavy load of books, headed for "A.L.B.S.,

The Abraham Lincoln Book Shop at 18 East Chestnut

18 E. Chestnut." The caricature is titled "Book Toter." Meyer remembers that after the books were all in place, "Newt" Farr treated the movers to dinner in a restaurant on Chicago Avenue located in a building he owned.[11]

A "Railroad Fair" was one of the highlights of Chicago's summer of 1949. It was held in Grant Park and Soldier Field, and featured a pageant called "Wheels A-Rolling." This was the first Round Table event to which women were invited. They continued to be barred from membership. Barbara Long Pleiter, widow of historian E.B. (Pete) Long, remembers it: ". . . It was a marvelous railroad fair. It featured a pageant with real trains going across the stage. . . . There was one car with Lincoln and Civil War displays. . . ."[12] The Round Table

attended a performance and held a meeting at the Fair on August 30. Robert S. Henry spoke on "The Railroads of the Confederacy."

On October 17, 1949, The Civil War Round Table was incorporated as a perpetual organization, under the General Not For Profit Corporation Act of Illinois. The incorporators were Alfred W. Stern, Joseph L. Eisendrath, William Herzog, and Lloyd D. Miller. The first board of trustees under the corporate status was: Lloyd D. Miller, John G. Graef, Verne Miners, Raymond J. Friend, and William H. Hazlett. The "perpetual" office was listed as 18 East Chestnut Street, and its agent, Ralph G. Newman.[13]

Its stated purpose was : "To promote social, historical, educational, and literary activities by its members, and particularly the study and analysis of events and personalities associated with the period of the war between the United States, commonly known as the 'Civil War'; to engage in the study of historical characters and events associated with the period; to foster and create publications of literary and historical value dealing with the history of the United States and particularly the Civil War period of that history. . . ."[14]

The year 1950 brought several very notable speakers to The Round Table. Louis A. Warren spoke on "The Lincoln Political Puzzle." In April, Allan Nevins' topic was "Could the Civil War Have Been Avoided, and If So, How?" The first talk to be tape-recorded was Benjamin P. Thomas' September 22 address on "Freedom's Firebrand—Theodore Weld."

Colonel Robert R. McCormick, *Chicago Tribune* publisher and Civil War buff, spoke on October 26. He had written a book, *The War Without Grant;* the topic of his address was "The Fight for the Border States." The evening is recalled with some amusement by those who were present. Apparently, the Colonel's skill as a businessman was not matched by eloquence as a speaker. Having been asked to speak for forty minutes, he walked to the podium, began *reading* from the galleys of his book, and ended promptly at forty minutes—mid-sentence. He permitted some questions, but not too many.[15]

Beginning with the September 1950 meeting, the form of meeting notices was changed. The growth and progression of the organization called for a more thorough and formal monthly announcement than the double postal cards which had served the purpose in the past. Beginning with the ninety-fifth meeting, and continuing for the next nine years, Ralph Newman wrote, and his administrative assistant Margaret April prepared for mailing, french-fold notices. Printed on quality paper stock, these announcements provided extended information about the meetings and speakers. The new no-

William B. Hesseltine

tices featured The Civil War Round Table heading in a distinctive type associated with the Civil War period.

Joseph L. Eisendrath, president of The Round Table for the 1950-1951 term, was asked to review The CWRT's first decade. Among his recollections was the attendance at a Round Table meeting by Captain Thomas M. Ambrose, Chicago's last Civil War veteran, at the age of ninety-six. Ambrose died just past the century mark. Eisendrath continued his reminiscences: "Who will ever forget Carl Sandburg's appearances and repeated arguments about Abraham Lincoln? . . . Our discussion period often has led to some heated arguments. . . . Dr. Louis A. Warren of Fort Wayne was called on the carpet to back up his famous criticism of William H. Herndon's contributions to the Lincoln story."[16]

No longer a fledgling organization, The Civil War Round Table concluded its first decade exhibiting growth in numbers, spirit, and recognition in the historical community. The first address of the second decade was given on December 7, 1950 by renowned historian William B. Hesseltine, author of many books, including *Lincoln and the War Governors* (1948) and *Confederate Leaders in the New South* (1950). His topic was "Davis vs. Lee: Postwar Careers of the Confederate Leaders."

Chapter 4 ☆ *Early Milestones:*
The 100th Meeting and the
First Battlefield Tour

T HE CIVIL WAR ROUND TABLE held its 100th meeting
on February 16, 1951 at the University Club of Chicago.
It was indeed a special occasion. After dinner, Round Table
President Joseph L. Eisendrath, Jr. provided a "Historical
Review" of the organization. In his remarks, he noted: "I think
that background in American history has much more of a
contemporary effect than we commonly realize. We are part
of what we are; inquiring into the origins of our country isn't
merely a hobby.... Much of this interest of Round Table
members is purely romantic, of course, but it is not impractical.
You can't live intelligently now without also living the past
that has brought this present into being." "So I feel," Eisendrath
continued, "and I am sure most of you feel that perhaps even
the history of The Civil War Round Table should be taken
seriously."[1]

The address that evening was given by Robert S. Henry,
who spoke on "Rehearsal in Mexico: Trial by Battle of Civil
War Leaders." In his address he said that, "The focus of
American history is the war of 1861-1865. By arbitrament of
arms that war determined the fundamental nature of the
United States as a nation rather than a federal compact...."[2]

Elmer Gertz wrote an article about the 100th meeting in
the Summer 1951 *Lincoln Herald*. He reported that "One hundred or so members attended the 100th meeting of The Civil
War Round Table (actually there were two or three in excess
of the century mark, but the legend will grow that 100 attended the 100th meeting). Eight states and the District of
Columbia, twenty-two cities and various suburbs of Chicago
were the points from which those in attendance journeyed."
He went on to talk about how some of the earlier members
had begun to lose interest over the past few years and thus
their attendance at meetings had become sporadic. But many
of them came to the 100th meeting and it served to revive their
enthusiasm. Afterwards, they began to attend meetings more
regularly. Gertz observed: "They now show off the group to
their friends. They bring in new members." He went on to

Program	Retrospect
Dinner *Introductions* *Historical Review* JOSEPH L. EISENDRATH, JR. ADDRESS *"Rehearsal in Mexico"* ROBERT S. HENRY *Discussion*	THE CIVIL WAR ROUND TABLE *held its first meeting on December 3, 1940. Nearly all subsequent meetings have followed the pattern established at that time —a talk by an informed speaker and a free discussion of his subject. The meetings have given many students, both professional and avocational, an opportunity to present the results of research, while to others they have been the means of enlarging knowledge and clarifying understanding. The success of the Civil War Round Table may be measured by its present membership of one hundred eighty five, and by the fact that its example has led interested groups in several other cities to form similar organizations.*

make a prediction, a much too modest one as history would prove. He said: "This is likely to continue until the 150th meeting and perhaps even the 200th session."

Percival G. Hart, founding member and speaker at that first meeting, had moved to California and was unable to attend the celebratory gathering. He wrote a letter to Ralph Newman expressing his "deep regret" at not being able to attend. He went on to say: "It seems only yesterday that you and I and a handful of our good friends and fellow students met at the Bismarck Hotel to assist in the delivery of the infant organization." Referring in jest to his 1940 address, he said: "To stretch the metaphor, we might say that I administered the anesthetic." "From the beginning," he continued, "The Round Table's membership [has been] characterized by its love of the study of the Civil War period and by the active participation of each and every one [of its members]."[3]

A major development occurred in the spring of 1951— and it was a *major* development. The first annual Round Table battlefield tour took place from May 31 through June 3. The idea to sponsor a tour of Civil War battlefields was conceived by Ralph Newman. The idea was accepted with enthusiasm by the rest of the membership.

The itinerary for that inaugural battlefield tour was very

ambitious. It included Nashville, Franklin, Stone's River, Chickamauga, and the Cumberland Gap, and culminated in a meeting at Lincoln Memorial University in Harrogate, Tennessee. On that first tour, and continuing for a few subsequent tours, Round Tablers traveled by railroad in private cars. Member Elmer Gordon, then general passenger agent for the Chicago & Eastern Illinois Railroad, made the transportation arrangements. Ralph Newman's new administrative assistant at the book shop, Margaret April, applied her superb managerial and organizational skills in working out all the fine details of travel timing, lodging, and meals—though, as a woman, she was not permitted to go on the tour.

Prior to the trip, *Chicago Tribune* writer and Round Table member A.E. (Abe) Geldhof wrote a story about it for his newspaper. It appeared in the Sunday, May 27, 1951 edition. He reported that: "Government park service superintendents and historians at the various parks will act as guides and quizmasters, special buses taking the visitors to the most remote parts of each field. The visitors will travel at night, making the railroad sleeping cars their headquarters during the day."

Round Table member E.B. (Pete) Long, author of several books on the Civil War and the man who did much of the historical research for Bruce Catton's books, wrote a story about that first tour for the Fall 1951 *Lincoln Herald*. He called it a "second invasion of the South by Yankees." This is part of what he had to say: ". . . After weeks of planning, the forces gathered on the evening of May 31. There were no blue woolen army uniforms in sight at Dearborn station that night, but there were excited men from many businesses and professions clad in sports clothes and armed with Civil War maps and books, long stored up knowledge of their favorite conflict, and the desire to see the scenes of the great struggle of the 1860s in Tennessee and Kentucky. . . . The commanding officer was newly elected President Seymour Frank, Chicago attorney and one of the founders of the Round Table. . . . At a special desk in the redecorated Dearborn station the invaders checked in, received tickets and reservations and headed for two special Pullman cars which were to be their home for three-and-a-half days. After greeting their comrades and depositing their luggage, they gathered for an informal session of talk in the club car as the C.&E.I. *Dixie Flyer* pulled out of Chicago heading south."

The group attending that initial tour included such eminent historians as Allan Nevins, Stanley F. Horn, Paul M. Angle, and Benjamin P. Thomas. Also present was then new member C. Robert Douglas—who, at 26, was one of the youngest members.. Recalling that experience, Bob Douglas remarked: "Because we were the original Round Table, we were treated as royalty at the national battlefield parks. Because we had in our company such people as Allan Nevins and Stanley Horn, we were not minor leaguers. We represented some very prestigious people."[4]

Thirty people participated in the entire tour; others joined for parts of it. The trip culminated in a gathering at Lincoln Memorial University, where Round Table member Allan Nevins was awarded the L.M.U. Diploma of Honor for the Outstanding Contribution to Lincoln Scholarship in 1950. The 104th meeting was held the evening of June 2. The next morning the Round Tablers attended the Baccalaureate services of the Sixtieth Commencement at L.M.U.

In an article in the Fall 1951 *Lincoln Herald*, Dr. Robert Kincaid, then president of L.M.U., told about the battlefield tour group's arrival for the June 2 meeting: "The thirty excursionists began to trail into the crowded Lincoln Room, hot, perspiring, and disheveled. In the scramble for seats, each person took his own vantage point. Dr. Paul Angle, appropriately enough, perched himself upon the desk Lincoln had used in the Illinois Legislature. Dr. Ben Thomas, quiet and modest, sat close by like an attentive school boy. Dr. Allan Nevins, calm and undisturbed, took his place near a long case of Lincoln books. The newly-wed Dr. Harry Pratt (Illinois State Historian), with his wife, cuddled nearby.[5] Colonel William Herzog, treasurer of the group, stood with military mien back among the crowded seats . . ." Round Table President Seymour Frank made a few remarks and then "surrendered his prerogatives to Ralph G. Newman, the secretary," who "twitched his stubby black mustache, and started the proceedings. . . ."

The tired, disheveled group had a treat in store for them. Next on the program was a talk delivered by attorney, author, Lincoln collector, lecturer, and raconteur William H. Townsend of Lexington, Kentucky. They would have the opportunity to hear him again in sixteen months when he would address a Round Table meeting in Chicago.

According to Pete Long's *Lincoln Herald* article, enroute home on their special Pullmans, now attached to the *Southland*, "all members agreed that the first Civil War Round Table battlefield tour had been a tremendous success and they would do everything possible to see that it was not the last such trip. In appreciation of the hospitality afforded them at Lincoln Memorial University, the sum of $1000 was collected and telegraphed from Cincinnati to Dr. Kincaid for use in the school's scholarship fund."

Participants in that first tour shared their impressions with Pete Long. Bob Douglas felt that "the pictures of the little

Warren Reeder (right) with Jerry Warshaw

barefoot boy who was an unofficial guide on the Pinacle and teenager Peter Perkins Minton, who carried a map for all to study at Franklin, are among his most treasured memories. . . . Warren Reeder of Hammond, Indiana, says that the trip impressed upon him the importance of the western battles, even though the conflict in the east seems to have held more interest for the casual observer. 'In short,' Reeder says, 'I am ready for the next trip.'" Thirty-nine tours later, anyone who is privileged to participate in an annual battlefield tour of The Civil War Round Table is always "ready for the next trip." (See Appendix C for a list of battlefield tours.)

Chapter 5 ☆ *The Second Battlefield Tour,*
A Visit to Lincoln's New Salem,
and "The Lion of Whitehall"

THROUGHOUT the remaining months of 1951 and the beginning of 1952, the Round Table continued to grow and blossom. Meeting speakers through these months included two of its founders. Seymour J. Frank spoke in September on "We'll Hang Jeff Davis from a Sour Apple Tree." In January, Elmer Gertz's topic was "Charles A. Dana: The Eyes of the Government at the Front." Pete Long talked, on April 11, about "Ulysses S. Grant: The Man Behind the Memoirs."

The folks who were "ready for the next trip" got their chance in June of 1952. "The call for volunteers came early this year," Pete Long noted in the Summer 1952 *Lincoln Herald* "and there was no need of a draft as recruits came in from many sections of the country. The occasion was the Second Annual Battlefield Tour of The Civil War Round Table."[1] The itinerary was another ambitious one: Antietam *and* Gettysburg *and* Harpers Ferry. The dates were June 19 through 22.

Eighty-two men participated in this second expedition. Elmer Gordon once again arranged for the railroad transportation. Again, Margaret April put many hours of work into coordinating all the arrangements to ensure a smooth-running trip. Long wrote that: ". . . As the three special Pullmans of the *Columbian* left Chicago heading east, the campaigners had dinner in their private dining car. Talk centered upon what each wanted to see at the battlefields and enthusiasm, as usual, was high."

After visiting the Harpers Ferry and Charles Town areas, the group checked in at the Francis Scott Key Hotel in Frederick, Maryland. That afternoon they toured the Antietam battlefield, site of the bloodiest day in American history. The dinner speaker that evening was Otto Eisenschiml who gave what Long described as "a provocative talk" on "Gettysburg: The Most Inexcusable Battle."

The next day they were off to Gettysburg. The first day of that battle was covered by afternoon. The main speaker at the evening dinner was Bruce Catton, author of *Mr. Lincoln's*

Army (1951). Although he had invited him to speak, Ralph Newman had never met Mr. Catton. "When I arrived at the Hotel Gettysburg," Newman recalled, ". . . there was this mild, scholarly looking man sitting in the lobby. I recognized him from his photograph on the cover of *Mr. Lincoln's Army*, introduced myself, and we promptly moved to the bar for martinis (a maneuver to be repeated many times across a period of almost thirty years) . . ." Included in Sunday's tour, covering the second and third days of the battle, was a visit to the Eisenhower farm, where the group was met by General Arthur Nevins, brother of fellow Round Tabler Allan Nevins. (General Nevins was the manager of the farm.)

Long wrote that: "Everyone felt the trip had been well planned and smoothly run. President Elmer Gertz particularly deserves praise, and many members were very appreciative of the fine packet of printed material he distributed before the trip began . . ." This was the beginning of the now familiar battlefield tour kits.

Summing up the tour, Long observed that: "In short, those on the trip seemed unanimous in the feeling that even though many of them had seen these battlefields before, each experienced a new feeling of companionship in a common interest, learned from each other and came home with a warmth for the people of Gettysburg, Sharpsburg, Frederick, Keedysville, and other communities visited."

"It occurred to several members of the Round Table," President Gertz wrote in the Fall 1952 *Lincoln Herald*, "that, between journeys to distant points, we ought to visit some of the hallowed ground of our own state—the New Salem and Springfield area." Once again, as it was during the Railroad Fair, the "men only" rule was retracted. Over sixty men and women traveled by automobiles to central Illinois over the weekend of August 23-24, 1952. According to Gertz, "all returned feeling that similar summer outings should be a regular feature of Round Table life."

Enroute to New Salem, the Round Tablers stopped at the campus of Lincoln College in Lincoln, Illinois—the first college and town named for our sixteenth president. On August 27, 1853, Abraham Lincoln christened the new town of Lincoln with the juice of a watermelon. On February 6, 1865, the Illinois General Assembly approved legislation establishing Lincoln University, the charter under which Lincoln College continues to operate. Gertz wrote that: "There, Round Table member Raymond Dooley, president of the College, arranged a full program for us, which included an examination of the College's Lincoln collection, a buffet luncheon, appropriate songs by a choral group, and several brief, easy-to-take speeches."

Bruce Catton in 1966

At New Salem State Park, Dr. and Mrs. Harry E. Pratt, Mr. and Mrs. Benjamin P. Thomas, and Mrs. Henry E. Pond, historian of the New Salem League, acted as the group's guides through the recreated scenes of Lincoln's young manhood. A high point was the evening performance of Kermit Hunter's "Forever This Land" at Kelso Hollow Outdoor Theater. "No one," Gertz reported, "will ever forget the long shadow of Lincoln across the stage in the last moments of the pageant."

Some members of the group spent the night in the New Salem area and journeyed to Springfield in the morning. Others, including President Gertz and Secretary Newman, drove to the Illinois capital that night. After midnight, both of these men ran out of gas on the highway and had to be rescued. The next day, Gertz wrote, "Harry Pratt spread out for us a memorable exhibition at the Illinois State Historical Society in Springfield's Centennial Building. It included the items purchased for the state at the Barrett sale[2] and other priceless manuscripts, printed matter, and relics. All of us were brought closer to our great heritage there and when we visited the Lincoln tomb."

October 17, 1952 is a special date in Round Table history. Colonel William H. Townsend, who had spoken to the group at Lincoln Memorial University during that first battlefield tour, came to Chicago to give his rousing talk on

William H. Townsend, probably on the 1953 battlefield tour

"Cassius Marcellus Clay: The Lion of Whitehall." (It had originally been scheduled for the previous May 7 but, due to illness, Townsend had been forced to reschedule.) Many who were present that evening mention Townsend's talk as the most memorable Round Table address they've ever heard.[3] The subject matter was rich. That Lexington citizen of another era, friend of Abraham Lincoln, early leader in the abolitionist cause, champion of womanhood, diplomat, bowie knife artist, and soldier was surely "one of the most colorful figures ever to march across the pages of American history."[4]

The speaker was also a colorful figure. Ralph Newman talked about William H. Townsend of Lexington, Kentucky in a 1983 lecture: ". . . One of the nation's leading attorneys, he assembled a remarkable [Lincoln] collection, mainly from the 1920s to the 1940s. He was the author of many books, the most significant of which was *Lincoln and His Wife's Home Town* (1929), which appeared years later in revised and expanded form as *Lincoln and the Bluegrass* (1955). . . . One of the first Lincoln books he read was [William Eleazar] Barton's *The Paternity of Abraham Lincoln* (1920). When Townsend sent the volume to Dr. Barton for an inscription, it began a friendship which resulted in the two men journeying through Anderson County, west of Lexington, in search of the history of the Sparrow and Hanks families. He became a close friend and adviser to Emilie Todd Helm, Mary Lincoln's half-sister and the widow of Confederate General Ben Hardin Helm. He ultimately became the owner of Helm Place, the perfect place for a great collection of Lincolniana. . . ."[5] In this lecture, Newman said of Townsend that "those who knew him can still hear his voice and be reminded of another Kentuckian who would lean back in his chair and say, "That reminds me of a story. . . ."[6]

The October 17 meeting was held in the bungalow apartments on the roof of the Sherman Hotel, twenty-five floors above Chicago's loop, "with a longer cocktail hour than usual embellished with hors d'oeuvres."[7] The "unusually large number"[8] of 121 members and guests (including the owner of the Sherman) attended. In introducing Townsend, President Gertz said: "This isn't going to be simply a talk. This is going to be an event."[9]

An article in the Fall 1952 *Lincoln Herald* gives an account of the talk. In part, it says: "Colonel Townsend, after first belittling his own ability as a speaker before any but 'a small and compulsory audience of twelve,' proceeded to eat his own words by holding his hearers spellbound for an hour-and-a-half while he told in simple, forceful, and graphic terms the life story of Cassius Marcellus Clay, the 'Lion of Whitehall' and President Lincoln's chief supporter in holding

Kentucky for the Union. . . . As he described General Clay's prowess with the bowie knife and the many times in which he was compelled to wield it in duels, Colonel Townsend drew from a scabbard at his belt the actual weapon, flourishing it to his audience. When he spoke of Clay's carved-ivory handled special bowie knife that he used only on dress occasions, the speaker pulled that out too. And when he told of the immense horse pistol that President Lincoln had presented to Clay, out of Colonel Townsend's holster came that weapon. The effect on his listeners of this dramatic realism can be imagined."

"The Lion of Whitehall" talk was later produced as a long-playing record. Currently available on tape cassette,[10] it is as compelling and entertaining as it was the night it was delivered thirty-eight years ago.

Chapter 6 ☆ *The Third Battlefield Tour:*
J. Ambler Johnston and the
Last Public Address of
Douglas Southall Freeman

F ROM THE FALL OF 1952 through the spring of 1953, The Round Table presented such speakers as Benjamin P. Thomas ("The President Reads His Mail," November 7, 1952), Harry G. Hershenson ("Thaddeus Stevens: Thorn in Lincoln's Side," January 16, 1953), and Donald W. Riddle ("Congressman Lincoln," February 13, 1953). On April 30, Bruce Catton spoke on "Phil Sheridan and G.K. Warren and the Battle of Five Forks." For this occasion, the group met in the Lincoln Room of the Congress Hotel on South Michigan Avenue.

"Old campaigners" from the past two springs had marked May 7-10 on their calendars months before. The time arrived for the third annual battlefield tour. The 1953 tour focused on "The Peninsular Campaign, Richmond, and Williamsburg." This year the Round Tablers traveled to Richmond on a chartered DC-6 United Airlines plane. Thirty-seven members were aboard the plane. Others joined the tour later. Sixty members registered at the meetings. Members of the Richmond Round Table who joined the tour group made the total number of participants considerably larger.

A.E. (Abe) Geldhof wrote about the trip in the Summer 1953 *Lincoln Herald:* "The flight from Chicago was smooth and so pleasant that the tourists were enabled to mingle in the aisle and debate Civil War problems with each other. Harpers Ferry was reached before Pilot Charles McKenna, himself a Civil War fan, found a hole in the clouds through which he could drop the big plane."

"Dropping to a low altitude and handling the ship like an observation plane, he showed his passengers the battle-field of Antietam (Sharpsburg to the Richmond hosts), spread out below, describing the terrain over the plane's public address system. Gettysburg, he explained, had been under too heavy a cloud cover to make a visit there worthwhile.

"McKenna turned back to Harpers Ferry. After giving the party a look at Fredericksburg and the Rappahanock River, he came in for the landing at Richmond, with everybody aboard keen with anticipation of the pleasures in store during the next three days. . . . Buses were waiting at Byrd Field, and the 1953 battlefield tour began at once with a visit to Chimborazo Hill, the famous bluff overlooking the James River, which figures in every Civil War novel based on the battle for Richmond. Here the party looked down on the site of Tredegar Iron Works, where the Confederacy made its munitions. Then, after stopping at St. Paul's Church and viewing the pew from which Patrick Henry delivered his deathless oration in which he cried, 'Give me liberty or give me death!' the group was taken to the state capitol, once the capitol of the Confederacy, where, seated in the hall where the Confederate Congress met, the visitors were welcomed by Attorney General [of Virginia] J.L. Almond, Jr., on behalf of Governor James Battle, who was out of the city."

Other stops that day included the White House of the Confederacy, maintained as a museum, and the site of Libby Prison—which was at that time what was described as a "well-filled junk yard."[1] At the White House of the Confederacy, many of the tour group "went around to the porch, now in the rear of the house, to view the balcony from which Jefferson Davis' little son fell to his death."[2]

The Richmond News Leader carried an editorial on May 7, with the headline: "This Time, It's 'Welcome Yankees!'" The editorial closes by stating: "In all seriousness, there is much to be gained from the sort of study The Civil War Round Table is making of the American past. To keep alive the military history is of value in itself, for today's tacticians can learn many a lesson from the campaigns of 1861-65, but there is a deeper significance to be drawn from the nature of the combat. In the relationship of the Federal government to the States, in the terrible conflicts of States' rights and human rights and property rights, students of the Civil War period can find much of value to apply to the great issues of 1953. But this is intended to be a word of welcome, not a solemn discourse: We hope our visitors find their stay a profitable one, and that they will come back (which is more than we might have said to Mr. Grant) again."

The high point of the tour's first day (perhaps of the entire tour) was the evening dinner address by Douglas Southall Freeman, noted biographer of Washington and Lee. He spoke about the reliability of witnesses and writers on the Civil War and on the task of the historian. The title of his address was "Critique and Character in the Civil War." A recording was made of the speech and it was printed in Volume I of *Civil War History* (March 1955).

Joseph T. Marsh wrote an article about Dr. Freeman in the Spring 1953 issue of the *Lincoln Herald*. In the article Marsh noted that though Freeman had devoted a lifetime to writing about Civil War leaders and military science and tactics, most of the writing had been done in his "spare time." Marsh continues: "His work schedule would put most of us to shame, although few would likely envy his 2:30 a.m. rising hour. But the 2:30 a.m. to 8:00 a.m. schedule he keeps enables him to wring the maximum number of working hours out of each day and still get enough sleep. . . . A sign above his wall office clock, when he was editor of *The Richmond News Leader*, stated: 'Time Alone Is Irreplaceable. Waste It Not.'" Frank Vandiver recalled how the presence of this sign "made you feel that if you stayed ten seconds, you were really in trouble with him, although [Freeman] "himself was always the model of Southern courtesy."[3]

In Marsh's article, he noted that "Freeman served as editor of the afternoon paper from 1915 until his retirement on June 30, 1949. But for Dr. Freeman it was not a retirement, simply a 'changeover' to writing history and biography instead of newspaper work. . . . Upon 'retirement,' he retained his 8:00 a.m. daily news broadcast but dropped a noon news spot. An Associated Press news ticker brings the latest news dispatches right into his home.

"His respect and admiration of General Robert E. Lee caused Dr. Freeman to salute the Confederate chieftain's statue each morning as he drove down Monument Avenue to his editor's post. . . . It was Dr. Freeman who first suggested to Eisenhower that Ike run for President, Eisenhower disclosed in a Richmond campaign speech last Fall. . . . When Eisenhower in 1946 accepted an invitation to receive an honorary degree from the University of Richmond, he wrote that he was accepting because his mother was a Virginian and because 'I am such an admirer of Dr. Freeman that I am always disposed to conform instantly to any suggestion he makes.' . . . Dr. Freeman was rector of the University for sixteen years until 1950, when he resigned."

Freeman traveled extensively throughout the country to fill speaking engagements—sometimes averaging 20,000 miles a year. He was dubbed the "flying professor" by Columbia University in the 1930s, when he was a visiting professor of journalism. As early as 1908, he edited *Collection of Confederate Papers* and served as editor of *Lee's Dispatches* in 1915. His four-volume biography of Lee, on which he worked twenty years, won him the Pulitzer Prize in 1934.

Friday's tour schedule included a luncheon at White Marsh Plantation, a trip to Colonial Williamsburg, and dinner at the Wiliamsburg Inn. Charles E. Hatch, Jr., historian for the Colonial National Historical Park, was the dinner speaker.

Saturday's tour of the Richmond area battlefields was

led by Dr. Freeman's close friend, historian J. Ambler Johnston. An article in the May 7 edition of *The Richmond News Leader* states that: "The white-haired Johnston, considered by many as the dean of Richmond architects-engineers, conducted numerous tours of Richmond battlefields . . . prior to World War II. His last conducted tour was about three years ago."

The article continues: ". . . Johnston disdains professional guides with their fixed routine and their repetitious banter. . . . Occupying a seat in a car equipped with a public address system, he will lead a caravan of buses bearing Round Table members from North and South and interested members of the general public to the key points about Richmond.

"Johnston has had a lifelong interest in the Civil War because of his father's participation in it. The father, Nathaniel Burwell Johnston, was a seventeen-year-old Confederate private who fought at the Wilderness, Cold Harbor, and Fort Harrison, and was surrendered and paroled at Appomattox."

Johnston's interest in preserving Civil War battlefields began around 1915. "I ran across the old breastworks and moats at Fort Harrison," he remembered, "so covered with honeysuckle and a second growth of pines that it was difficult to get to them." In 1917, he told his friend Dr. Freeman about the condition of Fort Harrison. This led to an inventory by Johnston and Freeman "nearly every Sunday morning for several years" of the condition of Richmond area battlefield sites. Johnston reflected on that period of time: "In the early 1920s, the fields were completely unmarked, overgrown with timber, no roads, no markers, nothing to indicate where the engagements were, and you had to learn to know your way around. Roads were put through and numbered afterward to make a battlefield route."[4]

Dr. Douglas Southall Freeman addressing The Round Table on the lawn of his home in 1953. Also pictured is Stanley Horn

Freeman and Johnston went to the Rotary Club in 1924, presenting to that organization the problem of the unmarked battlefield sites. This resulted in the Rotary Club heading up a fund collection drive to mark the sites. The Richmond Battlefield Markers Corporation, of which Johnston was secretary, carried out the marking project.

The placing of the markers in the 1920s engendered interest in the battlefields to such an extent that when the Fort Harrison land was placed on sale for the lumber on it, a small group of men—Freeman and Johnston among them—borrowed money, bought the property, and formed the Richmond Battlefield Parks Corporation. The corporation made a public appeal to raise $45,000 and started a program to acquire deeds to points of interest in the major battlefields.

Johnston recalled: "We never had a case of anyone holding us up on the price. . . . We were able to buy at twenty-five cents on the dollar value of the land." More than twelve owners donated their land and the corporation eventually acquired almost 700 acres. In 1932, the corporation turned the land over to the state of Virginia for use as a park. Subsequently the battlefield sites were given to the Federal government and the land is now known as the Richmond National Battlefield Park. Thus, it is due to the efforts of J. Ambler Johnston and Douglas Southall Freeman that the battlefield sites around Richmond exist today. And it is perhaps a fruit of their pioneering that we have preserved additional Civil War battlefield sites.

Saturday evening after dinner, the Round Tablers heard an address by Virgil C. (Pat) Jones, Washington correspondent for the *Saturday Evening Post*. Jones was the president of the Civil War Round Table of the District of Columbia and had written *Ranger Mosby* (1944), a biography of the daring Confederate Partisan Ranger leader John S. Mosby.

On Sunday, the group toured the Petersburg National Military Park and enjoyed an al fresco luncheon on the lawn of the Crater Museum before returning to Richmond. The concluding event was a garden party on the lawns of Dr. Freeman's estate in suburban Richmond. Dr. Freeman had written Ralph Newman, saying, "I hope you gentlemen will be my guests for tea on Sunday." Newman recalls: "On the plane one of the main topics of conversation was whether, when Dr. Freeman said 'tea,' he meant 'tea,' because we knew he did not drink alcoholic beverages. When we walked into his garden, however, all our fears were dispelled, because there in the garden were two long tables, each manned by red-jacketed waiters. At one table they dispensed mint juleps; at the other you could call your shots."[5]

Virgil C. (Pat) Jones

Abe Geldhoff wrote about the gathering in the Summer 1953 *Lincoln Herald*: ". . . President Elmer Gertz[6] presented to Dr. Freeman a recording of William T. Townsend's talk on Cassius M. Clay, and was presented in turn with an autographed private edition. . . ." The host gave a brief talk on General Lee's meeting with General Pickett after the war, after which he invited his guests into his library and study where he showed them some of his impeccably written manuscripts. With some reluctance, the group departed and headed for the Richmond airport.

The address to The Round Table on May 7 was to be Dr. Freeman's last public address. Five weeks later, on June 13, 1953, at the age of sixty-six, Dr. Freeman was dead. Elmer Gertz attended the funeral as the offical representative of The Civil War Round Table.

Chapter 7 ☆ *The Growing Years:*
The Round Table's Adolescence

SEVERAL ROUND TABLE MEMBERS traveled to New
York City on November 1, 1953, to attend the New York
Civil War Round Table's observance of the eighty-eighth
birthday of Frederick Hill Meserve. Ralph G. Newman and
Allan Nevins served on the Committee for Arrangements, as
did Carl Haverlin, president of Broadcast Misic Incorporated
and member of both the Chicago and New York Round
Tables.

Meserve, the noted collector of Lincoln photographs,
was the author, with Carl Sandburg, of *The Photographs of
Abraham Lincoln* (1944). Ralph Newman wrote in the meeting
notice that: "The Meserve Collection, comprising in entirety
more than a hundred thousand items, includes many of the
priceless original Brady portrait negatives, taken in the New
York and Washington Brady studios during the 1850s and
1860s. Dr. Meserve is arranging a display of photographs for
exhibition on the day of our meeting." Carl Sandburg wrote of
Meserve: "Down in the teeming, bustling wholesale textile
district of the island of Manhattan you might have found most
any day of the last four decades a quiet-spoken businessman
who had what some people would construe as a hobby—just
a hobby. But he was no hobbyist. Instead of a hobby it was a
passion that quietly, incessantly moved him in a work he had
conceived. It took time. It took sustained effort and true
devotion to carry on the conception. As the years passed, he
wrought it out—and became the acknowledged foremost
authority on the photographs of Abraham Lincoln."[1]

On February 19, 1954, Ralph Newman, now Round
Table vice president—the following September he would
begin the year of his presidency, during the 1954-1955 term—
served as moderator for a panel discussion on "Has The
Lincoln Theme Been Exhausted: A Reappraisal." The topic
was inspired by a paper delivered eighteen years earlier by
the late James G. Randall, Lincoln scholar, author, and Round
Table member. In the meeting notice, Newman observed

that: ". . . Dr. Randall pointed out most vividly that the Lincoln theme had not been exhausted. He outlined many projects to be done and led in showing the way. . . . The Round Table is proud to try to carry on the analysis of the Lincoln literature as it stands today . . . " He urged members to give thought to the theme and "to come prepared." "Let's have an old-fashioned Round Table discussion," he urged. "We can," he said, "in this manner, show our appreciation of the great work of Dr. Randall . . ." Panel participants, in addition to Newman, were Joseph L. Eisendrath, Jr., Seymour J. Frank, Elmer Gertz, Ralph Korngold, William Herzog, and E.B. (Pete) Long.

The years 1954 and 1955 saw some of the established historians of the day as well as some of the promising new ones speaking at Round Table meetings. T. Harry Williams, distinguished author and professor of history at Louisiana State University, spoke on "The Patterns of an Historian" in March of 1954. He addressed the group again fourteen months later; his topic then was "Beauregard the Man." "Around the Circuit with Lincoln and Davis" was Chicago attorney Willard L. King's topic on May 20. The talk was a preview of his soon-to-be-published biography of the former associate of Lincoln's and United States Supreme Court justice, *Lincoln's Manager, David Davis* (1960). Harold M. Hyman spoke in November on "The Loyalty Oath in the Civil War." His book, *Era of the Oath: Northern Loyalty Tests During the Civil War*, was published that year. Such respected and renowned historians as Bruce Catton, R. Gerald McMurtry, and Benjamin P. Thomas were Round Table speakers in 1955.

A joint meeting of the Chicago and Milwaukee Round Tables took place in the fall of 1954. It was billed as "a weekend of Civil War and football." Included on November 5 were a luncheon, an open house at the State Historical Society of Wisconsin, and a dinner followed by an address by Harry Barnard on "Rutherford B. Hayes and His America." The next day the Illinois and Wisconsin Round Tablers attended the Wisconsin-Northwestern football game. The meeting notice said that "the Simon House has assured us of late operations to accommodate those who wish to continue the talk on either the Civil War or football." The cost of Friday's dinner is listed as $5.00.

Two events honored the seventy-fifth birthday of founding member Otto Eisenschiml in June of 1955. On the 16th he was the speaker at the regular monthly dinner meeting held in the Wedgwood Room of the Pearson Hotel. Ralph Newman wrote in the meeting notice: "An eminent chemist and businessman, Dr. Eisenschiml began as what we would call an amateur in history, but in the best sense of the word he has long since become a true historian. Still, through it all is the humor, the clarity, the enthusiasm of the man who loves his avocation. Not that all of us agree with his findings entirely, but we respect them, and Dr. Eisenschiml himself would be the last to ask us to side completely with him. Now, as he reaches seventy-five, we have this opportunity to honor one of the founders of The Civil War Round Table, a man who has added so much to its reputation for straight-shooting, hard-fighting history." Eisenschiml's topic that evening was, appropriate to his reputation, "An Unorthodox View of the Civil War."

On the 19th, Round Table members held a special "75th Birthday Tribute to Otto Eisenschiml" at the South Shore Country Club. Carl Haverlin, making a special trip to be present for the occasion, took an early flight to Chicago that day and headed for the Abraham Lincoln Book Shop. He and Ralph Newman decided to pool their mental resources and devise some inventive addition to the evening's program. Newman fondly recalls the results of their brainstorming: "Carl and I came up with a gag presentation. We went through the book shop looking for something and we discovered a *carte de visite* photograph of an unknown Civil War soldier. We developed a script and that evening I went up on the podium and said that, knowing this important birthday of Otto's was coming up, we had been engaged in a search for the last year or so to find something significant we could give him—perhaps some new bit of evidence on the Lincoln murder that had somehow escaped his attention—as a token of our affection. Leading the search, I announced, has been Carl Haverlin who has come in from New York to make this presentation.

Carl Haverlin

"Carl got up and said, 'I have here a photograph of Jonathan K. Smith, private, 93rd Maine Volunteers.' (There were no 93rd Maine Volunteers.) Embellishing the story, Carl continued, 'Private Smith, on the evening of April 14th, 1865, sat in Row C, Seat 14 at Ford's Theater. Till the day he died, in January of 1904, he maintained that he hadn't the slightest idea what had happened in the Presidential Box that night.' He then presented, with much flourish, the *carte de visite* to Otto. Everyone laughed and applauded. The next day, Otto called me. He said, 'How did you ever find that thing? That's great!' He hadn't gotten the gag. He believed the whole fabricated story and I didn't have the heart to tell him any differently. He continued to believe it was authentic."[2]

Though women were still not admitted as members, a special "Ladies Night" was held on December 9, 1955, at the Svithiod Singing Club. Civil War movies, provided by the State Historical Society of Wisconsin, were shown and songs were sung by balladeer Keith Clark of Ottowa. "Ladies Night" became an annual event through 1977.

On October 8-9, 1955, members and ladies joined in the annual meeting and tour of the Illinois State Historical Society at Galena. New CWRT President E.B. (Pete) Long conducted a panel and discussion on "Galena's Influence on Ulysses S. Grant" and Elmer Gertz spoke on "Galena's Other Generals."

The Round Table celebrated its 150th meeting, on April 1, 1956, with a special meeting. Eminent historian, teacher, and writer William B. Hesseltine spoke on "The Prison at Andersonville." The dinner was held at the Pearson Hotel and featured entertainment by folksinger and Round Table member Win Stracke. Honorary Life membership awards were presented to Dr. Hesseltine and to Dr. Avery O. Craven. (See Appendix D for a list of Honorary Life members.)

The battlefield tours continued to be welcomed events each spring. From May 13-17, 1954, the group toured Shiloh and Vicksburg as well as some additional Civil War sites in surrounding areas. At Jackson, Tennessee, T. Harry Williams spoke on Beauregard and his part in the Battle of Shiloh. At Vicksburg, Bell I. Wiley discussed "On the Trail of the Confederacy." Eva W. Davis, curator of the Old Court House Museum, and women from the Warren County Historical Society were hostesses to the Round Table members at a coffee hour. On the tour's final day, the campaigners lunched on the riverboat *Sprague*, the historic "Big Mama" sternwheeler of the Mississippi River, and enjoyed motor launch rides on the Yazoo Canal.

The itinerary for the 1955 tour included Fredericksburg, Chancellorsville, The Wilderness, and Spotsylvania. Approximately seventy-five Round Table members flew to Washington, D.C. in two chartered planes, where they were met by buses which took them to the tour sites. Thursday night's speaker was Ezra J. Warner, who would later write *Generals in Gray* (1959) and *Generals in Blue* (1964).

Ezra J. Warner speaking during the 1955 tour

The group saw the spot where Thomas "Stonewall" Jackson was fatally wounded at Chancellorsville, where his arm is buried, and the house in which he died. During this day of the tour, historian J. Ambler Johnston provided a moving, even spine-tingling, demonstration of "living history." At the very spot where Robert E. Lee and Jackson held their conference before Jackson left on his now famous flank attack, Johnston told the story of that meeting. He concluded by saying, "Jackson then got out his watch to verify his time with Lee." At that point, he pulled out of his pocket the actual watch of "Stonewall" Jackson. Johnston had persuaded the board of directors of the local museum which owned the

The 150th meeting on April 12, 1956 at the Pearson Hotel

watch to release the item in his care for twenty-four hours. (He would repeat this demonstration for the Round Table tour in 1968.) For lovers of history, moments like this are thrilling reminders that we are part of our past and that the past is relevant to the present.

The 1955 tour was the first year for the Baffartt Award, created by Ralph Newman and Jerry Slechta, with "tongues-in-cheeks" for "excellence in imbibing." The acronym deciphered is: "Best Armful for the Annual Round Table Tour." On the actual trophy the name of each year's winner was engraved. (It was passed on from one year's winner to the next year's.) Each winner also received a hollow cane, containing vials capable of holding liquid refreshment.

J. Ambler Johnston speaking to The Round Table in 1966

The first "honoree" was John "Rebel" Peacock of North Carolina. Peacock was quite a character. He carried a supply of pencils to distribute on his journeys. On each pencil was imprinted: "John R. (Rebel) Peacock, unpardoned, unrepentant, unreconstuctible. Save your Confederate money, boys. The South shall rise again." Several Round Table members promised his pleading wife to try to see that John stayed straight during the tour. This proved to be a formidable and impossible task. John was very ingenious and totally unreconstructed. Bob Douglas remembered the sighs of relief when several Round Tablers finally managed to get him on the plane at the tour's end. The relief was short-lived. As the plane prepared for take-off, they looked out the window to see John on the apron of the airport, waving goodbye to his Round Table "buddies."[3]

The Baffartt was awarded during thirteen consecutive tours. It was discontinued after 1967, as its appropriateness had diminished by that time. (See Appendix E for a complete listing of Baffartt Award winners.)

Round Tabler Gilbert (Gil) Twiss, a *Chicago Tribune* copy editor, wrote in the Fall 1956 *Lincoln Herald:* "Chattanooga-Atlanta Campaign, Sixth Annual Tour, 1956, The Civil War Round Table,' the big blue and gray name badges read. The tour began in Chicago on Wednesday, May 16, and was eventful every moment until the campaigners returned on May 21. Forty occupants of the three special Pullmans got their first surprise when *The Georgian* of the Chicago and Eastern Illinois Railroad made a half-hour stop at Evansville, Indiana at 10:20 p.m.

"The din of a caliope, bugles, drums, cannon shots, and firecrackers introduced Bish Thompson and a gang from the Civil War Round Table of Vanderburgh Court House, Inc. Carrying signs and dressed in uniforms and stovepipe hats, they passed out reprints of the July 18, 1862 Newburgh (Indiana) *Register* and visited with the campaigners

*The welcome at Evansville
on the way to Chattanooga
for the 1956 tour*

until the train left.

"Awakening in Chattanooga, the first attraction was 'The General,' engine of 'The Great Locomotive Chase,' in the station of the Nashville, Chattanooga, and St. Louis Railway. Sixteen more campaigners joined the tour at breakfast in the Reed House. Miss Drue Smith of station WDEF conducted interviews for radio and television.

"Two Greyhound buses, placarded 'Leonidas Polk' and 'General McPherson'—the heroes who were killed at Pine Mountain and Atlanta—took the party aboard . . ." This began the now fondly cherished tradition of naming tour buses for Civil War generals. The pre-tour announcement informed its readers that: "Five previous battlefield tours have always proved that campaigners get more than their money's worth. $160 from Chicago includes train, Pullman, and bus fares; all meals except breakfasts; and admissions to meetings and parks."

"An innovation to this trip," Twiss noted in the *Lincoln Herald* article, "was the presence of Margaret April . . ." For the first time, a woman was allowed to go on a Round Table battlefield tour. Margaret April remembers it well: "The Round Table had several private cars on the train that year. But they said that I could not be in one of those cars because . . . it was no place for a woman. So, I decided that if I couldn't ride with the group, I wouldn't take the train; I'd fly."[4]

She flew to Chattanooga where she was met by several tour members who had arrived early. The next day, they met the group at the train station. She said that she had never before or since seen such a disheveled group of people. The effects of staying up most of the night on their journey was quite evident. "As I recall," she continued, "at that time there was a hotel on top of Lookout Mountain. That's where we stayed. They drove me in the tour bus to Lookout Mountain, dropped-off me and their baggage, and then the group went sightseeing. I wasn't with them for the first half-day. I took care of getting everyone's baggage put in their rooms and so forth. That was what they wanted me along for. Thereafter, I worked it down to a fine art so that I did not have to stay behind."[5]

Speakers during the tour included Dr. Frank E. Vandiver, of the history department at Rice University; Colonel Allen P. Julian, director of the Atlanta Historical Society; and Dr. Bell I. Wiley, of the history department of Emory University and author of, among other books, *Billy Yank* (1952) and *Johnny Reb* (1943). Twiss wrote in the *Lincoln Herald*: "The party stopped at White Columns, the new home of WSB Radio and WSB-TV in Atlanta. Carl Haverlin, president of the Civil War Centennial Association, presented J. Leonard Reinsch, director of the station, with a scroll honoring the placing of a historic marker at White Columns, the site of a southern camp on the eve of the Battle of Peachtree Creek. Members of The Round Table were interviewed for radio and TV."

Writing about the Saturday night activities, Twiss continued: "Then, at Brookhaven Country Club, there was 'Fun Night.' The program was arranged by Marcus Bartless, program director of WSB-TV. A high point of the evening was songs by the special mixed choir of forty voices from North Fulton High School, directed by Bob Lorenz. . . . Phil and Nancy Erickson presented make-believe songs. Warren Foster as monologist was the master of many voices.

"The climax was a special preview showing, for our tour, of the documentary film on Gettysburg, photographed on the battlefield. Campaigners were pleased to see the name of an old friend, Dr. J. Walter Coleman, as technical adviser for the film. At the Brookhaven meeting, incoming President Harold (Hal) Hixson of the Chicago Round Table, presented CWRT pins[6] to Colonel Julian, Beverly Dubose, and Wilbur Kurtz, Jr., from Atlanta for their parts in making the tour a success." In his summation of the tour, Twiss noted that: "Ralph Newman, Carl Haverlin, Pete Long, and Hal Hixson were in demand for radio and television interviews. The local press of Chattanooga, Atlanta, and Marietta gave good coverage to the tour. The national press associations sent out some stories. An advance story on the tour was widely printed."

Thus, by the spring of 1956, The Civil War Round Table was a stable and growing organization. It was not only recognized and respected by the historical community but had gained considerable attention in the local and national media. And another significant milestone had been reached: a woman had actually been allowed to be a participant in an annual battlefield tour—even if she was there primarily to work.

Chapter 8 ☆ *The Pre-Centennial Years: The Round Table Begins to Blossom and Mature*

THE ATLANTA HISTORICAL SOCIETY'S Colonel Allen P. Julian—companion, lecturer, and guide from the past spring's battlefield tour—came to Chicago in October of 1956 to talk to The Round Table about "The Savannah Campaign." (The group was seeing a lot of Colonel Julian. Prior to the tour, he had spoken at the regular May meeting on "The Atlanta Campaign".) The second annual "Ladies Night" was held on December 7, again at the Svithiod Singing Club on Wrightwood Avenue. Bish Thompson, a columnist for the *Evansville Press* and commanding officer of the Civil War Round Table of Vanderburgh Court House, Indiana, advised the group "How to Enjoy a War." It was Bish who had led the exhuberant and noisy group which greeted The Round Table tour train as it passed through his town the previous spring.

The 157th meeting on January 17, 1957 was indeed a memorable one. Ralph Newman wrote in the meeting notice: "Robert E. Lee was born 150 years ago on January 19th, so our next meeting . . . will be largely devoted to his great biographer, Douglas Southall Freeman, who so generously entertained us on the Richmond trip of 1953. . . . His friend of many years, J. Ambler Johnston, will tell some of his experiences

J. Ambler Johnston, Mrs. Douglas Southall Freeman, Jerry Slechta, and Ralph Newman at the 157th Meeting

with Dr. Freeman during the years of research and writing *R.E. Lee* (1934) and *Lee's Lieutenants* (1942-1944), as well as other things bearing on Freeman as other than a historian . . ." The title of Johnston's address was "Lee and Freeman." The meeting was held in the Georgian Room of the Pearson Hotel.

Johnston, who had been Freeman's friend since both were in their late twenties, had been of invaluable assistance in the author's research for his books. Freeman, of course, recognized and appreciated this. Round Table President Harold (Hal) Hixson noted in his introduction of Johnston that night that: . . ."On the flyleaf of Volume I of Freeman's *Lee*, he, in his meticulous hand, inscribed the following: 'To J. Ambler Johnston, friend of many years, companion in studying the battlefields named in these pages. A candid counsellor, a prudent critic, a true southerner.'"[1] Together, as fellow-pioneers, Freeman and Johnston had begun the fight for the preservation of our Civil War battlefield sites. In his address, Johnston observed: "It would be hard to make you realize the condition of the fields around Richmond when the preliminary work was done on Freeman's *R.E. Lee*."

A story that Johnston related that evening, in discussing the historical research for Freeman's books, pointed out how serendipitous the finding of some crucial historical fact can sometimes be: "An amusing incident in connection with Mrs. Lee is referred to in a footnote on page 254 of *R.E. Lee*, Volume II. At Freeman's Current Events class one night, he dwelt at length on how a historian sometimes runs against a blank wall. Mrs. Lee left the White House when McClellan came up the peninsula, and some weeks later the records, both Federal and Confederate, were complete on her passing through the Federal lines into Confederate territory. 'Where,' asked Freeman, 'had Mrs. Lee been meanwhile?' He had exhausted every available source of information. It was a total blank.

"After the meeting, I went home and my mother, eighty-two years of age at the time, and sharp as a briar, asked, as she did every Monday night, 'What did Dr. Freeman talk about tonight?' I told her, to which she replied, 'That's perfectly ridiculous. Anyone with his knowledge should have known where she was. She was at Malbourne. She occupied the front room on the left at the head of the steps on the second floor. I remember so well the day she went through the lines. They had no carriage at Malbourne, so they sent over to Ingleside to borrow ours, and I remember Uncle Albert, the coachman, fixing a white flag on a stick and putting it in the whip socket. I rode over to Malbourne with him, and stayed there until the carriage came back after it had taken her down to the lines.'

"I asked, 'Mother, why haven't you told me this before?' And she replied, 'Why, you never asked me.'

"I immediately went to the phone and called Freeman. Mrs. Freeman answered the phone and said, 'I am sorry but Douglas has gone to bed.' 'Wake him up,' I said. 'I might die tonight and I am going to get this information over to him at once.' She woke him up."

Johnston concluded his talk with this observation: ". . . An author of long ago lives when his writing guides us. And when we study the lives of great and good men, we come under their influence. May it not be possible then, at this very moment, right here and now, that we are in touch with immortality?"[2] At the meeting's end, J. Ambler Johnston was awarded an Honorary Life membership in The Civil War Round Table.

Pete Long gave 1957's February address on "Lincoln and Fort Sumter." On April 12, a special meeting was held at the Lincoln National Life Foundation in Fort Wayne, Indiana. Bruce Catton spoke on "Lincoln as Commander-in-Chief."

The seventh annual battlefield tour traveled to the Shenandoah Valley. The group departed on May 14 aboard New York Central Train Number 4, the *James Whitcomb Riley*. Among the places visited were the Virginia Military Institute; Washington and Lee University; and the battlefields of Port Republic, New Market, Cedar Creek, Winchester, Antietam, Ball's Bluff, and White's Ferry. They also visited Harpers Ferry, Shepherdstown, and the Luray Caverns. Speakers included Lee Bushong of the Winchester Civil War Round Table and Rev. Joseph T. Durkin, S.J., professor of history at Georgetown University and author of several books on the Civil War.

A joint meeting of the Chicago and Springfield Round Tables took place on September 28, 1957. The afternoon session convened in the Illinois State Historical Library, then located in the Centennial Building (constructed on the site of the Ninian W. Edwards home—where Abraham and Mary Lincoln first met, were married, and where Mary died) in Springfield. The group viewed the Horner Collection and attended the formal dedication of the collection of Round Table member and past President Alfred Whital Stern.

The featured speaker at the dinner held at the Illini Country Club was Governor William G. Stratton, a member of both Round Tables. In the meeting notice, Ralph Newman wrote that Governor Stratton had ". . . long been identified with the subjects of Lincoln and the Civil War. His middle name is Grant, after the general. The governor's father, William J. Stratton, was an admirer of Grant, an interest which the governor also possesses. The governor was instrumental in authorizing the restoration of the Grant home in Galena and participated in its rededication."

The Arts Club was the site for the third annual "Ladies Night" on November 1. Harnett T. Kane spoke on "The Gallant Mrs. Stonewall," the title of his latest (1957) novel. The novel on Mary Anna Morrison Jackson was written as a companion work to Kane's *The Lady of Arlington* (1953) about Mary Lee and *Bride of Fortune* (1948) about Varina Davis.

The year 1958 got off to a good start for The Civil War Round Table. A.E. (Abe) Geldhof wrote in the Spring 1958 *Lincoln Herald*: "A record attendance of 162 for a regular meeting turned out on January 24 at the club's old meeting place, the Maryland Hotel, to hear that always interesting speaker, Dr. Frederick Tilberg, historian of the Gettysburg National Battlefield Park, discourse on the second and third days of the Battle of Gettysburg. Overcoming electronic difficulties, Dr. Tilberg used a graphic series of screened maps to illustrate his step-by-step description of Longstreet's attack on Sickles' advanced line on July 2nd and Pickett's drive on the 3rd."

Geldhof added that: "President [Marshall W.] Rissman made a full report of his attendance a few days previously at the meeting of the Centennial Commission in Washington. He was a little fearful that the Commission may be drifting too far afield in its far-flung program. . . ." R. Gerald McMurtry, director of the Lincoln National Life Foundation, spoke in February on "Lincoln's Address at Gettysburg." Bell I. Wiley came in April to talk about "The Confederate Congress." In May, Otto Eisenschiml returned to The Round Table podium. He spoke on the subject matter of his new book, *Why the Civil War?* (1958). Ralph Newman wrote of Eisenschiml in the meeting notice that: ". . . His favorite position has been the unorthodox and the provocative. There has never been a dull moment and great has been the discussion stimulated." Otto Eisenschiml was never known to disappoint his audience.

Fort Donelson, Nashille, Franklin, and Stones River were on the agenda for the eighth annual battlefield tour. The campaigners departed on May 15 on the Chicago and Eastern Illinois train, *The Dixie Flyer*. One of the speakers that year was Round Table member and noted Confederate historian Stanley F. Horn. Author of *The Army of the Tennessee* (1941) and *The Robert E. Lee Reader* (1949), Horn was editor of *The Southern Lumberman*. Horn's father-in-law, Sims Crownover, a Nashville attorney, also addressed the tour group. Horn's topic was "The Battlefields Around Nashville." Crownover talked about "The Battle of Franklin." Friday night's dinner was held in the Club Room of the historic Maxwell House, where The Round Table members were the guests of the Tennessee Historical Society. A reproduction of an 1879 Maxwell House menu was given as a souvenir of the evening.

Al Meyer (right) with Arnold Alexander on the 1963 tour to Richmond

There were a couple of innovations during this tour. On the front page of the newsletter announcing the tour, in bold print, were these words: **"Ladies are invited on tour."** The other new development was the assignment of "bus marshals." Gil Twiss wrote in the tour newsletter: "The tour schedule is such that prompt unloading and boarding of buses will be necessary. Marshals to keep the show 'on time' on the road will be Al Meyer and George Donovan. They will also cue the 'auto train' traveling in the wake of the buses." Al Meyer would become famous for the whistle he carried around his neck to effectively round-up his troops.

The Lincoln-Douglas Debate Centennial was commemorated in Galesburg, Illinois on October 4 through 7, 1958. This provided an occasion for a joint meeting of Civil War Round Tables and the Illinois State Historical Society. The itinerary was crammed-full; nearly every hour of the four-day celebration was taken up with speeches and activities. Speakers included Allan Nevins, Willard L. King, Bruce Catton, Carl Sandburg, E.B. (Pete) Long, and William B. Hesseltine. Tuesday, October 7, was "Centennial Day." At 3:00 p.m., attendees could view a reenactment of the Lincoln-Douglas debate of that date 100 years earlier. On the platform were Carl Sandburg, Illinois Senators Everett M. Dirksen and Paul H. Douglas, and narrator Ken Carpenter. This was one of those once-in-a-lifetime experiences in which Round Table members were privileged to participate.

Round Tablers traveled by plane, bus, and boat during the ninth annual battlefield tour to Charleston and Savannah

Preparing to depart for Charleston

(April 29-May 3, 1959). According to the tour newsletter, $190 covered the costs for "plane, bus, and boat fares; hotel (two to a room with bath); all meals (except where stated); admission charges where required; tour literature; taxes and tips." A single room for the length of the tour would cost an additional $12. "Ladies" were again invited, as they would be for all subsequent tours.

Major General Ulysses S. Grant 3rd, U.S.A., Retired, grandson of the Civil War hero and president, was chairman of The Civil War Centennial Commisssion. Karl S. Betts, founder and past president of the Washington, D.C. Civil War Round Table, was executive director of the Commission. Both men spoke at the 181st meeting of The Civil War Round Table, on May 20, 1959, at the St. Clair Hotel. Ralph Newman wrote in the meeting notice: "The two men who direct the Civil War Centennial Commission will speak to us on "A Centennial for All Americans." Civil War Round Tables and Centennial Commissions of the middle west are invited to send representatives to this meeting to hear the report of programs, plans, and aims of the national commission. . . ."

Gilbert (Gil) Twiss

Over the past year, more "newsy" items of value to people with an interest in the Civil War had begun to appear as part of the meeting notices. In September 1959, a brand new publication was born. The newsletter of The Civil War Round Table, in the professional format that we know today, appeared for the first time. It was the work of Gilbert (Gil) Twiss, Round Table secretary for the 1959-1960 term. Twiss, a *Chicago Tribune* copy editor, continued as editor of the newsletter until his death in 1968. He generally wrote his copy on his typewriter at a desk that Ralph Newman provided in a corner of the Abraham Lincoln Book Shop. The newsletter of The Civil War Round Table in Chicago remains the preeminent newsletter of all the Civil War Round Tables throughout the world.

Jerry Slechta began his term of presidency (1959-1960) on a high note. Not only could he boast of his organization's slick new monthly newsletter, but his first speaker was Allan Nevins, whose September talk was titled "The Darkest Hour of the War in the Northwest."

The first Civil War Tour of Chicago occurred on Sunday, October 18. Included on the itinerary were a brunch at the Lincoln Inn on LaSalle Street; an address at the Chicago Historical Society by Director (and Round Table member) Paul M. Angle; and stops with informative talks at Rosehill Cemetery, the Lincoln Statue on Lincoln Avenue, the tomb of Stephen A. Douglas, and Oak Woods Cemetery. The day concluded with cocktails and hors d'oeuvres at the Abraham Lincoln Book Shop.

Round Table president Jerry Slechta (left) with Chicago Police Commissioner Timothy J. O'Connor on the 1959 tour of Chicago

The tour had a police escort, led by Chicago Police Commissioner Timothy J. O'Connor. Twiss wrote in the newsletter that O'Connor was "one of the city's outstanding students on Camp Douglas and Confederate prison camps . . ." He joined the group at the Chicago Historical Society, participated in the discussions along the way, and spoke at Oak Woods Cemetery. This tour served as 1959's "Ladies Day."

Civil War scholar and author Stephen Ambrose addressed The Round Table on November 12. His topic was "Old Brains: the Civil War Career of Henry Wager Halleck." This had been the subject of Ambrose's master's thesis, written while he was a teaching assistant to T. Harry Williams at Louisiana State University.

Ambrose was the author of an article on the Round Table movement, which had been published the previous summer in the *Wisconsin Magazine of History*. Titled "The Civil War Round Tables," the magazine editor called it: "An illuminating account of an increasingly popular movement—which at home and abroad is making America's Irrepressible Conflict one of the best-studied wars in history."[3]

Ambrose concludes the article by observing that: "Round Tablers share a deep and abiding belief that the Civil War is the central theme in American history. Their feelings are well expressed in the opening statement of the 1956-1957 Washington Round Table yearbook: 'The fifty years preceding the great conflict sounded only the opening chords in the prologue to the dramatic events of the Sixties.' The Round Tables are another evidence that the quiver has not yet subsided, and that a catastrophe which divided the nation a hundred years ago is, today, through the Civil War Round Tables, helping to unite it."[4]

Chapter 9 ☆ *Centennial Years*

A S THE ROUND TABLE ENTERED THE 1960s, interest in the era it studies was surging—the years of the Civil War Centennial were at hand. Civil War Centennial Commissions were forming—nationally, state-wide, and in many large cities. Round Table members participated in the work of these commissions. Ralph Newman served as chairman of the Civil War Centennial Commission of Chicago and vice-chairman of the Illinois Commission.

Battlefield tours took on a special meaning during these years. Gil Twiss wrote in the 1960 battlefield tour edition of the newsletter: "The tenth tour probably will touch more points of historic interest than any previous tour. . . . Previous tours have covered most all major Civil War battlefields. This tour will furnish an opportunity for discussion of the tour schedule for the four centennial years."

Richmond and Manassas were the major sites to be covered in 1960. In April, Ralph Newman served as moderator for a Round Table "Symposium on Battlefields of Virginia to be Visited on the Tenth Annual Battlefield Tour." On the panel were Otto Eisenschiml, E.B. (Pete) Long, and John Patrick Hunter. The dates for the annual pilgrimage were April 27-May 1. According to the tour newsletter, check-in time was "7:45 a.m., Central Daylight Time, Wednesday, April 27, with Registrar Margaret April in American Airlines waiting rooms at Midway Airport. . . ." By that time, Registrar April had put in many hours of effort in planning the logistics of the trip, as she had done each year since 1951 and would continue to do until she turned the job over to others in 1985. She was also in charge of seeing that the tour kits were stuffed and transported to the airport. She recalled that: "We had someone decide which reading material would be useful. I would order the tour kits and the badges and would arrange for someone to come in to the book shop on a Saturday morning to stuff the kits, and then we would all go out to lunch."[1]

After a luncheon at the Princess Anne Hotel in

Fredericksburg, Virginia, that Wednesday, the group checked in at their "command post," the John Marshall Hotel in Richmond. By 3:30 p.m., they were off for their first stops of the tour—Battle Abbey, the White House of the Confederacy, and the Capitol. Dinner speakers that year included Francis Wilshin, Superintendent of Manassas National Battlefield Park, and Governor J. Lindsey Almond, of Virginia.

A committee composed largely of Round Table members and friends threw a birthday party for Otto Eisenshiml in June. An item in the June 1960 newsletter mentions that: "Dr. Otto Eisenschiml will be honored by a group of friends on the penthouse terrace of the Sherman Hotel the evening of Sunday, June 19. Taking note of his familiar initials, the committee in charge has tagged the party 'O.E. at 80.' . . . To us of The Civil War Round Table, there is no higher figure than Otto. He is a founder, an honorary award member, a diligent researcher and writer, and a speaker who will rise at the drop of a questionable statement." The engraved invitation stated that the dinner was "celebrating the eightieth birthday of the incredible and inimitable Otto Eisenshiml." A souvenir booklet was prepared for the event, containing extracts from tributes from O.E.'s friends, including Carl Sandburg, Judge Abraham Lincoln Marovitz, and Governor William G. Stratton. Ralph Newman wrote the introduction.[2]

C. Robert Douglas, president for the 1960-1961 term, had the honor of presiding at the Twentieth Anniversary meeting of The Civil War Round Table on November 4. Gil Twiss wrote in the newsletter: "The Twentieth Anniversary dinner of The Civil War Round Table will present the same speaker in the same locale as the first meeting in 1940. The

"O E at 80"

Being the committee for a dinner
celebrating the eightieth birthday
of the incredible and inimitable
Otto Eisenschiml

June 19, 1960

Dinner Committee

Paul M. Angle	Dr. Robert L. Kincaid
Margaret April	Irv Kupcinet
Rabbi Louis Binstock	E. B. Long
Dr. Preston Bradley	Herb Lyon
Bruce Catton	Judge Abraham L. Marovitz
Edward Cavenaugh	David C. Mearns
Ellen Cozzens	Dr. Karl A. Meyer
Dr. Raymond Dooley	N. Floyd McGowin
C. Robert Douglas	Dr. R. Gerald McMurtry
Robert Elson	Dr. Allan Nevins
Newton C. Farr	Ralph G. Newman
Dr. Bernard S. Friedman	Norman Ross
Elmer Gertz	Carl Sandburg
Seymour Goldfarb	Jerome M. Slechta
Nate Gross	Dr. Charles Stevens
Gertrude Gscheidle	Walter Trohan
Dr. Walter Guthman	Dr. Frank E. Vandiver
Robert Selph Henry	Dr. Clyde C. Walton
Judge Harry G. Hershenson	Tony Weitzel
Stanley F. Horn	B. C. Yates

You are cordially invited to attend a
Buffet Dinner
in honor of
Otto Eisenschiml
on Sunday evening, the nineteenth of June
nineteen hundred and sixty
Skyline Terrace, Sherman Hotel
Chicago, Illinois

R.s.v.p.
Ralph G. Newman
18 East Chestnut
Chicago, Illinois

Cocktails at five-thirty

Percival G. Hart speaking at the 20th Anniversary Meeting of The Round Table on November 4, 1960

group gathered then was the forerunner of a spontaneous movement that has now grown to about one hundred-twenty Civil War Round Tables in the United States and abroad."

Founding member Percival G. Hart, returning to Chicago from his home in California for the event, spoke in the Walnut Room of the Bismarck Hotel on "The Campaign of Chancellorvsille." Recalling the founding of The Civil War Round Table, Hart said: "My own connection with the group came through my lifelong friend Newton Farr, who first steered me to Ralph Newman's Home of Books on Madison Street, across from the LaSalle Hotel . . ."[3] After moving to the west coast, Hart was instrumental in forming the Civil War Round Table of Southern California. Recalling the founding of that Round Table, he stated that: ". . . we arranged for the first meeting in January 1955, with Irving Stone as speaker. We are enjoying an interesting and prosperous career, with about one-hundred active members. I was honored to serve as the first president."[4] One hundred-thirty men attended the Twentieth Anniversary meeting.

News from across the Atlantic Ocean appeared in the November 1960 newsletter: "A letter from Patrick C. Courtney, secretary-treasurer of The Confederate Research Club of England said: 'Steps are being taken to bring about a change of constitution of the CRC, which will, subject to the necessary number of votes being cast by the membership, change its name to THE AMERICAN CIVIL WAR ROUND TABLE, U.K. (United Kingdom). All being well, this change is scheduled for January 1, 1961. It marks a change in policy which will bring a better understanding of the Civil War, and it will come at an appropriate time at the beginning of the Centennial.'

"Mr. Courtney said 'we shall cease to use the Confederate Battle Flag as our emblem.' He requested permission of the Chicago CWRT to use our lapel pin and shoulder patch. Samples of these have been sent to Mr. Courtney with the information that American CWRT, U.K. members are welcome to use the design, as many Round Tables in this country already are doing.

"Chicago CWRT members who are also members of the British group include W. Norman FitzGerald, Richard B. Harwell, Carl Haverlin, Colonel Robert S. Henry, Stanley F. Horn, E.B. Long, Ralph G. Newman, and John R. Peacock."

The American Civil War Round Table, U.K., in 1990, is still going strong. The organization publishes a newsletter, which is sent to the editor of the Chicago newsletter. Chicago Round Table members have attended and addressed meetings of their sister group when visiting in London.

People were getting "geared-up" for the Civil War Centennial in this country and around the world. This item appeared on page one of the January 1961 newsletter under the headline, "Ike's Centennial Appeal": "In a proclamation on December 7, President Eisenhower asked the American people to take a direct and active part in the centennial of the Civil War and commemorate a conflict he called the United States' most tragic experience. He requested all federal, state, and local government agencies 'to encourage, foster, and participate' in the centennial observance."

Round Table members were taking time to develop some of their special interest areas. This is from the February 1961 newsletter: "Joseph L. Eisendrath, Jr., who is working on a study of Civil War weather and is enlisting helpers, has prepared some cards for recording data: date, place, time, temperature, wind, barometer, ground condition; author, title of work, page, and quotation." Persons who wished to help work on the project were urged to contact Joe Eisendrath.

News regarding a growing interest in and movement towards battlefield preservation began to surface in the newsletters in 1961. January's issue reported on the first annual meeting of the Gettysburg Battlefield Preservation Association. Its executive director "reported that the association 'has managed to save two of the most important sites on the Gettysburg Battlefield from commercialization.'" (The sites referred to were the 55-acre Wolf tract adjoining Devil's Den and the 118-acre Meals Farm area.) Information about battlefield preservation has continued to be an intergral part of the newsletter up to the present.

In the March newsletter, Gil Twiss informed readers of Illinois Senate Bill Number 39, which would provide $1,015,000 for the purchase and restoration of the Old State Capitol in

Springfield—where Abraham Lincoln gave his House Divided speech and where his body had lain in state. "Your support of this bill," Twiss advised, "can be expressed in a letter to your state senator."

The Civil War Round Table was coming into full bloom as it entered the first year of the Civil War Centennial. Twiss reported in February that there were "323 paid members as of January 1, 1961." Nearly every issue of the newsletter carried reports of other Round Tables around the country and world, as well as informing readers of various Centennial plans in other states.

The Civil War Round Table celebrated its 200th meeting on April 7. The man chosen to speak for this special occasion was an old friend—Frank E. Vandiver, who had "quivered in his boots" as an awestruck young scholar of twenty-two when he addressed the group in 1947. (His record as the youngest Round Table speaker remains unchallenged today.) Vandiver, who was in 1961 a professor of history at Rice Institute in Houston, spoke on "The Confederacy and the New South." "Our April 7 meeting," Gil Twiss reported, "is a big round number—200. And, there's something else that's special about it. The speaker, Frank E. Vandiver, is an old time member and longtime friend. He was something of a 'boy wonder' back in the late 1940s when he could stump our older members with his knowledge of the Civil War. Since then, he has many a book, article, and lecture to his credit." "The meeting drew ninety-five," Twiss reported, and "was like old home week."

That "time for the next trip" came up from April 26-May 1. The 1961 focus was on the Vicksburg Campaign. The transportation to Mississippi was via train—the *Panama Limited*. Friday night's dinner was enjoyed aboard the riverboat *Sprague*. Round Tablers saw a melodrama titled "Gold in the Hills" and a performance by the Dixie Showboat Players.

Albert W. Banton, historian of the Vicksburg National Military Park, served as chief guide and lecturer for the tour. "He will be aided," Gil Twiss noted, "by Jerry Schober, assistant historian, and Edwin Bearss, regional research historian who two years ago was our speaker in Chicago on the battle of Champion Hill." Ed Bearss would become, over the years, a familiar and integral part of battlefield tours and a beloved friend of The Civil War Round Table.

Since the summer of 1959, The Round Table had been sponsoring annual golf outings. A special July newsletter in 1961 informed members that: "The third annual Mid-West Civil War Round Table golf outing will be held Saturday, July 15, 1961—and again on the pleasant and beautiful layout of the Meadow Springs Golf Club at Jefferson, Wisconsin.

Left Photo: *1961 Vicksburg tour campaigners (from left) Ned Julian, Hal Hixson, Wilson Smith, Frank Welcher, Brooks Davis, and a local guide*
Right Photo: *During the 1961 Vicksburg tour, Round Table president Bob Douglas (left) presented a check to Park Service historian Ed Bearss to support the raising and restoration of the* Cairo

"Though sponsored by the Chicago CWRT, invitation and welcome is extended to Round Tablers and friends from Milwaukee, Madison, Rockford, the Quad Cities, Peoria, Springfield, and in fact, Round Tablers from any-where. . . . President Gerhard P. Clausius will convene a meeting of Chicago CWRT officers and executive committee, but it will be tailored to fit into the day's activities and allow time for golf." The host was former President Jerry Slechta.

Otto Eisenschiml gave what was to be his last address to The Civil War Round Table on September 15, 1961. His topic was "Ethics and the Civil War Historian." In the next month's newsletter, Gil Twiss noted that: "Stirring discussion followed Dr. Otto Eisenschiml's paper. . . . After citing various historical writings, Dr. Eisenschiml proposed a code of historical and ethical 'don'ts.' They drew a quick reaction from the floor.

"Two motions were presented and the one adopted was by Judge Joseph Burke. This provides that Dr. Eisenschiml's proposed code be 'referred to the Executive Committee with directions to submit a report on the adoption of a suggested voluntary code for historical writers.'"[5]

Another item in the October newsletter noted that Illinois Governor Otto Kerner signed the measure for the state's purchase of the Old State Capitol building in Springfield for restoration as a permanent shrine to Lincoln. The restored building would house the state historical library and society and a Lincoln collection.

Round Tablers had a busy October in 1961. The regular meeting on the 12th featured Harold M. Hyman, speaking on "Lincoln's 'Mars': The Lincoln-Stanton Relationship." This was a preview of his soon-to-be-published book on the controversial cabinet member *Stanton: The Life and Times of Lincoln's Secretary of War*, with Benjamin P. Thomas (1962).

The Civil War Round Table sponsored a dinner as one event of the Northwestern University Civil War Centennial Symposium held on October 18 and 19 in Evanston. Northwestern had scheduled as speakers several premier Civil War scholars, such as Paul M. Angle, Bruce Catton, David Donald, Ralph G. Newman, and T. Harry Williams. The Round Table's dinner for symposium participants was held on October 19 at the Town House Restaurant at 6935 North Sheridan Road in Chicago.

On October 28 and 29, 1961, The Round Table sponsored its second tour to historically restored Galena, Illinois—where Ulysses S. Grant had lived for several years. Gil Twiss wrote: "Headquarters will be at the DeSoto House . . . [which was] Grant's campaign headquarters for the presidency . . ." The DeSoto House had been visited by both Abraham Lincoln and Stephen A. Douglas. The November 2 issue of the *Galena Gazette* carried a front page story on the Round Table's visit.

A "Ladies Night" was held on November 16 at JAZZ, Limited., featuring "Songs of the Civil War" performed by some of the city's top jazz musicians. Gil Twiss wrote that: "Ralph Newman will give a commentary on each of the Civil War songs. These include songs by Root & Cady, Chicago publishers who were kings of the Civil War Tin Pan Alley. Some of the original scores will be exhibited, from the collection of Broadcast Music, Inc. These were assembled by member Carl Haverlin, who is president of B.M.I." The *Chicago Tribune*, on Sunday, November 26, printed a story, with pictures, about the event. Under the headline "Swingin' to Civil War Jazz," writer Mary Middleton observed that there were ". . . no long, gray beards among these Civil War savants—a few mustaches perhaps—and no longhair music for the boys who marched off to battle 100 years ago either." The Round Table would return to JAZZ, Limited for a repeat performance in November of the following year.

The January 1962 newsletter carried a report of a change in the leadership of the national Civil War Centennial Commission. Major General U.S. Grant 3rd and Karl Betts were being replaced as chairman and executive director, respectively, by Allan Nevins and James L. (Bud) Robertson, Jr. Major General Grant was being retained as chairman emeritus. Gil Twiss wrote that: "Dr. Nevins, historian and Pulitzer Prize winning author, announced a deemphasis on battle reenactments, which he said will be left to local groups. . . . 'Above all, our central theme will be unity, not division . . . We shall allow the just pride of no national group to be belittled or besmirched,' Dr. Nevins said. . . . Battle reenactments were one point of dispute which led to a series of resignations from the commission in September. . . . Dr.

Nevins said that in the next two years special emphasis would be placed on the Emancipation Proclamation. . . ."

Ralph Newman observed that: "The Civil War Centennial was a strange mixture of intelligent and scholarly events and embarrassing 'reenactments' and poor planning. It all began with the first meeting at Charleston on the 100th anniversary of the firing on Fort Sumter, 12 April 1961. The leadership of the National Commission planned to have the first meeting at the Francis Marion Hotel. Then they acted surprised when they learned that black members of some state commissions would not be welcome at the hotel because of its segregation policies.

"When this was called to the attention of President Kennedy, he appointed Allan Nevins to become national chairman. . . . and the meeting was moved from the hotel to the Naval base in Charleston Harbor. I covered the meeting for the *Chicago Tribune* and also attended as vice president of the Illinois Civil War Centennial Commission. The opening lines of my story were censored by the *Tribune* copydesk: 'Because of segregation policies which prevented black members of some state commissions from attending the meeting at the Francis Marion Hotel in Charleston, the meeting was moved to the Naval base in the harbor where a different type of segregation was in effect—*a man could not sleep with his wife* in the quarters provided for us.'"[6] Under the leadership of Dr. Nevins and Dr. Robertson, the work of the Commission was accomplished with more ease and grace. Nevertheless, as Glen Wiche noted, "the Civil War Centennial mirrored some of the unsettled issues that the war itself tried to solve a century earlier."[7]

The time for the twelfth annual tour arrived. The dates were April 25-29; on the agenda were Gettysburg, Antietam, and Harpers Ferry. The transportation to and from the east was by plane. A high point was the "Antietam Free-for-all" discussion on Friday night, for which Pete Long served as moderator. Panelists were Edward Stackpole, Willard Webb, and Lloyd Miller. The superintendents and historians of the Gettysburg, Antietam, and Harpers Ferry sites served as commentators.

Something new was added to the battlefield tour badges that year: pendant ribbons listing all previous tours. Members were provided with gold stars to affix beside each tour in which they participated. Newton Farr, Hal Hixson, and Ralph Newman were the only ones who could claim a star for each of these tours.

The September 1962 newsletter carried the following item: "At the June 15 meeting, incoming President Warren A. Reeder, Jr. presented outgoing President Gerhard P. Clausius with a gavel—a tradition—and a rare document, a form signed by General Stephen A. Hurlbut, a Clausius favorite." Dr. Clausius (an optometrist from Belvidere, Illinois, home of his hero) would later be instrumental in providing a proper tombstone for General Hurlbut.

The September meeting was held at the Chicago Historical Society where Bell I. Wiley spoke on "Kingdom Coming," in honor of the centennial of the Emancipation Proclamation. Ladies were invited to this event. The preceding dinner was held at the Germania Club. Attendance was 140. In the October newsletter, Gil Twiss noted that: ". . . President Warren Reeder, Jr. introduced a number of guests, among them Representative Corneal Davis, chairman of the American Negro Emancipation Centennial Commission, and Representative William Robinson and Mrs. Edith Sampson of the Commission. . . ." Mrs. Sampson would later be appointed by the President of the United States as a delegate to the United Nations.

Dr. Gerhard P. Clausius, 1962-63 President, in 1981

The 214th regular meeting of The Civil War Round Table on October 26, 1962, took place in Springfield as part of the first Assembly of Illinois Civil War Round Tables. The speaker was James I. (Bud) Robertson, Jr., editor of *Civil War History*, executive director of the National Civil War Centennial Commission, and noted Civil War author and editor. His topic was "Billy Yanks from Iowa: An Example of Midwestern Gallantry."

The Civil War Centennial Commission of Illinois, on December 6, 1962, granted its Award of Merit to The Civil War Round Table of Chicago "for stimulating a deeper understanding of the Civil War period, for contributing to the general knowledge of the era, for encouraging patriotism, and for inspiring pride in our great American heritage." The award was signed by the Commission chairman, Senator Hudson R. Sours.

Members of The Round Table were invited to a special meeting on January 13, 1963 at the Lincoln Federal Savings and Loan Association to view an exhibit of member Arnold Chernoff's collection, "Firearms of the World." Chernoff gave a "descriptive speech" about his collection and refreshments were served. Member Frank J. Kinst, who hosted the event, was presented with The Civil War Round Table's Distinguished Service Award, "not just for the meeting and refreshments, but for that and numerous other good deeds he has done for our organization."[8] (The February 1963 newsletter noted that: "Other recent recipients of the Distinguished Service Award were Art Thorsen and John Mies, of station WBBM, for their radio programs dealing with the Civil War.")

In February The Round Table had as its speaker David Chambers Mearns, the chief of the manuscript division and holder of the Chair of American History of the Library of Congress, and author of numerous books and articles on the Civil War era. He spoke on "The Gettysburg Address: The Mysteries of the Manuscripts." That evening Mearns was awarded an Honorary Life membership in The Civil War Round Table.

An off-beat topic was presented at April's meeting. Robert W. Waitt, Jr., a Richmond publisher who was also vice president of the International Manuscript Society and active in numerous historical organizations, spoke on "Sin and the Civil War, or The Kinsey Report of the War." Gil Twiss wrote in the newsletter: "About his talk to the Chicago CWRT, Bob says, 'It will feature that heretofore little discussed, but entertaining pastime of Civil War soldiers: sex. It will include quotes from soldier letters, diaries of prostitutes, and newspaper accounts. It will not go into combat details, but will describe the armies involved and the battlefields they used.'" Writer John Justin Smith, who was present that evening, wrote about the meeting in his April 15, 1963 *Chicago Daily News* column.

In April, it was "on to Richmond" for the thirteenth annual battlefield tour. From the 24th through the 28th, the campaigners traversed the battlefields in and around Richmond, Virginia. J. Ambler Johnston spoke at Wednesday night's dinner and provided the group with his unique, unparalleled expertise on the Richmond battlefields throughout the tour. United States Senator Ralph W. Yarborough of Texas was Friday night's dinner speaker.

The flag of The Civil War Round Table made its debut in a photograph in the May 1963 newsletter. Gil Twiss wrote that: "It measures three-by-five feet. The upper half is blue and the lower half gray.; the upper lettering gray and the lower blue. The center design is principally white, red, and gold. The flag's fringe is gold. The design was by Ralph Newman."

Bruce Catton opened the 1963-1964 term, under the presidency of H. George Donovan, with an address on "Politics and the Army of the Potomoc" on September 26 at the St. Clair Hotel. A total of 169 members and guests attended. Gil Twiss wrote that "this was one of the largest [meetings] in our history."

The September newsletter announced the winners of a "Write a Letter to Mr. Lincoln" contest The Round Table had sponsored for children under fifteen years of age living in Illinois, Indiana, and Kentucky. The contest was part of the dedication program of the Lincoln Heritage Trail at New Salem State Park on the previous August 3rd.

New Civil War Round Tables were continuing to

The Round Table flag,
designed by Ralph Newman

spring up around the country, including one in the Virginia State Penitentiary. J. Ambler Johnston and members of the Richmond Civil War Round Table had helped to launch the group by providing speakers and materials. In a request that the group be added to the mailing list for The Round Table newsletter, Johnston said: "They seem to be so appreciative of any recognition from the outside and it would give them quite a lift to receive your publication. . . . Their library has available space, but is pathetically meager as to books on our subject and so if you have any that you feel disposed to send them, it will be highly appreciated by the group and I believe a real contribution to rehabilitation."[9]

The following news on the Prison CWRT is found in 1963 newsletter issues: ". . . Members of the Prison CWRT can't visit battlefields as others do. Recently dirt was brought into the penitentiary for a fill in the recreation yard. When the dirt was being raked, up came grape shot, a hand-forged hook, a hand-forged wagon spike, and a shell fragment. The dirt had been hauled in from an area of the Seven Pines battlefield." "[The] Prison Civil War Round Table has taken a step up to printer's type for its newsletter. . . . The newsletter expressed gratitude to Chicago CWRT for the Distinguished Service Award. Photocopies of the award were made for members to have or send to relatives or friends."

In November 1963, distinguished Civil War author Shelby Foote spoke on "Grant's Seven Failures Above Vicksburg." Also at that meeting Ralph Newman told how Illinois would present its story at the upcoming New York World's Fair. (Newman was chairman of the Illinois Commission for the Fair.) Twiss reported that: ". . . One feature is a lifelike (audio animatronic) figure of Abraham Lincoln created by Walt Disney . . . A sound track will play excerpts from many Lincoln speeches. . . . The Lincoln figure will only be a portion of the Illinois exhibit . . ."

For the December 8 "Ladies Night," Round Table member Win Stracke, founder of the Old Town School of Folk Music, prepared an evening of musical entertainment and comedy which was presented at the Chicago Press Club. The festivities were clouded, however, by somber news. Twiss wrote in the next months's newsletter: "The Ladies Night program . . . was saddened by the deaths, within the previous twenty-four hours, of Otto Eisenschiml and William Hesseltine. Ralph Newman made the announcement which many persons had not known until that time. The shock was apparent from the buzz of voices. Win Stracke called for a moment of silence and then sang 'Tenting Tonight' as a memorial to both men."

January 17 provided a special treat for Round Table members—the first address before the group by John Y. Simon. John was an old friend of The Round Table. He had spent the summers of his undergraduate years working as a stock clerk at the Abraham Lincoln Book Shop before going on to Harvard to earn his masters and doctoral degrees. Twiss wrote that: "Joe Eisendrath, a past president of The Civil War Round Table, asked and received the privilege of introducing Simon. Joe had John as a guest at a meeting when John was thirteen years old." Executive director of The Ulysses S. Grant Association since 1962 and editor of *The Papers of Ulysses S. Grant* (16 volumes published, 1967-1988), Simon's topic that evening was "From Galena to Appomattox: Elihu B. Washburne and Ulysses S. Grant."

Another Simon spoke in February—State Senator Paul Simon. His talk on "Lincoln the State Legislator" was a preview of his forthcoming book, *Lincoln's Preparation for Greatness* (1965), the only book that has been written to date about Lincoln's years in the Illinois legislature. On February 12, Ralph Newman and Pete Long participated in a discussion on Abraham Lincoln on NBC-TV.

The March 1964 newsletter carried a report of a second Prison Civil War Round Table being formed at The Maryland Institution for Men. Members of the Hagerstown Civil War Round Table were instrumental in its formation. According to the report, the group was "limited to thirty, selected from a screening of applications."

The battle sites of Louisiana were visited for the first time during the fourteenth annual tour (April 29-May 4, 1964). The group headed south via Pullman cars on the *Panama Limited*. On Thursday night, they enjoyed cocktails and snacks as the guests of Dr. and Mrs. T. Harry Williams. Port Hudson, Fort Jackson, Fort St. Henry, and the Confederate Memorial Hall were among the places visited. The Fun

Night (traditionally, the Saturday night of the tour) dinner was at the elegant, world-famous Antoine's. On the menu were Oysters Bourguignonne, turtle soup, pano pailotte, pommes soufles, green salad, and crepes suzette.

This was a special tour for Betsey and Brooks Davis. They joined the tour as the conclusion of their honeymoon. Betsey compared it to Brooks "taking me home to meet the family."[10] She had been presented with a white orchid corsage as a "wedding bouquet" the night of the formal dinner at Antoine's. In keeping with wedding bouquet traditions, Betsey threw her orchid into the group—and it was caught by Newton Farr, who had eluded marriage all his life. Though "Newt" wore the corsage proudly the remainder of the evening, he retained his status as one of Chicago's most eligible bachelors.

Another near-crisis occurred when Betsey accidentally packed Brooks' and her train tickets in their suitcases, which had been taken to the train with all the other tour luggage earlier to be placed in the baggage car. Registrar Margaret April used her powers of persuasion to talk the railroad officials into holding the train while the matter was resolved. Betsey and Brooks convinced the officials that they were, indeed, telling the truth—and the *Panama Limited* headed north with all Round Tablers aboard.[11]

Betsey Davis at the 400th Meeting in 1981

John Hope Franklin, distinguished scholar of the Civil War and Reconstruction periods and professor of history at the University of Chicago, on October 16, 1964, became the first African-American to address The Civil War Round Table. He spoke on "The Military Occupation of the South, 1865-1866." As the country was in the midst of what some have called "the second Civil War" during the civil rights revolution of the 1960s, it was most fitting to welcome a black scholar to The Civil War Round Table.

The October 1964 newsletter reported on a new award to be offered by The Round Table: "The terms of a $3000 Fellowship award were announced at the September 17 meeting. To encourage significant research into fundamental questions on the causes, conduct, and results of the Civil War, The Civil War Round Table, starting in 1965, will award one or more fellowships annually to qualified graduate students for the completion of dissertations in Civil War history.

"Initially the award is made possible through the generosity of Lloyd D. Miller, a past president of The Civil War Round Table, in the tradition of cooperative inquiry between professional and non-professional Civil War historians, which has marked the course of The Round Table. . . ." The idea for a fellowship was conceived by Ralph Newman. (See Appendix F for a list of Fellowship Award recipients.)

Lloyd Miller (right) with Jerry Slechta

Lloyd D. Miller addressed the 235th meeting in November on the topic of "The Battle of Franklin." Gil Twiss wrote in December's newsletter that Miller had "used a new six-by-eight-foot map board, drawn by Barbara Long. Lloyd had special lighting for the board and used markers, which he moved into proper position on the magnetized board. He also had some of the charts he had used in his speech on the same subject on February 28, 1945." Miller, who missed being a founder by four months, has been described as a "big, blustery fellow" with a heart of gold.[12] He often enlivened the question and answer periods with his provocative and persistent questions.

The Round Table's good friend Edwin C. Bearss, National Park Service regional historian and battlefield tour guide, spoke in January 1965 on "The Ironclad Gunboat Cairo." It was Bearss, with two others, who had rediscovered the sunken Union vessel in the Yazoo River and was spearheading efforts to raise and salvage it. Ed Bearss was awarded an Honorary Life membership in The Civil War Round Table that evening.

February's meeting—a "Ladies Night"—took place at three sites. An autographing party, in honor of Alice Hamilton Cromie's *A Tour Guide to the Civil War* (1964), preceded dinner at the Racquet Club. This was followed by a viewing of *The Red Badge of Courage* at the Chicago Historical Society and a visit to the Society's Lincoln and Civil War exhibits.

The official Civil War Centennial was fast drawing to a close. April's newsletter carried news of ceremonies to be held in Virginia: "Commemoration of the surrender of Robert E. Lee and the Army of Northern Virginia to Union General

Ulysses S. Grant will be held at the restored Appomattox Court House on April 9. Major General U.S. Grant 3rd of New York and Robert E. Lee IV of San Francisco will cut the ribbon dedicating the court house."

Victor Searcher, author of *Lincoln's Journey to Greatness* (1960) and *The Farewell to Mr. Lincoln* (1965), spoke on April 9 on "Lincoln's Last Journey." The meeting was preceded by a reception hosted by DePaul University to show their appreciation to The Civil War Round Table for the gift to the University Library of the Otto Eisenschiml Collection. Both events were held at the St. Clair Hotel. ("Ladies" were allowed to attend the reception, but not the meeting.)

It was time for the concluding event of the Civil War Centennial. (The battlefield tour—for the first and only time—was moved up to October, due to the scheduling of this event.) "The four-year Civil War Centennial observance," Gil Twiss wrote, "will culminate April 30-May 4 in Springfield, with commemoration of the Abraham Lincoln funeral. Centennial commissions, Civil War Round Tables, and the Illinois State Historical Society will participate . . ." The Round Table hosted a large reception the evening of May 1 for members of the assembly of the National Commission. Ralph Newman recalled that Governor Kerner had "turned the governor's mansion over to us as a command post. He told us we could use the mansion any time we wanted to."[13]

The list of speakers at the various events was awesome. It included: historians Allan Nevins, James I. Robertson, Jr., Paul M. Angle, Clement Silvestro, T. Harry Williams, Floyd S. Barringer, Bell I. Wiley, Richard N. Current, Avery O. Craven, Harold M. Hyman, E.B. Long, Shelby Foote, Clyde C. Walton, Ralph G. Newman, John Y. Simon, Frank E. Vandiver, Haskell Monroe, George F. Markham, and Bruce Catton; poets

Alice Cromie (seated) with Joyce Warshaw, Marshall Krolick, and Ver Lynn Sprague on the 1974 tour to Chattanooga

Gwendolyn Brooks and Mark Van Doren; Congressman Paul Findlay (Illinois); and United States Senators Paul H. Douglas (Illinois) and Ralph Yarborough (Texas).

Governor Otto Kerner spoke on "We Are Not Enemies But Friends" and made the presentation of a Lincoln funeral arrangement document to Robert Todd Lincoln Beckwith, the great-grandson of Abraham Lincoln, who was visiting Springfield for the first time. Norman Luboff, nationally acclaimed composer, conducted a group of local choirs in a stirring production of "The Lonesome Train" by Earl Robinson in the Jack Kelso Theater at New Salem, with Ralph Newman as narrator.

On May 4, the Illinois House of Representatives and Senate met in joint session at the Old State Capitol and adopted resolutions honoring Abraham Lincoln and Stephen A. Douglas. The gathering then moved to the Lincoln Tomb at Oak Ridge Cemetery. With Governor Kerner presiding, Adlai E. Stevenson III, a state representative, read a memorial by his father, the ambassador to the United Nations.

Actor Sidney Blackmer read Carl Sandburg's "There Was a Funeral . . ." from *Abraham Lincoln: The War Years* (1939). Members of the National Commission spoke some final words. It was singularly moving—and symbolic of the struggles of the 1860s and the 1960s—that, at the 100th anniversary of Lincoln's burial, the final prayer was offered by Deacon Corneal Davis, an African-American state legislator who was the grandson of a slave. Before delivering his benediction, he had this to say to those gathered at the tomb of the Great Emancipator: "You have heard a United States Senator, an Illinois Supreme Court Justice, a Governor, and other dignitaries speak. Now the grandson of a slave will pray for you." [14]

Chapter 10 ☆ *The Round Table Moves Ahead: From "Burying" the Centennial to Building "Toward the Second Centennial"*

T HE CURTAIN HAD FALLEN on the Civil War Centennial, the concluding ceremonies had been held; but—in the minds of a couple of members of The Civil War Round Table, at least, one final act had yet to be performed. "When Win Stracke and I made our 'cultural' tour of Europe with Paddy Bauler," Ralph Newman reminisced, "I conceived the idea of Centennial Park to bury the Civil War Centennial." It was decided to designate the little (fourteen-by-twenty feet) patch of green in front of the Abraham Lincoln Book Shop "Centennial Park." Stracke composed the lyrics and music of "The Biggest Little Park in the World (Centennial Park on Chestnut Street)." (See Appendix G for the lyrics.) Newman recalled how this idea had developed: "It was inspired by a newspaper article relating how Bernard Baruch, the philanthropist, had donated a small plot of land to New York City for a park. . . . [We] thought that Chicago should have a similar recreational facility in front of the Abraham Lincoln Book Shop."[1]

A "Centennial Marker" stone was made by a friend of Jerry Slechta's—"Scratchy" Neis, a Wisconsin tombstone maker. Unveiling ceremonies were set for October 6, 1965. Betsey and Brooks Davis were living in an apartment above the book shop at the time. Betsey remembers: "I kept hearing Brooks and Ralph talking about this event they were planning. They'd say things like: 'We'll go out and block off the street, the governor will come up, and then we'll undrape the stone,' and so forth. I thought, 'Oh, they're mad!' Then, on the appointed day, Margaret [April] walked up to our apartment and said: 'Well, are you ready? The governor is just coming in now.' I looked out the front window and Otto Kerner was walking up the street, the street was blocked-off, there were policemen on motorcycles in front of the building, there were flags flying. . . . I never believed it would happen. But, after that, I believed!"[2]

Gil Twiss wrote about the festivities in the November newsletter: ". . . [Round Table member] Ver Lynn Sprague, of

Win Stracke sings "The Biggest Little Park in the World" at the dedication of Centennial Park on October 6, 1965

the Department of Tourism and Development, was master of ceremonies. He was flanked by a large sign of the Lincoln Heritage Trail with the additional wording 'Unofficial Tour Detour.'

"Sprague introduced the landlord, Ralph G. Newman, who said the park was in answer to Mayor Daley's plea for more small parks. A neighbor, county Commissioner George Dunne, requested permission to name his adjoining lawn Centennial Park West. Governor Otto Kerner unveiled the marker and said it was the zenith in his career of dedications, but that this was the last Civil War Centennial activity he expected to be connected with. Milton Pikarsky, Chicago public works commissioner, was present to see that all things were properly done and blocked off parking meters on the street for the occasion.

"Sergeant Ron Persenico, of the reactivated 104th Illinois Infantry, was in command of a one-man squad and ordered the firing of a volley over the stone—a one-gun salute. . . . Sprague called on Round Table President Brooks Davis to plant a symbolic Abraham Lincoln tulip, adding to the forty-nine he had already planted. He also planted two Abraham Lincoln roses donated by Peggy Lebold [widow of early Round Table member Foreman "Mike" Lebold]. Davis was introduced as caretaker and night watchman of the

Governor Otto Kerner dedicates Centennial Park

(From left) Lester Joseph, Hal Hixson, Brooks Davis, Al Meyer, Griffin Martin, Pete Johnson, and Dr. Gilbert Govan listen to Hobart Cawood, chief historian at Chickamauga National Military Park, during the 1965 tour.

park. . . . Win Stracke capped the ceremonies by singing 'Centennial Park.'" NBC newscaster Len O'Connor broadcast the ceremonies on network radio.

Thereafter, Betsey Davis gave a few whimsical "garden walks" of the park, while standing in a stationary position. And for awhile, "Centennial Park" was a stop on the Chicago tour bus schedule. The original stone (all 400 pounds of it) was stolen. Its replacement was also stolen, but the culprit only got as far as a short distance away on State Street before abandoning it. The stone was then firmly installed in the ground by city workers.

The dates for the postponed 1965 battlefield tour were October 13-17. Chattanooga and Atlanta and the road connecting them were the objectives of The Civil War Round Table's fifteenth annual battlefield tour. Speakers included authors Gilbert E. Govan and James W. Livingood and The Round Table's old friend Colonel Allan P. (Ned) Julian. The talented Win Stracke was the master of ceremonies for Fun Night. The travel was by air and bus.

The Civil War Round Table marked its twenty-fifth

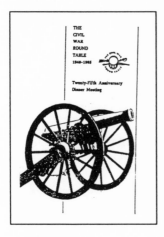

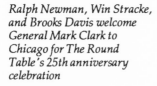

anniversary with a dinner at the Knickerbocker Hotel on December 14, 1965. The evening was designated as a Round Table "Ladies Night." Ver Lynn Sprague presented a brief talk on the history of The Round Table. The men who had begun the group twenty-five years earlier were honored. (By this time, five of the original sixteen had died.) The principal speaker was General Mark Clark.

The *Chicago Tribune*, on December 12, ran a story about The Round Table as it reached its quarter-century mark. Writer Percy Wood noted that: "The Round Table's historian, Gilbert Twiss, a copy editor for the *Tribune* and former president of the Illinois State Historical Society, says that its members have written more than 250 books and that the overall value of their collections total several million dollars."

Touching on the motivation for The Round Table, the article continues: ". . . Why does the Civil War, more than 100 years ago, hold such a fascination? 'There are many reasons,' [Ralph] Newman said yesterday. 'By all odds, it's the most romantic period of our history. Winston Churchill called it 'the last war fought between gentlemen.' Studying the careers of Lincoln, Lee, Grant, Sherman, or Forrest is as exciting as fiction.

"'Stonewall Jackson marching victoriously up and down the Shenandoah Valley, Phil Sheridan at Winchester, the great locomotive chase, the battle between the *Shenandoah* and the *Kearsage*—all are thrillers. But, best of all, they're true.

"'Yet the Civil War means more than that. When 600,000 men in a nation of thirty million died as a result of the war, one cannot escape wonderment that the nation survived—and in surviving, grew within a century to be the world's greatest power. No American can contemplate that fact without emotion.'"

The title of General Clark's address was "America's Wars." Elmer Gertz remembers the evening well: "General

Ralph Newman, Win Stracke, and Brooks Davis welcome General Mark Clark to Chicago for The Round Table's 25th anniversary celebration

Clark was so charming at our pre-meeting cocktail hour. And then he gave the most blood-thirsty talk. He wanted us to go to war with Russia and China forthwith. It was dreadful." Following the address, Win Stracke courageously provided some political balance by singing an anti-Viet Nam War peace song he had composed. (See Appendix H for the lyrics of "Part of Me.") "If I had to pick the single most interesting Round Table meeting," Gertz observed, "this would be it, largely because of the contrast between Mark Clark's bellicose speech and Win's peace song." Asked what General Clark's views were about the music which had followed his talk, Gertz said that "If he had any, he didn't express them to us."[3]

As Gil Twiss noted in the next month's newsletter, a highlight of the anniversary dinner was the souvenir which was given to each person attending—a "muster roll done in Civil War style and containing the names of the 303 members and Honorary Life members. These were in the center spread of the twenty-one-by-thirty-two-inch fold-out. A brief history of The Round Table was embellished with cannon from the head of the newsletter, and with other battle scenes and figures. The front had the evening's program in Civil War era typography. Inside were lists of current officers, founders, past presidents, and honorary award members." The muster roll was the creation of member Jerry Warshaw, who was its designer and typographer. Member Al Meyer provided the printing services.

Messages of congratulations to The Round Table on its quarter century anniversary came from former President Harry S. Truman, Illinois Governor Otto Kerner, many eminent historians, and Civil War Round Tables across the country. President Truman said that he hoped The Round Table would continue its "deliberations and studies in depth of this historic turning point in the evolution of this nation . . ."[4]

The following item appeared in the February 1966 newsletter: "While men were at the meeting, about a dozen ladies gathered at the Abraham Lincoln Book Shop to hear the tape recording of Shelby Foote's speech on Vicksburg, then had dinner at Armando's restaurant, and finally joined the men at the Press Club." This was the beginning of the "ladies auxiliary" of The Round Table, which they, tongues-in-cheek, named "The Camp Followers."

The Camp Followers was a group of wives of Round Table members who wanted something to do while their husbands were at Round Table meetings. Margaret April remembers those days: "A group of us would get together— originally on the second floor of the book shop. The women would make little talks. We outgrew that, and started going to restaurants." Asked if these women resented not being

Barbara Long (left) with Lloyd Miller and Betsey Davis at a meeting of The Camp Followers in 1966

allowed to join The Round Table, she replied: "At that point, it was a matter of custom and it didn't bother them. They just accepted it."[5] Concurring with this observation, Betsey Davis stated that "Camp Followers were not adamant about wanting to be able to join The Round Table; they were wives, not independent women . . ."[6]

Barbara Long Pleiter recalls a Camp Followers talk she gave on "Swords, Roses, and Vitriol," about Southern women and their hatred of Yankees. Betsey Davis gave a talk on Varina Davis. Ella Clausius spoke about Mary Todd Lincoln. Joyce Warshaw's topic was "Lincoln—the Long Way Home." "Outside" speakers also appeared before the group. Round Table members—such as Lloyd Miller, Pete Long, and Bill Sullivan—addressed the ladies group during the years of its existence (1966-1977), in some cases "trying out" a particular talk before delivering it to The Round Table.

One of the more amusing Camp Followers stories is the one involving Barbara Long's attempts to serve Mary Lincoln's famous white cake. She recalls: "I had a recipe for what was called Abraham Lincoln's favorite cake. It was a very heavy cake, with three or four cups of flour, a lot of baking powder, and plenty of nuts. I baked it and brought it to a Camp Followers meeting. I had it in a case that was supposed to have a lock on it. When I got out of the car, I picked up the case. The lock didn't work and the cake went down into the gutter, which was full of muddy water. The cake was still on the plate—which broke. We [Pete and Barbara] retrieved the cake, which looked surprisingly good. Mud was all over the bottom, but the top was fairly pristine. We placed it on top of a nearby trash bin. I remember thinking that some bum might come by and think he'd found a treasure, only to be sadly disappointed when he discovered it was full of muddy water.

"Sometime after that, I made a second attempt. This time

I got it to the book shop just fine. I was so careful. When the time came to serve it, I went to the kitchen to bring it out, as we were going to cut it on the coffee table. I don't know what happened. I was wearing a solid navy blue dress, and—all of a sudden—I was wearing the cake on my chest and I was full of white frosting, all the way down to my shoes. I did keep it from hitting the floor, but I was a mess. We collected what hadn't been harmed and ate chunks of it."[7] Margaret April also remembers the cake and recalls that it tasted very good, in spite of its sloppy appearance by the time it was served.[8]

Barbara Long Pleiter remembers the way the Abraham Lincoln Book Shop was then, and especially the area on the second floor: "It had a club-like atmosphere. There was a kitchen on the second floor and Ralph even had a sort of bar where people could get a drink if they wished. People congregated there. The Camp Followers met there sometimes. [On several occasions, these quarters were the setting for CBS and NBC television shows.] The book shop was the catalyst that held The Round Table together."[9] The pleasant, welcoming ambience that Ralph Newman had created and sustained attracted people to both the book shop and The Civil War Round Table.

Another gala event took place on April 6, 1966. The Civil War Round Table celebrated its 250th meeting; this coincided with the centennial date of the founding of the Grand Army of the Republic, the Civil War veterans' organization. The dinner was held in the Beaubien Room of Stouffer's restaurant in the Prudential Plaza. The newsletter informed that: "Ladies and guests are welcome." Three-hundred people attended.

Gil Twiss wrote in the newsletter: "There will be a short program at the dinner. Past presidents of The Round Table and their ladies will be introduced. Copies of 'Part of Me,' the

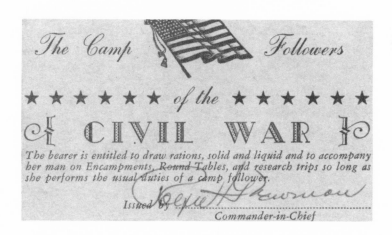

Camp Followers membership card

song that Win Stracke composed for and sang at the twenty-fifth anniversary meeting . . . will be distributed. An additional souvenir will be copies of *Lincoln Raises an Army*, by Don Russell, published some years ago by The Round Table. Round Table historical material will be on display."

The group then moved to the G.A.R. Memorial Hall in the Chicago Public Library. Ralph Newman introduced Chief Librarian Gertrude Gscheidle who told of the meaning and background of the G.A.R. and its significance to the library. The main address was given by Sir Denis Brogan, professor of political science at Cambridge University in England, and "outstanding British student of America and the Civil War."[10] His topic was "The War as a War."

Former President Eisenhower sent a message to The Round Table to be read at its 250th meeting. In it he said: "With all who believe that knowledge of our history is a rich source of strength and wisdom to every American generation in the meeting of its problems and trials, I salute the contribution made by you of The Chicago Civil War Round Table to the revival of Civil War study."[11]

On April 30, The Round Table held an auction at the Furniture Club on Lake Shore Drive to benefit the Fellowship Award Fund. After the 7:00 p.m. dinner, a number of items were auctioned: books, flags, weapons, uniform parts, and other Civil War-related items. Joe Eisendrath and Marshall Krolick served as co-chairmen for the event. According to the May 1966 newsletter, the auction "drew one-hundred to an excellent dinner in the Furniture Club and raised a handsome sum for the college Fellowship Award fund . . ." The total amount netted was $1,433.95.

"The Sixteenth Annual Battlefield Tour, May 26 to 30," Gil Twiss wrote in the newsletter, "will offer a thorough look at Washington, D.C.—Civil War aspects and modern—and outlying battlefields and an inspection of the John Wilkes Booth escape route after the assassination of President Abraham Lincoln.

"For the trip to Washington, the White Sox DC-7 plane has been leased. Going east it will be the 'General Abner Doubleday Special' and returning, the 'John A. Logan Special.'"

Marshall Krolick recalled The Round Tablers' landing in Washington aboard the Chicago White Sox plane and their de-planing: "The White Sox owned an airplane which they used to fly the team to games around the country. Between trips, they would charter it. Bill Wilson arranged for The Round Table to use it in 1966. It said 'Chicago White Sox' all over it. The airport at which we landed in Washington didn't have a jetway; you just got out and walked down the stairs to

The Chicago White Sox plane was used for the 1966 tour to Washington, D.C. and the 1968 tour to Fredericksburg

the runway and into the airport building.

"The White Sox were not very successful that year. They had a bad ball club. As we were getting off the plane, there were some people standing on the runway. (Keep in mind that, at that time, most of The Round Table members were probably between fifty and seventy.) As we were getting off the plane, a guy who was waiting to service the plane was heard to say, 'I heard the White Sox had a bad team, but this is ridiculous!'"[12]

Tour guides included Colonel J. Gay Seabourne and Elden (Josh) Billings of the Washington, D.C. Civil War Round Table and John Divine of the Loudon County Historical Society. During this time, Ralph Newman had been working with President Lyndon B. Johnson on the appraisal of his presidential papers. Thus, The Round Table was given a V.I.P. tour of the White House on Friday, May 27. The group was shown not only the first floor rooms, but also was given "an exceptional visit to the second floor rooms, including the Lincoln bedroom."[13] At the conclusion of the White House tour, in the state dining room, the Round Tablers were greeted by President Johnson, who posed for a picture with Robert Todd Lincoln Beckwith, great-grandson of President Lincoln and a member of the battlefield tour party for two days.

It had been discovered that the monument of General

The Round Table, led by Ver Lynn Sprague, dedicated the monument to General John A. Rawlins in Washington, D.C. in 1966.

John A. Rawlins, General Grant's chief-of-staff from Galena, Illinois, had never been dedicated. The Round Table determined to assume this belated duty that Friday afternoon after their White House visit. Gil Twiss wrote that: "The White House visit lasted so long that Representative John B. Anderson of Rockford, Illinois, had departed from the General John Rawlins monument before we arrived there. However, our group carried out a dedication ceremony (an eighty-year omission). Ver Lynn Sprague presided at a wreath-laying ceremony and Mrs. Ward Smidl directed a group in singing 'The Battle Hymn of the Republic.' A luncheon arranged by our member Senator Paul Douglas was held in the Old Senate Office Building. Then, in the manuscript division of the Library of Congress, John Sargent, president of Doubleday Publishers, Bruce Catton, and E.B. (Pete) Long presented to the library the nine million words of research that Pete had prepared for Catton's *Centennial History of the Civil War* (1961-1965). Quincy Mumford, librarian, accepted the gift. Others present included David Mearns, chief of the manuscript division of the library, Roy Basler, and Lloyd Dunlap. A Distinguished Service Award was presented to the library."

J. Ambler Johnston and Edwin C. Bearss served as guides for the latter part of the tour. Fun Night was held at the Command Post, the Marriott Twin Bridges Motor Hotel. The entertainment was provided by well-known political satirist Mark Russell. Following Russell's performance, Round Table member Miles Janousek sat down at the piano and led a sing-a-long. Before heading back to Chicago on May 30, the Round Table party had front section seats in the Arlington Cemetery Amphitheater to hear President Johnson deliver his Memorial Day address.

The 1965-1966 term concluded on a high note, with Frank

Pete Long presents the nine million words of research for Bruce Catton's Centennial History of the Civil War *to Library of Congress librarian Quincy Mumford as Bruce Catton looks on.*

E. Vandiver speaking on "Toward the Second Centennial" on June 10 at the Wardroom of the United States Naval Armory on Lake Michigan at the foot of East Randolph Street. Seventy-five members and guests were present. Gil Twiss reported that "President Brooks Davis reviewed the 1965-1966 year. He then introduced the new officers . . . and presented the gavel to [new] President Michael S. Lerner. On the call of Maurice Fisher, there were three lusty cheers for Brooks."

Frank Vandiver remembers this Round Table talk as the one he had the most fun with, "because it was a humorous assessment of the build-up to the second Centennial." He recalls talking about "all the nonsense that was passing for good work" that had surfaced during the first Centennial.[14]

Miles Janousek leads a sing-along during the 1966 tour

In his address, in addition to providing a touch of humor, Vandiver emphasized the amount of work still to be done in Civil War scholarship. "We still haven't all the basic sources for study," he noted. "We need more biographies of political figures. . . . The navy is neglected in Civil War writing. . . . Civil War biographers have neglected a whole group of people—men of letters, musicians, and artists. . . . We need to know more about what went on in Southern cities, population shifts, class support of the war, effect on the national economy, and such things as the founding of the Academy of Science, the Homestead Act, and the College Land Grant Act . . ." "Let us go forward," he urged, "firm in our affection for the Civil War and honest in our studies."

Chapter 11 ☆ *Concluding the 1960s and Beginning the 1970s: The Round Table Marches Into Its Third Decade*

D R. FRANK L. KLEMENT, PROFESSOR of history at Marquette University, delivered the main address at the 256th meeting. (His topic was "Vallandingham and the Civil War.") But there was another element of significance in the December 8, 1966 meeting. It was the evening that The Civil War Round Table showed its appreciation and affection for founding newsletter editor Gil Twiss.

Twiss wrote about it in the next month's newsletter: "Behind the speaker's table was a banner reading, 'The Civil War Round Table Salutes Gil Twiss.' At the beginning of the meeting, President Mike Lerner spoke in complimentary terms of the CWRT newsletter.

"Charles Wesselhoeft, chairman of the awards committee, then presented to your editor the certificate of Honorary Life membership in The Round Table. Jerry Warshaw had centered the certificate in a collage of various issues of the newsletter. This was placed under glass in a frame of Civil War style.

"Ralph Newman read a paper, which he said required much research, and turned up the Civil War career of one Ebenezer Twiss, a cavalryman and relative of your editor. Thereupon, Ralph presented a two-foot high metal figure, the plaque reading, 'U.S. Cavalry 1865.'

"Another presentation was a case of what is reputed to have been U.S. Grant's favorite, Old Crow. A telegram from Camp Followers expressing their 'ladylike sentiments and our gratitude' was read. Elmer Brinkman and Pete Long were the spokesmen.

"As your editor said then, and repeats now, we were overwhelmed by the friendship and honor; we're eternally grateful, and we thank you one and all."

In addition to being a designated "Ladies Night," a woman delivered the address at the February 14, 1967 meeting! Alice Hamilton Cromie, frequent battlefield tour participant and author of *A Tour Guide to the Civil War*, spoke on "Serendipity and the Civil War." The meeting was held at the

Ivanhoe Restaurant and Theater. After the dinner and address, the group saw the play *Jane,* starring Joan Bennett.

In February 1967, Henry W. McGee, postmaster of Chicago, became the first African-American member of The Civil War Round Table. Although a number of African-Americans had attended Round Table meetings and participated in special events over the years (and there had never been a membership restriction for any group of people—except women), McGee was the first to join the organization.

On the seventeenth annual battlefield tour (April 20-23), campaigners headed for Missouri and Arkansas. Wilson's Creek, Pea Ridge, Prairie Grove, and Westport were among the sites on the itinerary. On Sunday, the group made stops at former President Harry Truman's home and the Truman Library in Independence, Missouri. It seems to have been the usual convivial crowd on this tour. Gil Twiss noted in his tour wrap-up that: "April 21 was a drizzly day. Some bridges were too weak for the buses to cross . . . [and] passengers got out and walked. At one, Tour Chairman Charles Falkenberg declined to dismount, saying, 'No, I'll go down with my bus.'"

Only three days after returning from the battlefield tour, Round Tablers had another big event on their schedule. A special reception occurred prior to the April 26 meeting, to celebrate the publication of the first volume of *The Papers of Ulysses S. Grant,* edited by The Round Table's good friend, John Y. Simon. "Ladies" were invited to the reception, held on the seventeenth floor of the Furniture Mart, but not to the meeting and dinner which followed. (Women of the Camp Followers had dinner in a separate room.) The speaker that evening was Fred G. Benton, Jr., of the Baton Rouge Civil War Round Table, who spoke on "The Battle and Siege of Port Hudson."

Another auction to benefit the Fellowship Award Fund was held on June 4—this time at "Centennial Park." In his letter to fellow members, Marshall Krolick, chairman of the fundraiser, assured his readers: "The personalities of our auctioneers are guaranteed to provide plenty of fun and there will be enough variety of items on sale to satisfy everyone's special interest."[1] The auction was the first Round Table event in the tenure of new President Ver Lynn Sprague.

The November 10, 1967 "Ladies Night" at the Kungsholm Restaurant featured a talk by Ralph Newman on "Readin' Writin' and Round Tables." This was followed by a performance of the famous Kungsholm Puppets.

The year 1967 ended on a sad note for The Round Table. December's newsletter carried the obituary of founding member Newton C. Farr. "Though he was senior to most of us

Jerry Warshaw, 1968-69
President

in The Civil War Round Table," Ralph Newman wrote, "he was young in heart, youthful in his interests, modern in his approach to business and education, and progressive in all community activities. . . . That we shall miss him would be one of the understatements of the age; that we shall remember him, in Jefferson's words, is a fact that is self-evident."

The Round Table began the new year with an appropriate topic, given that 1968 was the year of Illinois' Sesquicentennial. Dr. Glenn H. Seymour, former president of the Illinois State Historical Society, spoke on "Illinois in the 1850s" on January 12. Some Round Table members were quite involved in Sesquicentennial activities. Ralph Newman served as chairman of the Sesquicentennial Commission and Ver Lynn Sprague was its executive director. Jerry Warshaw designed the Sesquicentennial flag. Camp Follower Joyce Warshaw was Newman's administrative assistant for the work done on planning and executing the various Sesquicentennial activities which took place throughout the year.

Also in January, the restored Ford's Theater in Washington, D.C. was opened to the public. There had been no public performances there since that fateful night on April 14, 1865. A number of Round Table members attended the grand reopening performance, featuring many top stars of stage and screen, on January 30.

The high quality of Round Table speakers continued. Lloyd Ostendorf—photographer, artist, Lincoln collector, and the recognized authority (since the death of Frederick Hill Meserve) on the photographs of Abraham Lincoln—spoke on February 9 on "The Faces of Abraham Lincoln." Renowned Civil War author Shelby Foote gave an address titled "Grant Comes to Washington" on March 8.

Round Table members participated in joint meetings of the Illinois State Historical Society and the Illinois Sesquicentennial Commission, which took place from April 18 to 20 in Chicago. (A number of members also traveled to Springfield to participate in the rededication of the Old State Capitol in August of 1968.)

"The eighteenth annual battlefield tour [to Fredericksburg], May 2 to 5, was one of the finest," Gil Twiss reported, "blessed with good weather and everything running smoothly throughout. Registration for all events was nearly a hundred. Sixty persons rode the chartered White Sox DC-7; others joined the party in Washington, D.C. and Fredericksburg. . . . For the campaign, the buses were named Alexander Schimmelpfennig and Carnot Posey. Marshall Krolick, Richard Cohen, Charles Wesselhoeft, and H. George Donovan were the bus marshals. . . ."

J. Ambler Johnston, honorary chairman of the tour, was

presented with a Distinguished Service Award. Historian Ralph Happel, Ranger Ralph Bullard, and that popular fountain of Civil War knowledge Ed Bearss served as tour guides and lecturers. The Fun Night program included some humorous responses to questions assigned to various campaigners (for example, Glenn Wiche's assignment was to provide a reply to "how I would have advised Burnside"). Following the program, "Miles Janousek sat at the piano and played endlessly for song and entertainment."[2]

A veteran member spoke for the first meeting of the 1968-1969 season, the term of Jerry Warshaw's presidency. Lloyd D. Miller, "a vigorous and cogent speaker," according to Gil Twiss, talked about "The Union Left—The Second Day of Gettysburg." Twiss reported that: "For member Miller, this is a repeat performance of a talk he delivered to the 114th CWRT meeting on May 27, 1952, when seventy-two members heard his presentation. It might be noted that of that 1952 group, only twenty-six are active members now, nineteen are deceased, and twenty-seven are 'gone with the wind,' as Miller puts it. At that appearance, Miller pioneered the use of a magnetic map board to illustrate the progress of the battle. He will again use a magnetic board at the September 13 talk, but this one is five times larger, weighing some 300 pounds. 'It takes four guys to carry it before we make it rigid,' Miller explains, 'but it provides an opportunity to show movements of the bodies of troops on a scaled map of the Gettysburg battle area. . . .'"

Another "first" for the Round Table occurred at the September 1968 meeting: the beginning of the dinner meeting quiz, the creation of Marshall Krolick. Though the responsibility for its preparation has changed hands over the years, it remains a popular feature each month. The first question on that first quiz was: "Grant's first attempt to capture Vicksburg ended in failure in 1862 because of the destruction of his supply base. Name the supply base and identify the Confederate cavalry leader who destroyed it." (The answers are: Holly Springs and General Earl Van Dorn.)

The newsletter continued to carry news of battlefield preservation work. This is from the September 1968 issue: "The 'Second Battle of Antietam'—over a large aluminum refinery at Doubs, Maryland—has just about been settled. The first plan of the Potomac Edison Company was to run high-tension transmission lines one mile south of the Antietam battlefield. That aroused Civil War fans. Heeding the protests, the Department of Interior effected a compromise. The power lines will now run north of the battlefield, approaching it no closer than two miles, and, the route will follow valleys and other low points as much as possible.

Towers will be reduced from 110 feet high to between 80 and 90 feet. The 'Second Battle of Antietam' is thus not an un-qualified victory for the conservationists, but it is not a total defeat either."

In the October 1968 newsletter, the first mention of the Monday Lunch Group appears: "All CWRT members are welcome to attend the meeting of the Unofficial CWRT Board of Directors and Chowder and Marching Society held each Monday noon in our special (?) CWRT room in Chodash Restaurant, 312 West Randolph Street." The Monday Lunch Group is still thriving, though they have changed meeting places numerous times.

December's newsletter carried news of other Round Tables. The group in Milwaukee (the second CWRT to be formed) had their 200th meeting; Pete Long was their speaker for the occasion. The CWRT of Kentucky had observed its fifteenth anniversary the previous month. The Hamilton (Ohio) CWRT celebrated its second year, and the Cincinnati group was planning a spring battlefield tour to Fredericksburg.

Four Round Table members appeared on the WLS-TV program "Exposure" on December 15, talking about the Civil War and Round Table activities. Ralph Newman, Pete Long, Jerry Warshaw, and Dick Bjorklund were interviewed by Shari Blair.

The Civil War Round Table suffered a grevious loss on December 23, with the death of Gil Twiss, at the age of sixty-one. Tributes were paid to him at the January 1969 meeting and contributions were made in his name to the Fellowship Award fund. His final editorial, in December's newsletter, had been a plea for battlefield preservation. Dick Bjorklund assumed the position of newsletter editor.

January's newsletter also carried the sad news that founding member Vernon Hanson had died. (Mr. Hanson's death had occurred in April, but was not mentioned until the notice appeared in the January issue.) His death, Dick Bjorklund noted, reduced the number of surviving founding members to ten.

Perhaps the most elegant event in Round Table history was planned for Valentine's Day, 1969. On February 14, (a "Ladies Night"), The Round Table held a Grand Review Ball, featuring the 1st Brigade Band and craftsman-historian E.J. Kupjack who spoke on "History in Miniature." Held in the Case and Cover Room of the Furniture Club in the Furniture Mart, black tie was "acceptable," but the guests were "en-couraged to appear in period costume."[3] The announcement called for "dancing in the Civil War manner." A story about the ball appeared in the society pages of the February 13 *Chicago Tribune*. In the March newsletter, Dick Bjorklund

The head table at the 1969 Ladies Night Grand Review Ball. From left: Betsey Davis, Marshall Krolick, Roberta Krolick, Mrs. E.J. Kupjack, Jerry Warshaw (President), E.J. Kupjack (speaker), Joyce Warshaw, Clyde Walton, Mrs. Walton and Brooks Davis

reported that: "More than one-hundred members, their ladies, and their guests" attended. "Many members," he added, "turned out in uniform with their ladies clad in Civil War era dresses." The Round Table had demonstrated yet another way to have a good time with history.

The nineteenth annual battlefield tour (May 1-4) went to Shiloh and Northern Mississippi. Sites visited included Shiloh, Iuka, Corinth, Holly Springs, Brice's Cross Roads, and Tupelo.

Jerry Warshaw titled his final remarks as Round Table president "Old Presidents Never Die, They Merely Reminisce." In it, he thanked all those who had assisted him and said that he was "torn between being sorry and happy that the year is over." He gave special thanks to "my Devil's Advocate, Marshall Krolick who kept the club and president on an even keel, and who really deserves more praise than I can give for the magnificent job done over the years as treasurer. A most remarkable fellow."[4] The Round Table has attracted a number of "remarkable fellows"—and since 1977, remarkable people of both sexes. Warshaw passed the presidential gavel to Clyde Walton that June.

"Another 'first' in the history of The Civil War Round Table will be marked Friday, December 12," Dick Bjorklund wrote, "when our speaker will be the current holder of the CWRT Fellowship Award, Okron E. Uya . . . Professor Uya, now teaching in the department of history of the University of Wisconsin, will speak on the career of Robert Smalls, a one-time slave who became a distinguished figure in the Civil War and Reconstruction periods." Professor Uya thus became the second person of African descent to address The Civil War Round Table.

On February 13, 1970, The Round Table presented a "Gala Four-Star Ladies Night Program" at the Chicago Public

Stanley Horn speaking during the 1969 tour to Shiloh.

Library. Dr. Philip D. Jordan, an authority on Civil War and Western folklore, told some "lively yarns of the war era." Dr. Preston Bradley, founder of the People's Church of Chicago, spoke on "If Lincoln Were Here." Bruce Catton was there as a special guest to receive a testimonial from The Round Table. The fourth "star" was "the Central Building of the Chicago Public Library, now nearly one-hundred years old, which will house its first dinner party in almost a century of service to Chicago." One hundred forty dinner guests attended.

In March, the group began meeting at a new place, the dining room of the Chicago Bar Association on LaSalle Street. April and May of 1970 offered interesting events for Round Table members. On April 10, John Y. Simon spoke at the 290th meeting on "Grant at Belmont: Victory or Blunder?" Maps drawn by Barbara Long were distributed to everyone prior to Simon's address. Dick Bjorklund notes in the newsletter that: "Grant's papers, when all are published, will reach at least fifteen volumes, according to the editor, Dr. Simon." (This would prove to be quite an understatement. Currently, Dr. Simon is at work on Volume 17 of a projected twenty-six. Grant, apparently, had a lot more to say than anyone had realized.)

The twentieth annual battlefield tour (April 30-May 3) journeyed to the areas around Savannah and Charleston. Included in the itinerary were Fort Pulaski, Beaufort, and Fort Sumter. Among the speakers were Federal Judge Alexander A. Lawrence and Warren Ripley, state editor of the *Charleston Evening Post*.

"Past President Jerry Warshaw," Dick Bjorklund reported, "will present a . . . Round Table 'first' on Friday, May 8, when he will show some gems from his collection of Civil War films." "Augmenting Jerry's films and narrative," Bjorklund continued, "will be authentic nickelodeon music by Arnold Alexander, a reformed lawyer [and former Round Table president] who will return to his original trade as an itinerant piano player."

Popcorn was served as the group enjoyed such classics as:

- D.W. Griffith's 1911 *The Battle;*
- *The Drummer Boy of the Eighth,* produced in 1913 by Thomas Ince;
- *Life of Lincoln,* produced by the Edison Company in 1915 under a commission from the state of Illinois to mark the fiftieth anniversary of the death of Abraham Lincoln; and
- *The General,* produced by and starring Buster Keaton, a 1927 full-length silent movie about the great railroad chase of the Civil War.

A.P. Andrews spoke on "Major General Earl Van Dorn:

Saint or Sinner?" at the June 5 meeting. That evening, the president's gavel was passed to Dan Lapinski.

In September of 1970, Don Russell took over as editor of the newsletter. In the December issue, he reported that: "The November meeting was cheered by the presence of two CWRT veterans returning from far places. E.B. (Pete) Long, who left us last summer to become professor of history at the University of Wyoming, Laramie; and Ver Lynn Sprague, CWRT president, 1967-1968, from the Isle of Capri, Naples, Florida. Pete was returning from the Conference of Southern Historians at Louisville. Ver Lynn had cooked up some business in Chicago, and saw that it coincided with the date of a CWRT meeting."

The March 1971 newsletter carried an interesting article, nearly a page long, about black sailors in the Civil War. It detailed the heroic deeds of African-American sailors John Lawson and Robert Smalls and featured a photograph, noting that: "Black Navy men were an integral part of a ship's crew a century ago, as evidenced by this U.S. Navy photo of the Civil War era."

Dan Lapinski, 1970-71
President, in 1981

The American historical community lost a giant on March 5, 1971. Allan Nevins, the great Pulitzer Prize winning (twice)[5] biographer and Civil War historian died at the age of eighty in Menlo Park, California. "Allan Nevins," Don Russell wrote, "was a thorough student, and was thoroughly approachable. He was a great inspiration to many of us, and many counted him as a good friend and good companion."

The 300th meeting was celebrated on April 2, 1971 (a "Ladies Night"), when Round Tablers and their guests were treated to a "gourmet French-accented dinner at 7:30 p.m. at the Cafe LaTour." Don Russell added, in the newsletter's meeting preview, that: "A piano and bar will be available after the formal program." The Round Table's old friend Colonel Allen P. Julian delivered the main address, on "Margaret Mitchell and *Gone With The Wind*." Ralph G. Newman gave a brief talk, titled "The Civil War Round Table—We Point with Pride."

"The twenty-first annual battlefield tour [April 29-May 2] . . . will take our campaigners to the historic Shenandoah Valley," Marshall Krolick wrote in the special tour newsletter, "with stops en route at Harpers Ferry and 2nd Bull Run." "Our traveling," he continued, "will be by United Air Lines jet and air conditioned Greyhound highway cruisers, complete with the most modern conveniences and necessary refreshment. . . . Innovations on this year's tour include a system of inter-bus communication, a permanent guide on each bus . . . , and the services of a bugler, who will summon us to mess, to the buses, etc. with the calls heard on those same fields over a hundred years ago. . . . Ed Bearss and Preston Smith, who will also act as two of our guides, will address us on Friday night . . ." Krolick and Lloyd Miller were co-chairmen for the 1971 tour.

Fun Night was quite memorable that year. Brooks Davis was the chairman for the evening program. He had brought with him a copy of a 1961 *New Yorker* article, "Tuckertee Ridge (A Handy Account of an All-Purpose Civil War Battle),"[6] which had been whimsically purported to be intended for use by speakers during the Centennial when they ran out of anything else to say. "It was an account of a fictional battle, a parody of Civil War talks," Krolick recalled. "It used such phrases as 'The mess handed Grant the order. Grant read the order. He immediately picked up his gloves, put on his beard, and mounted his horse. . . . Much of it was subtle; you really had to listen to realize what it was."

Davis and Krolick decided to try to attempt a "believable" presentation of "Tuckertee Ridge." "I called Ed Bearss," Krolick related, "explained the situation, and asked him if he could come up with someone who was a Civil War person that nobody in our group would know. I would introduce him as professor so and so, as if he were to give a serious talk. . . . Well, Ed sent us a man from the National Park Service, who really looked the part of my mythical professor—horn-rimmed glasses and all. And he had memorized the *New Yorker* piece.

"I introduced him as a professor from the University of Virginia. 'I know this is Fun Night and normally we have a little frivolity—and we will have that—but we have with us tonight a new history professor at the University of Virginia whom most of us have not had the opportunity to meet. He did his undergraduate work under T. Harry Williams at LSU and his graduate work under Frank Vandiver at Rice. I know you'll all enjoy hearing him and hope you'll all forgive us if we have a few serious moments—for about twenty minutes or so—while he describes a very little-known battle, but an important battle, that occurred right here in Virginia.

"The guy got up and gave his speech. He was terrific! Sitting at the head table, I could see the whole room. The first person to get it was Charlie Wesselhoeft, and he started to laugh. Slowly, other people started to realize that they were being had and started to chuckle. This ripple grew into gales of laughter half-way through the speech. But the guy never stopped. He didn't pause, he didn't blink. He just kept reciting this cockamamie speech until he was done. When he had finished, he received a standing ovation.

"At the end, Ver Lynn Sprague got up. With his booming voice, he said, 'Mr. Chairman!' 'Yes, Ver Lynn,' I replied.

Will Leonard (left) and long-time member Charles Wesselhoeft

'Mr. Chairman,' he continued, 'will the speaker have time for some questions?' He then proceeded to ask this long, involved question that made about as much sense as the speech. Everybody cracked-up at that point, all over again."[7]

Will Leonard—Round Table member, battlefield tour companion, and columnist for the *Chicago Tribune*—wrote about the 1971 tour in his May 8 column: "HEREWITH WE SUBMIT our annual report on the springtime tour of historic battlefields by members of The Civil War Round Table of Chicago. This year the enthusiasts (how we hate that word 'buffs') trailed back and forth, hither and yon, along the deliberately confusing trails used by Stonewall Jackson in the Shenandoah Valley campaign of 1862. If Stonewall could have President Abraham Lincoln and the federals baffled, then you can imagine what he did to a hundred Chicagoans 109 years later. But we learned a few valuable things.

"Item: Sheridan wasn't 'twenty miles away,' as the poem says, when he rode from Winchester to Cedar Creek, to stem the good guys' retreat. It was about eleven-and-a-half miles.

"Item: At Port Royal, where Jackson did a Muhammad Ali (i.e., 'float like a butterfly, sting like a bee'), there's a Bing Crosby Stadium today. None of the guides could explain why.

". . . . Item: One of the tourists, sound asleep in a motel near Winchester, was wakened by a pounding on his door, and thought for a moment the end of the world was at hand. But it seems there are fireworks for sale in the Shenandoah Valley, and his buddies from Chicago were lighting a series of sparklers and stuffing them through the keyhole one after another. [The harshly-awakened tourist has been identified as Dan Lapinski, president of The Round Table for the 1970-1971 term.)

"Long ago, before we left Chicago, we had ascertained that eventually, the federal government defeated the Confederacy. Somehow, that was reassuring last week between the Appalachians and the Blue Ridge."

Veteran member Joseph L. Eisendrath, who missed being a founder by only one month, closed out the 1970-1971 season with an address, on June 11, on "The Lincoln Myths." Don Russell wrote about Eisendrath in the June newsletter: ". . . He was president of The CWRT in 1949-1950. He says he has 'a good working library on Lincoln and I have authored many Lincoln and Civil War articles. My biggest honor was [being a] footnoter and researcher for Otto Eisenschiml. He wanted me to do a book with him.'. . . Professionally, Joe Eisendrath is head of Banthrico, Inc., manufacturers of coin banks and die castings. He has engaged in numerous civic activities and admits to being a lousy golfer."

Russell reported in the September newsletter that, at the June meeting, "Joe threw out his twenty-five or so [Lincoln] myths and left it to members to decide which they preferred to discuss first, second, and thereafter.

The result was a lively discussion in which all participated, and we got around to most or all of the twenty-five." The installation of officers was another feature, as usual, of the June meeting. Dan Lapinski turned over the presidential gavel to Marshall Krolick.

In October of 1971, Jerry L. Schober talked about "Mary Ann Pitman, Rebel Soldier, United States citizen, and Patriot." Pitman was the young woman who—disguised as a man—enlisted in the Confederate Army, fought in the Battle of Shiloh, and rose to the rank of 2nd lieutenant prior to serving with distinction under the command of General Nathan Bedford Forrest. Curiously, there was no summary whatsoever of this talk, as is customary, in the following month's newsletter.

Charles Wesselhoeft delivered an address on "Civil War Railroads," an area in which he had done considerable research, at the November meeting. The year ended with what was billed as "A Double-header Evening" on December 10, 1971. The evening began with an autographing and cocktail party at The Book & Bottle (across from the Abraham Lincoln Book Shop) in celebration of the publication of Pete and Barbara Long's new book, *The Civil War Day By Day, An Almanac, 1861-1865* (1971). Bruce Catton said this of their book: "In all the vast collection of books on the American Civil War, there is no book like this one."[8]

Marshall Krolick, 1971-72 President

Following the party, Pete Long addressed the 306th meeting at the Chicago Bar Association. His topic was "War Beyond the River: The Trans-Mississippi in the Civil War and the Influence of the War in the West." The Round Table was delighted to have their former president and good friend back from Wyoming for the evening, and equally delighted to hear his address. Don Russell noted, in the newsletter, that: "To say that no one anywhere knows more about the Civil War than does Pete Long is no exaggeration, for who else has devoted to that subject a decade of full-time research?"

The Civil War Round Table was thirty-one years old now and entering the third year of the 1970s. It continued to thrive, presenting top-notch scholars at its meetings, fostering and encouraging new Civil War scholars, supporting the work being done to preserve our Civil War battlefield sites— and coming up with innovative ideas to support its objectives. And, in all of this, The Round Table kept proving that the study of history can be not only worthwhile and enlightening, but great fun as well.

Chapter 12 ☆ *1972 through 1977: From a Birthday Party for General Grant, to the Introduction of the Nevins-Freeman Award, to the Admission of Women as Members*

JAMES I. (BUD) ROBERTSON, JR. GOT 1972 off to a good start for The Round Table with a January 14 address on "The Stonewall Brigade." Don Russell wrote in the next month's newsletter that Robertson "apologized for addressing us for a second time . . . on "The Stonewall Brigade," but charged that Marshall Krolick would not let him talk about anything else. In this our president, who seldom can boast overwhelming support, had unanimous consent. After all, it was nearly twelve years since Bud was with us, March 11, 1960. Since then, he has written his book on the subject and obviously has added much depth to his knowledge of the Stonewall Brigade . . ."

The Round Table lost another of its founders in February. Don Russell reported that Charles Norton Owen had died, at the age of seventy-seven, in Evanston Hospital. There were now only nine surviving founders.

On April 21, The Civil War Round Table, joining with The Ulysses S. Grant Association, The Illinois Special Events Commission, and the Friends of the Chicago Public Library, held a 150th birthday commemoration of the birth of Ulysses S. Grant. Held at the Chicago Public Library, guests enjoyed cocktails and Civil War era music by JAZZ, Limited, a dinner, and an address by T. Harry Williams on "Grant as President." (This was a "Ladies Night.")

This evening was especially noteworthy for one Round Table member. Don Russell included this note in the newsletter: "While attendance at the Grant party was strictly limited, and late-comers were denied a reservation, invasion by a gate crasher was narrowly averted by the quick action of Ward and Edie Smidl. Appropriately named Sara Grant Smidl, all 6 pounds, 4 ounces of her, agreed to make her appearance at a nearby hospital at 11 p.m. the night of the party."

The twenty-second annual battlefield tour went to Vicksburg from May 4 through May 7. Though costs had risen a little since those first tours, it was still outrageously inexpensive (by today's standards) to go on a battlefield tour. $225 (two to a room) or $235 (single) *included:* round trip plane fare, bus ground transportation, hotel room, Command Posts (this meant free drinks), group service tips, group admission fees where required, and tour literature.

The dinner speaker for the first night was "the eminent expert of Vicksburg, Mr. Edwin C. Bearss."[1] The Friday night address was given by Lieutenant Colonel (retired) Henry Hanisee. Marshall Krolick remembers that evening: "The colonel's topic was "The *U.S. Rattler*." The *Rattler* was not an ironclad, but a gunboat. It was part of the Mississippi River squadron in the area of Vicksburg. This boat had done absolutely nothing of any significance whatsoever; but this guy had made a career out of studying the *Rattler*. He proceeded to give us well over an hour of: 'On Tuesday, the *Rattler* moved ten miles upstream and docked at the Jones plantation and on Wednesday, it moved eight miles downstream and docked at Smith's plantation.' and so forth. This went on for over an hour with this boat doing nothing but patroling the river. Who cared? People were nodding off and falling asleep. It was horrendous.

"Finally, the *Rattler* hit a mine the Confederates had lain in the river. He covered the explosion in precise detail, and went into great histrionics about the death throes of the ship. He ended his talk with the line: 'And, with the last shuddering gasp, the gallant ship *Rattler* slowly sank beneath the waves.' As he said 'beneath the waves,' Morrie Fisher [Round Table member Maurice Fisher], who was sitting right in front, said in a very loud voice, "thank God!' Everyone in the audience went into gales of laughter." Asked what the colonel's reaction was, Krolick replied that he just stood there, adding that he felt the man deserved any humiliation he suffered for putting his audience through such a tedious ordeal.[2]

Saturday's Fun Night that year was aboard the riverboat *Sprague* where the group saw a performance of "Gold in the Hills." Sunday's schedule included stops at the Chickasaw Bayou and a tour of the Old Court House Museum.

Taps were played for another Round Table founder on May 29, 1972. Monroe F. Cockrell, who was also the first Round Table president, died at the James C. King Home in Evanston, Illinois at the age of eighty-seven.

The Civil War Round Table, in June, presented Margaret April with a certificate of appreciation for the countless hours she had spent planning every minute detail of the battlefield tours since 1951. A parody of Lincoln's Gettysburg address, it noted that: "The membership will little note nor long remember what we say here, but it can never forget what she did to so nobly advance the success of our tours." "It is up to us," it continues, "to be here dedicated to the task of continuing this enjoyable search for knowledge and that in honoring Margaret, we take increased devotion to the cause for which she worked so many hours over so many years, and that we here highly resolve that her work should not be in vain and that this program shall continue to grow and that battlefield tours of the members, for the members, and by Margaret April shall not perish from the earth."

The Round Table sponsored their second Civil War Tour of Chicago on Sunday, June 25. Mike Lerner was chairman for the event. The group gathered for breakfast at the Pickle Barrel Restaurant at Howard Street and Western Avenue. (Participants brought their own lunches; cold pop and beer were packed on the bus.) Stops included Calvary Cemetery in Evanston; Rosehill and Graceland Cemeteries in Chicago; the Chicago Historical Society; the Stephen A. Douglas tomb; and Oak Woods Cemetery. At the Chicago Historical Society, Richard Blake entertained the group with his impersonation of Abraham Lincoln. There were 120 participants in the tour.

From September 29 through October 1, new President Charles Falkenberg, Jr. and Brooks Davis and Frank Rankin, tour co-chairmen, led the group in a special battlefield tour of the Kentucky Bluegrass area. Don Russell wrote in the special newsletter that The Civil War Round Table "tour members will be in Kentucky the last weekend in September, manuevering boldly in a way that Generals Braxton Bragg and Don Carlos Buell could never have imagined! Our fall 1972 special battlefield tour will arrive in Louisville early Friday afternoon following a group photograph taken at Chicago's O'Hare airport and a fast flight to the land south of the Mason-Dixon line . . ." Sites visited included Pleasant Hill, also known as "Shakertown," where members of that sect fed and lodged many Federal and Confederate troops, including John Hunt Morgan's men; the Perryville battlefield; Transylvania College; Mary Todd Lincoln's childhood home in Lexington; Whitehall, the home of Cassius Marcellus Clay; and Farmington, the Louisville home of Lincoln's dear friend Joshua Speed. A joint meeting with the Kentucky and Louisville Civil War Round Tables took place on Saturday night. On Sunday afternoon, Dr. R. Gerald McMurtry delivered an address on "Recollections of Judge William Townsend and his Cassius Clay Speech."

The first big event of 1973 came on March 9. Billed in the newsletter as the "319th Regular Meeting" and "18th Ladies Night," the Camp Followers sent out invitations which cordially invited its members, friends, and guests to attend "The

Campaigners prepare to depart for the special battlefield tour to Kentucky in 1972

Gentleman's Night Dinner and Meeting." The subject of Bell I. Wiley's address that evening was "Women of the Lost Cause." The Camp Followers' invitation noted that: "For seventeen years, the gentlemen of The Civil War Round Table have devoted one night a year to a program to which their ladies were invited. This year the tables are being turned and the ladies are taking over!"

Don Russell wrote in the March newsletter: "The 18th Ladies Night of The Civil War Round Table will be different, we are promised. For one thing, it will be in a different place from our regular meeting rooms. It will open with a reception in the Grand Army of the Republic Room of the Chicago Public Library. There will be special displays and, we are told, champagne will be served from an historic silver bowl. Dinner (with wine) will follow in the Tiffany Rotunda. We then move over to the Auditorium for the program, where Betty Walter, president of the Camp Followers, Alice Cromie, and others will have a part."

Russell wrote in the next month's newsletter that: "Ladies Night, taken over by the Camp Followers, who proclaimed it Gentlemen's Night, proved a huge and expected success . . . Champagne flowed, wine was poured, the food was good and plentiful, and the service was overwhelming. Betty Walter opened the program session, and Alice Cromie introduced the speaker, but the ladies stopped there and did not freeze out President Charles V. Falkenberg from his accustomed role as arbitrator, moderator, and presiding officer." Russell continued, reporting on Dr. Wiley's talk about the women of the Confederacy: ". . . It was a popular war and a women's war. Mothers urged their sons to enlist; belles ridiculed and discarded swains who did not wear the gray. A few women sought to take up arms and there were some who disguised themselves as men and joined the troops. It was recorded at one prison camp that an officer prisoner had given birth to a son! A few gained fame as spies—Rose Greenhow, Emma Samson, and Belle Boyd . . . Also heroic were those who stayed home and remained loyal despite the heavy losses . . . Among the real heroines were the poor women who kept farms and plantations going while the men were away. Only a few had slaves and many women plowed the fields, harvested the crops, cut and hauled the firewood, and ran their households. Because many essentials could not be bought after the war's second year, they had to make at home soap, candles, leather, cloth, and dyes . . ."

The twenty-third annual battlefield tour (May 10-13) in 1973 traveled to Gettysburg. It was billed in the newsletter as the "General Schimmelfennig Memorial Tour." Don Russell wrote about the Union general in an earlier newsletter: "Brigadier General Alexander Schimmelfennig has had unusual attention from CWRT members because of his name, and for this there is a precedent. There is a legend that President Lincoln, in signing his commission, said he knew nothing about the man but that his name alone was sufficient recommendation as obvious recognition of German immigrants. A two-page article about him in the February 1972 issue of *Civil War Times Illustrated* pictures his pigpen "headquarters" at Gettysburg. While trying to rally his troops in the town on July 1, the general was cut off by Confederates and was hit in the head by a gun butt. He feigned death and escaped to a pigpen. [He spent two-and-one-half days there.] Patricia Weaver of the magazine staff adds the detail that the pigpen was owned by her great-great-grandfather, John Henry Gerlach, and that Mrs. Gerlach fed and hid the general until the Confederates abandoned Gettysburg July 4 and he could return to his command."

During Friday afternoon, May 11, the tour stopped at the site of General Schimmelfennig's pigpen hide-away. Dan Lapinski had something special for Marshall Krolick, whose special area of interest and expertise in the Civil War is the Battle of Gettysburg. Lapinski attempted to present Krolick with a most appropriate and inventive memento of the "General Schimmelfennig Memorial Tour": a live baby pig! However, because he claimed that "the piglet had the quick-step,"[3] Krolick refused to accept it.

For this courageous—albeit not quite successful—at-

Dan Lapinski "attempts" to present a memento of the "General Schimmelfennig Memorial Tour" to Marshall Krolick at Gettysburg in 1973

tempt, Dan Lapinski became the winner of The Round Table's first Confederate Purple Heart, which was presented to him at 1973's Fun Night. The Confederate Purple Heart, given for gallantry above the call of duty during a Round Table battlefield tour, has become a tradition. The beautifully designed Purple Heart is passed on from one year's recipient to the next year's. The hand-painted, heart-shaped award, featuring purple backing and a Confederate flag and encased in a hand-carved wooden box, was the work of member Dr. John Magreiter. It is still in use and is currently in the possession of 1990's winner. (See Appendix I for a listing of Confederate Purple Heart winners)

For his "attempt" to present a live baby pig to Marshall Krolick, Dan Lapinski received the first Confederate Purple Heart at Gettysburg in 1973

Left photo: *Pat Newman with General Omar Bradley during the 1973 tour to Gettysburg*
Right photo: *1972-73 President Charles Falkenberg (right) with 1973-74 President Gordon Whitney*

There was a real-life drama during the 1973 battlefield tour. One participant, Dr. Raymond E. Mulrooney, suffered a stroke, followed by cardiac arrest, in the midst of the tour. Quick, heroic action by LaVerne Wesselhoeft, a registered nurse; Gordon Whitney, a firefighter; and Dr. John Magreiter, a physician from St. Louis, saved Dr. Mulrooney's life. Successful surgery was performed at Pennsylvania's Hershey Medical Center.

The final tour stop that year was the U.S. Army War College and Carlisle Barracks, where the group enjoyed a brunch and heard an address by Dr. Richard Sommers. General Omar N. Bradley, whose papers are part of the collection in the Military History Research Collection at the College, was The Round Table's guest of honor for the occasion.

A special award was presented at the June 8 meeting to George B. Hartzog, Jr., director of the National Park Service. He gave the address that evening on "An Endangered Species: Our Civil War National Parks." That evening, Charles Falkenberg relinquished the presidential gavel to Gordon Whitney.

The following announcement appeared in the June 1973 newsletter: "Ralph Newman announced a partnership with Daniel Weinberg in the Abraham Lincoln Book Shop at an open house commemorating the 184th anniversary of the inauguration of our first president, George Washington, Monday, April 30. The book shop also opened a new presidential department, displaying books, letters, and manuscripts relating to the presidents . . ."

A weekend tour of "Lincoln Country" was on the October Round Table schedule. On October 12 through 14, the group visited Lincoln College, Camp Butler, Lincoln's home in Springfield, the Old State Capitol, the Illinois State Historical Library, Lincoln's Law Office, and New Salem State Park. The

dinner speaker at Lincoln College in Lincoln, Illinois on
Friday was Paul Simon, former lieutenant governor.

Past President Dr. Gerhard P. Clausius finally got the
opportunity to deliver an address about his hero. He spoke,
on October 19, on "Lincoln's Friend Steve Hurlbut, hero of
Hatchie River." Dr. Clausius was an optometrist in Belvidere,
Illinois—the home town of Steven Augustus Hurlbut. Prior to
and following the evening of his talk, Dr. Clausius would
work General Hurlbut's name—somehow—into the question
he would ask of the speaker during the question and answer
period of nearly every Round Table meeting. (More to keep
the memory of Dr. Clausius alive than that of General Hurlbut,
Round Table members will still occasionally insert the name
of the Belvidere hero into their query to a speaker.)

*Ralph Newman, Dan
Weinberg, and long-time
Book Shop employee Dick
Clark outside the Abraham
Lincoln Book Shop*

Another past president, Ver Lynn Sprague composed the "Ballad of General Hurlbut" especially for the October 19, 1973 meeting. Prior to Dr. Clausius' talk, he led the audience in the singing of the ballad, (See Appendix J for the lyrics of this composition and "A Ballad to a Straddle Trench.")

In January of 1974, Marshall Krolick assumed a new job: editor of the newsletter. "To my immediate predecessor, Don Russell," Krolick said in the January issue, "I join with the entire membership in expressing our heartfelt appreciation for a job well done during the past three-and-one-half years . . ."

The February 8, 1974 "Ladies Night," held at the Como Inn, featured Dick Blake's "A Look at Lincoln" and a performance by the "Schimmelfennig Singers." Marshall Krolick wrote in the newsletter that: "Vocally and visually, Dick [Blake] creates the amazing illusion that the audience is actually in the presence of our 16th president. His warm portrayal depicts the essence of Lincoln as the Great Emancipator grew from a young politician to a war-weary chief executive." "To set the stage for Dick's presentation," Krolick continues, "we will first be treated to a program of "Songs of the Sixties" (1860s, that is) sung by four professional members of the Chicago Symphony Orchestra Chorus. This talented quartet, named the "Schimmelfennig Singers" in honor of our immortal hero, will include . . . The Round Table's own senior vice president, Ward Smidl . . ."

Marshall D. Krolick was the speaker at the March 8 meeting. His topic was "Lee and Longstreet at Gettysburg." "Guest Reviewer" Gordon Whitney said in the next month's newsletter summary that: "Marshall's presentation of an old conflict was admirably done with clear stated facts. He made you feel 'you were there.'"

Sad news appeared in the March newsletter: "Our dear friend and inspiration, James Ambler Johnston, died in his sleep Thursday, February 7, following a hip operation. Ambler, who would have been eighty-nine years old May 18, was buried among his friends in Hollywood Cemetery. The Round Table is sending a memorial to the History Department of his beloved Virginia State University, Blackburg, Virginia."

The destination of the twenty-fourth annual battlefield tour was Chattanooga and Chickamauga. Marshall Krolick noted in his review of the trip that: "A true highlight of the trip was the unique Chattanooga Choo-Choo Hilton, our headquarters during our four-day visit. Its fine dining facilities and shopping arcade are housed in the remodeled Southern Railway Depot. Parked on the tracks and extending from the former station are numerous Pullman cars which have been transformed into fully furnished rooms. Those who desired

At the Illinois Monument, Missionary Ridge—1974 Battlefield Tour

standard sleeping quarters were housed in the adjacent modern hotel building."

Stops on the tour included a visit to the "Confederama" electric map at the base of Lookout Mountain and a cable car trip to its top; Missionary Ridge; and Dug's Gap. Saturday's Fun Night program featured the Buster Keaton silent film classic, *The General*, with "brilliant narration by our own Jerry Warshaw, ably assisted by the piano mastery of Arnold Alexander."

Marshall Krolick reported in his review of the 1974 tour that: "This year's [Confederate Purple Heart] winner (?) of the priceless prize was our beloved Jack Kaluf, who had the honor to be advised by Delta Airlines officials that he had been bumped off our overbooked (by the airline) return flight. Jack's remarks, both on that occasion and on his being told of his selection as this year's recipient of the matchless medallion can best be described by the currently popular phrase 'expletives deleted.'"

The tour wound-up with a Sunday afternoon tour to the Tennessee Valley Railroad Museum and a steam locomotive train ride on a seven-mile journey through Missionary Ridge Tunnel. The *Chattanooga News-Free Press* ran a story about The Round Table's trip on May 5, under the headline, "Guns Still Blaze, Battle Shouts Still Resound."

"A most historic and gala evening," Marshall Krolick wrote, "is in store for Round Table members, their ladies, and guests on June 14, 1974. On that occasion, The Civil War Round Table will inaugurate what is to be an annual event, the presentation of the Nevins-Freeman Award to an individual who has made a distinguished contribution to our study and knowledge of the history and heritage of the Civil War . . ." The idea for this award was conceived by Ralph Newman and was named, of course, in honor of Allan Nevins and Douglas Southall Freeman.

Krolick wrote in the newsletter that: "Allan Nevins (1890-1971) and Douglas Southall Freeman (1886-1953) were both Honorary Life members of The Civil War Round Table. During their lifetimes, these two journalist-historians made significant and impressive contributions to the literature of American history and particularly to that of the American Civil War, 1861-1865. We were privileged to have both of these gentlemen and scholars in our midst on several occasions. Dr. Nevins appeared as a speaker before our organization and generously shared his valuable time in providing counsel and companionship to many of us. Dr. Freeman made his last speech about The War Between the States when he addressed us on the occasion of our battlefield tour to Richmond in 1953. He also was a most gracious host, entertaining

Allan Nevins in 1966

us at his home on the last day we were in the former Confederate capital."

Bruce Catton was chosen to be the first recipient of the Nevins-Freeman Award. The dinner was held in the rotunda of the Grand Army of the Republic Rooms of the Chicago Public Library; the program was held in the library's auditorium. Marshall Krolick wrote in the newsletter that: "Those participating in paying tribute to [Bruce Catton] included our own E.B. (Pete) Long and Ralph Newman, Samuel S. Vaughn, president of Doubleday Publishing Company, and, by means of telegram and appropriate gift sent from California, Carl Haverlin. Following their remarks, which detailed Mr. Catton's life and literary achievements, our guest of honor responded, expressing his thanks and relating several personal experiences which had a profound effect on his career."

Bill Sullivan recalls the evening as one of his favorite Round Table meetings: "A commemorative broadside was printed of one of Mr. Catton's poems. A copy was given as a souvenir to all who attended that evening. Few people knew that he had written poetry. He graciously stayed to autograph the copies. I think he signed everyone's twice. I was so impressed by the gentleness of this man and his genuine humility. That night he gave much of the credit for his books to [his researcher] Pete Long."[4]

"The award itself, which will be a permanent design and will be repeated each year," Krolick related in the September 1974 newsletter, "is approximately fifteen inches long and ten inches high. It consists of an appropriately engraved plate and a magnificent scale model of a Civil War artillery piece, complete with accoutrements, all mounted on a walnut base and covered by a removable transparent plexiglass case. It has been decided by the Executive Committee that the Award will be presented each year at the June meeting, which will also be the occasion of our annual Ladies Night."[5] (See Appendix K for a list of Nevins-Freeman winners.)

That evening Gordon Whitney surrendered the presidential gavel to new President Ward Smidl. Honorary Award Life Memberships were presented to Don Russell, Stan Kearney, Elmer Underwood, and Henry Bass for their support of and service to The Round Table.

The members of the board of directors of the Chicago Public Library—Ralph Newman was president of the Board—committed almost $12,000,000 for work on restoring the old central Library building and turning it into a "Cultural Center." In the September 1974 newsletter, Marshall Krolick reported that: They have indicated that they would welcome The Civil War Round Table. Our task would be to supply some book cases and furniture for the Civil War Library and

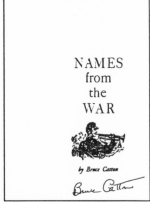

NAMES
from
the
WAR

by Bruce Catton

The cover of the commemorative broadside containing Bruce Catton's poem, "Names from the War" distributed at the time of the presentation of the first Nevins-Freeman Award to Bruce Catton in 1974

Ward Smidl, 1974-75 President, in 1981

for the establishment of an endowment fund to guarantee that all current and new publications would automatically be added to our collection. The library, in turn would place all of its rarer books on the Civil War in the same area. The entire collection would be non-circulating and so would always be intact and available."

The Round Table established a Research and Study Collection Fund, whose purpose was the creation of the Civil War room in the Chicago Public Library. In a letter to members in November, Arnold Alexander wrote that: "We are asking each of our members and friends, to the best of his ability and resources to make a pledge over the next three years to make this program possible."[6] The initial goal was to come up with $20,000; the ultimate goal was to raise $100,000.

The December 13 meeting was another "double-header." First on the agenda was a cocktail and autographing party at the Abraham Lincoln Book Shop, honoring Shelby Foote and celebrating the publication of the third and final volume of his *The Civil War: A Narrative* series, *Red River to Appomattox* (1974). Women were invited to the party. This was followed by the regular Round Table meeting at the Chicago Bar Association, at which Shelby Foote spoke on "Writing Civil War History" and to which women were not invited.

The Round Table was saddened with the loss of another of its founders in 1975. Alexander J. Isaacs, who was sixty-eight, died on March 18.

The Round Table chose the Richmond-Petersburg area for the site of its twenty-fifth annual battlefield tour (April 30-May 4). On Thursday, May 1, one of the stops scheduled was at the Massaponax Church on Old Telegraph Road near

The tour group at Massaponax Church before the "break-in"

Richmond. This was where Grant had held his 1864 Council of War and the names and regiments of Union soldiers, written on the walls of the church at that time, remained intact. Upon arriving, the Round Tablers were chagrined to discover that the minister who was to open the church was not there. Bill Sullivan remembers that people were "ambling around aimlessly" when he got the idea to try the back door of the church. Discovering that it might be eased open, he enlisted the assistance of Marshall Krolick and Raymond Jankovich, Jr. Krolick, using a credit card and a Swiss Army knife, performed the task in mere moments. The group had their tour, left a $50 check which had been prepared for the minister in the Bible on the lectern, and locked the doors of the church as they departed. During the Fun Night festivities on Saturday, Krolick was presented with some children's play tools—a "toy burglary set"—to commemorate his daring deed.[7]

The Fun Night program was highlighted by an impressive presentation by Harold Howard, then a college professor and now the guiding light behind the Virginia Regimental Series. Bill Sullivan recalls that Howard "was the first person I ever saw who did a real living history presentation the right way. He portrayed a soldier from The Army of Northern Virginia on the day after the surrender at Appomattox. He had a name, a history, a regiment, and a company. Howard had researched the diary of this soldier so well that he could answer a wide variety of questions as if he were that soldier. He could reply to queries about his equipment, whether he had been wounded and where, where he lived, whether he had a wife or children, and so forth.

"The audience was invited to try to trip him up by asking him questions that a soldier in Lee's Army couldn't possibly have known. But Howard was so well versed on his subject that he wouldn't attempt to answer questions that a Southern soldier in 1865 Virginia would not have been able to answer. People would ask him questions such as: 'What do you think about the situation in the Trans-Mississippi area?' He would reply that this was difficult to say because they hadn't heard from Texas in over nine months because the mail hadn't gotten through. It was the best portrayal of its kind I've ever seen."[8]

During this tour, The Round Table group was the guest of the Richmond Civil War Round Table at a reception at the White House of the Confederacy, where mint juleps were served on the lawn. In addition to Harold Howard, speakers included William Mallory and Hobson Goddin of the Richmond CWRT and Edwin C. Bearss and Joseph Cullen of the National Park Service. On Friday, Round Tablers had the option of taking a tour to Williamsburg in lieu of the day's battlefield itinerary.

Founding member Ralph G. Newman spoke at the May 9 meeting, when his topic was "The Last Full Measure of Devotion: Abraham Lincoln's Incredible Funeral." Mr. Newman was back on The Round Table podium the next month when he was honored as the second recipient of the Nevins-Freeman Award. The dinner was held on June 13— once again in the Grand Army of the Republic Rooms of the Chicago Public Library.

Marshall Krolick wrote in the newsletter that: ". . . Over one hundred and eighty members and friends gathered to pay tribute to this year's recipient, our own founder Ralph G. Newman. Ralph's great contributions to us and his many accomplishments in the field of Civil War study were described to those in attendance by the evening's principal speakers, John Hope Franklin, John Y. Simon, and Carl Haverlin. Entertainment was provided by the Civil War musical talent of Judy Plant. Also included in the program was the announcement that the Executive Committee had bestowed well-deserved Honorary Life memberships on three long and valued members, Arnold Alexander, Al Meyer, and Miner Coburn . . ." Another traditional ceremony occurred at the June meeting: Ward Smidl turned over the presidental gavel to Gerald M. Edelstein.

"Among the items on the agenda [for the September 1975 meeting]," Marshall Krolick reported, "was a presentation by Brooks Davis, co-chairman of the Research Center Fund, a check for $5000 to David L. Reich, chief librarian of the Chicago Public Library. This sum represented the initial installment of our commitment to secure the establishment of the Research Center . . ." A full-page explanation of what the Center would include was published in the October newsletter, along with a pledge form for members to fill out and return with the first installment of their pledge.

On October 10, Dr. Alfred C. Raphelson spoke on "General Alexander Schimmelfennig," covering the general's accomplishments before and after his prolonged stay in the Garlach family's pigsty at Gettysburg. Marshall Krolick admitted that "our preoccupation with the lighter side of the career of Alexander Schimmelfennig does not do justice to a brave soldier." On November 14, George M. Fredrickson spoke on "Lincoln and Racial Equality." The dinner was at the Blackhawk Restaurant; the meeting was held in at the G.A.R. Memorial Auditorium at the Chicago Public Library. This gave President Edelstein the opportunity to present a check for $5000 to Thomas Orlando, Special Collections Librarian. This gift represented the second installment and half-way point of The Round Table's initial commitment to fund the Research Center.

William J. (Bill) Sullivan opened the new year of 1976 for The Round Table with an address about "The Civil War on the Plains" on January 9. On February 13, James T. Hickey, curator of the Lincoln Collection of the Illinois State Historical Library, spoke on "Lincolniana in Illinois." Marshall Krolick noted that: "Under his [Mr. Hickey's] tenure, the State Historical Library has acquired approximately five hundered original documents in Lincoln's handwriting, as well as collections of pictures, relics, and broadsides related to our sixteenth president."

The 350th meeting on April 9 featured a symposium on "Where Goes the Civil War?" Chaired by E.B. (Pete) Long, the panel discussion brought together distinguished individuals from various segments of Civil War study. The panel consisted of: Ralph G. Newman, speaking for publishers, booksellers, and editors; Marshall D. Krolick, representing Round Table scholarship; and John Y. Simon, relating the opinion of the academician. The symposium concentrated on the status of Civil War writing in the 1970s, where it has gone in the recent past, and what its direction should be in the future.

Upon discovering that there was no headstone for the grave of Captain Marcellus E. Jones located in Wheaton Cemetery, Round Table members decided to do something to remedy that situation. Captain Jones, of the 8th Illinois Cavalry, while a lieutenant, had the distinction of firing the first shot at the Battle of Gettysburg. Ceremonies dedicating the headstone took place on Sunday, April 11, 1976. These ceremonies included a military honor guard and bugler and a

The headstone of Captain Marcellus E. Jones erected at Wheaton Cemetery by The Round Table in 1976

moving prayer by the Reverend Gene Winkler. The event received radio and television coverage.

From May 1-5, the twenty-sixth annual battlefield tour went to Manassas and Antietam. In addition to tours of the battlefields of Manassas and Antietam, the trip included stops at Harpers Ferry and Monocacy. On Sunday, May 5, the group toured Arlington Cemetery and the Washington D.C. area.

Bill Sullivan remembers Ed Bearss and Marshall Krolick running down, with few moments to spare before the bus left, to get Civil War era-like tintype photographs taken of themselves at a little shop in Harpers Ferry.[9] Sullivan also remembers "Will Leonard's great joust with the freight train." "During our trip to the Monocacy battlefield, we had to walk across a railroad bridge to get where we were going. It turned out that after most of us had crossed, we looked back and saw Will still on the bridge—with a train coming. Will was no spring chicken then. We couldn't get to him in time and he couldn't get to either end before the train came by. After the train had passed, we found him, with his rump edged between two of the ties on the double tracks to avoid being sucked under the train. Naturally, he was awarded with the Confederate Purple Heart that year."[10]

1976 Nevins-Freeman Award Recipient T. Harry Williams

The third annual Nevins-Freeman Award went to longtime Round Table friend and eminent Civil War scholar, T. Harry Williams. Following a reception at the Chicago Historical Society, the dinner and meeting was held at the Germania Club. Dr. Williams gave an address on "Why I Am Fascinated With The Civil War, or The Confessions Of An Addict." The president's gavel was passed from Gerald M. Edelstein to Terry Carr.

The June 1976 newsletter carried some sad news. The death of founding member Fred Evers was announced. Honorary Life member and former Governor Otto Kerner had also died.

Terry Carr, 1976-77 President, in 1981

The second annual Congress of Civil War Round Tables, sponsored by Jerry Russell's Civil War Round Table Associates, was held at the Army War College in Carlisle, Pennsylvania October 21 through 23. A number of top scholars participated. Marshall Krolick, who attended, reported in the November newsletter that: "Among the many resolutions passed at the Congress was one calling for the formulation, in each Round Table, of a Battlefield Preservation Committee

The November newsletter reported that: "The state of Illinois has recently received as a donation a collection of Lincoln memorabilia worth more than $100,000. The donor was Robert Todd Lincoln Beckwith, 72, the only living descendant of the sixteenth president."

The Round Table lost another valued member on January 6, 1977. Will Leonard, *Chicago Tribune* columnist, died at the age of sixty-four. Marshall Krolick wrote about Will in the February newsletter: "A regular attendant on our annual battlefield tours, his wit and companionship added immeasurably to the pleasure of all. . . . However, the twinkle of his eye and the ever-present smile of a leprechaun masked, but never hid, Will's serious appreciation of those who preceded us and what they accomplished . . ."

Middle Tennessee was the destination of the twenty-seventh annual battlefield tour (May 4-8). Sites visited included the battlefields at Stones River, Spring Hill, Franklin, and Nashville and Fort Donelson. Fun Night was held at the Grand Ole Opry.

Veteran member Lloyd D. Miller was honored as the fourth recipient of the Nevins-Freeman Award, on June 10, 1977, at a dinner in the Preston Bradley Hall of the newly restored Chicago Public Library Cultural Center. "A member of The Round Table since April 23, 1941, the date of the fifth meeting," Marshall Krolick noted, "Lloyd has not only served the organization in numerous capacities, but has consistently been the prime benefactor in any project designed to further the study of the events of 1861-1865. All of those who have been assisted in the past by our scholarship program or who will benefit in the future from the facilities of our Research Center owe to him a debt that can never be adequately repaid."

Miller was unique among Nevins-Freeman honorees in that he brought his own entertainment and music. The entertainment was in the form of movies he had taken of battlefield tours past. Bill Sullivan recalls the music: "Lloyd brought a lovely string trio (two violinists and a cellist) who went from table to table, playing beautiful classical music. He asked them if they could play "Marching Through Georgia"—and they did. This was probably quite an experience for those nice, very dignified ladies . . ."[11]

The Civil War Round Table and the Chicago Public Library co-sponsored a reception, on October 17, to dedicate the Civil War and American History Collection in the Cultural Center of the Library. On the same date, the "Treasures of the Chicago Public Library" exhibition was opened in the renovated Grand Army of the Republic Memorial Hall of the Cultural Center.

An issue which had long been bubbling beneath the surface finally came to resolution in 1977: whether to admit women to membership in The Civil War Round Table. Ralph Newman and others had for a long time advocated the admission of women. As noted previously, year after year,

Newman would propose the issue at Executive Committee meetings, Year after year, it was rejected. Adequate votes could not be garnered among members of the Executive Committee. Many of the men—especially the newer members, such as Dan Weinberg—were very embarrassed to belong to an organization which, in 1977, would refuse to admit women. Weinberg claims to have lost at least two women customers who left the book shop, enraged upon learning that they were not eligible for membership in The Civil War Round Table.[12] Most Round Tables around the country did have women members—but not the grandparent of them all.

Marshall Krolick, one of the leaders in the fight to continue to refuse membership to women, wrote an editorial in the newsletter back in January of 1975. A paragraph from that editorial perhaps best illustrates the point-of-view of the negative side of the argument: "For the record, and because we feel that fence-straddling will resolve nothing, it is the attitude of this column that The Round Table should not permit women members. After sincere reflection, we must conclude that to admit the ladies would, despite all good intentions, inevitably lead to an erosion of the purpose of this organization. With all due respect to those few serious female students of the Civil War, the undeniable truth is that most women could care less about the Battle of Antietam or Jackson's strategy in the Valley. The old argument that those ladies who are in the latter group would not come to meetings just doesn't hold water. They would come, regardless of the topic, if only to spend an evening out with their husband, boy friend, lover, or whatever. Soon the members themselves would, out of concern for the ladies' pleasure, reluctantly request meetings which would be more entertaining to the women. It is very easy now to say we will not change our format. Will it be so easy then?"

At the summer Executive Committee meeting in 1977, there were finally enough positive votes to pass a measure to at least propose the matter to the general membership. A procedure was set-up to resolve the issue. In accordance with the terms of this procedure, a discussion (announced in the September newsletter) was held at the September meeting, after which a vote was taken to determine whether the issue would be further pursued. By a vote of 38 to 34 at that meeting, it was decided that the issue would be pursued.

The next step was to poll all local members (those residing within two-hundred miles of Chicago) and former officers. Ballots, included in the October newsletter, were to be marked and signed by members, in order to certify their eligibility. (Given his views on the subject of female Round

Table membership, Editor Krolick is to be admired for including an item in that same October issue, which reads in part: "The Medal of Honor has been restored to Civil War surgeon, Dr. Mary E. Walker, the only woman ever to receive the honor . . . Dr. Walker's medal was withdrawn allegedly because she was a civilian and not a member of the military. However, the Army has now acknowledged that this was done probably as a result of sex discrimination . . .")

Apparently, not all eligible members voted because the final count did not equal the number of members.[13] (Perhaps the fence-straddlers kept straddling the fence.) The final tally, published in the December 1977 newsletter, was 97 to 58 in favor of admitting women to full membership in The Civil War Round Table, effective immediately.

The earth did not cease to revolve. The meeting topics were not watered-down. The Civil War Round Table now has a number of women members. For the 1990-1991 term, six women are serving as either officers, board of trustee members, or committee chairpersons.

The chairperson for the 1990 battlefield tour was Round Table Vice President Mary Munsell Abroe, who currently is writing her Ph.D. dissertation on the history of the preservation of the Civil War battlefield parks currently in the National Park System. The Battle of Antietam has been a subject of special study for Abroe for many years. The author of this book, who is also the current editor of the newsletter, is a woman.

Most encouraging of all, however, is the fact that Marshall Krolick, and others—such as Marvin Sanderman—who agreed with his position back in 1977, admit they were mistaken.[14] Having been shown that women can be every bit as interested, in a serious and scholarly way, in the study of the Civil War as men, they now welcome women into the membership of The Civil War Round Table.

Chapter 13 ☆ *From the 1970s, Into the 1980s: The Round Table Begins its Fourth Decade*

Margaret April speaking at the 400th Meeting in 1981

MARGARET APRIL WAS THE FIRST WOMAN to become a member of The Civil War Round Table. Considering all the work she had done for the group over the past twenty-seven years, this was very fitting. "I made it my business," April emphasized, "to see that no other woman got in before me."[1]

There was not any immediate surge, however, of women joining The Round Table. The 1978 roster lists only eight women. But, over the years, the number continues to grow.

Many of Marshall Krolick's editorial columns in the newsletter focused on battlefield preservation. "Probably no single issue is of greater importance today to students of the Civil War," he asserted in the March 1978 issue, "than that of battlefield preservation." He reprinted portions of an editorial which appeared in *Civil War Times Illustrated*, asking their readers to contribute whatever amount they could afford to The Civil War Sites Fund of the National Park Foundation. "Please take the time," Krolick urged, ". . . to reach into your pocket as deeply as you can. Neither you nor your children will ever be sorry."

The twenty-eighth annual battlefield tour (May 3-7) took the campaigners to the areas of Fredericksburg and Chancellorsville. Along with the two main sites, the group visited—among other places—Chatham, Kelly's Ford, Brandy Station, and the Wilderness. In his review of the tour, Marshall Krolick wrote that: "Evenings on the tour were a combination of scholarship and entertainment. Thursday night Bob Krick delighted all with an in-depth and oft-times humorous view of Confederate General William Barksdale, a man whose career and personality can only be described as unique." "And so the tour is over for another year," Krolick observed, "but the memories linger on. Good times, good friends, and a deep appreciation of the efforts put forth on our behalf . . ."

The 1978 Nevins-Freeman Award went to Bell I. Wiley on June 9. Dr. Wiley, who was the author or co-author of twenty-four books on the Civil War, wrote primarily about relatively unknown people. He became the foremost authority on the common soldier in the War. Wiley's *The Life of Johnny Reb* and *The Life of Billy Yank* were referred to as "the penultimate studies of what the War was like for the rank and file" in a booklet on the Nevins-Freeman recipients published by The Civil War Round Table in 1984.[2] His first book, *Southern Negroes, 1861-1865* (1938), was an expansion of his Ph.D. thesis at Yale University.

The program at the Chicago Public Library's Cultural Center was preceded by a dinner at the Blackhawk Restaurant. The evening concluded with a reception in honor of the opening of a major exhibit in the Civil War and American History Research Collection—"One Hundred Important Additions to the Civil War and American History Research Collection: An Exhibition of Acquisitions 1974- 1978." And the presidential gavel was passed from Myron (Mike) Cohn to Glen N. Wiche.

1978 Nevins-Freeman Award Recipient Dr. Bell I. Wiley

The world of Civil War studies was greatly diminished on August 28, 1978, when Bruce Catton died at the age of seventy-eight. Among his awards were the Pulitzer Prize, the National Book Award, the Presidential Freedom Medal, and the first Nevins-Freeman Award of The Civil War Round Table. There were many tributes. "Bruce Catton . . . has slipped away from us," George Craig, of the New York Civil War Round Table, said in a speech before the fourth annual National Congress of Civil War Round Tables a few weeks after Mr. Catton's death. "Bruce will be remembered," he continued, "as a calm, soft-spoken, reserved individual with a peculiar glint in his eye. Many of us gathered here owe our introduction to the Civil War from his various writings in the post-World War II period. His works heralded and stimulated a revival in the study of the Civil War."[3] "Bruce probably converted more individuals to the gospel of the Civil War," Ralph Newman observed in a eulogy printed in the October newsletter, "than any other person. He wrote from the heart and from the viewpoint of the common soldier. . . . He started out to be a novelist but found that in the Civil War truth indeed is stranger and more fascinating than fiction."

Myron (Mike) Cohn, 1977-78 President, in 1981

Beginning with the September 1978 issue, David R. Richert became co-editor (with Marshall Krolick) of the newsletter. Richert had served as assistant editor for the 1977-1978 term.

The Round Table sponsored a third Civil War Tour of Chicago on Sunday, October 15. The tour was led by Co-chairmen Brooks Davis and Ralph Newman. After a brunch at The Maven in the Allerton Hotel, buses departed from the Abraham Lincoln Book Shop. In addition to the customary

Glen Wiche, 1978-79 President, in 1981

cemeteries and monuments, this tour visited additional locations where important events in Civil War and Lincoln history took place, including the sites of The Wigwam, the Tremont House, and part of the route of the Lincoln funeral in Chicago.

Past President Brooks Davis wound-up 1978 by delivering the December 8 address. His topic was "The Perryville Campaign." There was news of another past president in the December issue. It was reported that: "Chicago Mayor Michael Bilandic has announced that founder and Past President Ralph G. Newman has been appointed to the newly created position of Chicago Archivist. Ralph will begin his new duties on January 1, 1979 . . ."

Old wounds from the Civil War were still being healed as 1978 drew to a close. An item in the newsletter noted that: "President Carter has signed the amnesty bill restoring full citizenship to Confederate President Jefferson Davis. In remarks delivered at the time of the signing, Mr. Carter noted that this action completes the long process of reconciliation that has reunited our country following the tragic conflict between the states. A similar action, taken by former President Gerald Ford in 1976, restored the citizenship of Robert E. Lee."

The Round Table continued to draw the top scholars of the Civil War era to the speaker's podium as it entered the new year of 1979. Mark E. Neely, Jr., Director of the Louis A. Warren Lincoln Library and Museum in Fort Wayne, Indiana, spoke on February 9 on "Lincoln's Image: Photos, Prints, and Cartoons of the 1860s." Noted Civil War scholar and author Herman Hattaway addressed the March 9 meeting; his topic was "General Stephen D. Lee." He had recently (1976) written a book of the same title. The meeting was preceded by an autographing party at the Abraham Lincoln Book Shop.

The February newsletter carried the news that "a Resource Exchange, which will make information about the Civil War interests and expertise of our members available to other members, and also will serve as the basis for a speaker's bureau, is being developed by The Round Table. According to co-chairman of the Exchange, Paul Kliger, it is designed to create a closer bond among members, enabling them to learn about the interests of others . . ."

Sunday afternoon, March 18, was "Civil War Film Day" for Round Table members. The afternoon began with a buffet lunch at the French Quarter restaurant in the Palmer House. Early films about the Civil War were shown at the G.A.R. Memorial Hall at the Chicago Public Library. A "Special Event Issue" of the newsletter was sent out, informing members that: ". . . You and your family are invited to cheer the heroes, boo the villians, and 'follow the flag' through these vintage motion pictures, produced just fifty years after

Appomattox. . . . Film enthusiast and fellow-member Jerry Warshaw will provide commentary for us. Among the great 'silents,' we will see are the melodramatic *Battle* of 1911, the earliest film biography of Abraham Lincoln and the first re-creation of the Andrews raid, *Railroad Raiders of '62*. . . . The Chicago Light Artillery Battery opens the festivities with a special Civil War color guard and appropriate ruffles and flourishes. . . . Complementing Jerry's films will be remarks on the G.A.R. and the Research Center by Round Table members and the reappearance of the Schimmelfennig Sing-ers under the able direction of 'Commander' Ward Smidl. . . ." The afternoon concluded with a reception in the Library Rotunda for the "Mr. Lincoln of Illinois" exhibit.

The next month campaigners were off to Shiloh and Northern Mississippi. The cover story in the tour newsletter informed members that: "A thorough review of some of the most important fields of the 'War in the West' is what you can expect from the Twenty-Ninth Annual Civil War Round Table Battlefield Tour, May 2-6, 1979. Truly this tour will have something to please everyone. Whether you are a battlefield purist who enjoys basking in history on the hallowed ground or an antebellum home devotee for whom musty smells are perfume, this tour is for you! New friends will guide us through the Corinth, Memphis, and Fort Pillow actions. These experts come with impeccable credentials regarding their respective fields. The total result will be an informative and pleasurable experience for all of our campaigners.

For those less historically inclined, there will also be an optional tour of antebellum homes and plantations. Even entertainment has not been forgotten, as Saturday night, Fun Night, will take us for a cruise down the Mississippi on an authentic paddle wheel steamer. On board we will enjoy our traditional command post and dinner to the accompaniment of a live Memphis-style band. . . ."

A story on The Round Table appeared in *The Daily Corinthian* in Corinth, Mississippi, on May 3. "Steeped in rich tradition," writer Irene Page noted, "The Round Table even has its own flags it carries with them on all trips. The flags became part of the group's tradition during a tour of the Shenandoah Valley battlefields. At a dinner in West Virginia all the decorations were Confederate flags. Considering themselves 'non-partisan,' the group decided 'no one would ever do that to them again.' [Since then, they have brought] their own Union and Confederate flags . . . as well as a Civil War Round Table flag.

"The current president of the organization, Glen Wiche, is only in his mid-20s and has attended meetings of the group since he was 12-years old. Wiche's father joined, although he was not interested in the Civil War, so Wiche could attend the monthly meetings as a guest in 1964 . . ." (Glen Wiche is, to date, the youngest person ever to serve as president of The Civil War Round Table.)

In the May newsletter, it was reported that The Round Table had presented an additional check in the amount of $5,000 to the Chicago Public Library Special Collections Division. The contribution was to be used for the purchase of research and reference sources and to provide for the restoration and preservation of Civil War artifacts and exhibit items.

On June 8, 1979, The Civil War Round Table awarded its Nevins-Freeman Award to its own E.B. (Pete) Long. Once again, the dinner was at the Blackhawk Restaurant and the program was held at the G.A.R. Rooms of the Chicago Public Library Cultural Center. Dave Richert wrote in the June newsletter that: "There is probably no one who knows more about the Civil War than Pete Long. He has . . . devoted his life to the study of the events of 1861-1865 and spent an entire decade in full-time research for Bruce Catton's Centennial History of the Civil War. For that work he collected, analyzed, and arranged more than nine million words of research notes on 26,000 pages while visiting some 125 university and historical libraries. A set of these notes was presented by

*1979 Nevins-Freeman Award
Recipient E.B. (Pete) Long*

Doubleday & Company to the Manuscript Division of the Library of Congress. Prior to that work, for five years, he aided Allan Nevins in a research and editorial capacity preparatory to the last two volumes of *Ordeal of the Union*."

Pete Long did not reach his position of accomplishment and respect in the historical community in the customary manner. When Long's college education was cut short due to lack of finances, he became a newspaperman. He wrote for the *Chicago Tribune* and the *Herald* in Morris, Illinois, before joining the Chicago bureau of the Associated Press, where he was employed from 1944-1952. He began his highly successful career in historical research and writing under the tutelage of Ralph G. Newman.

During the Nevins-Freeman program, tributes were paid to Long by Ralph Newman, John Y. Simon, and Long's wife Barbara. She talked about how Pete got into the field of historical research and writing: "When people ask my husband how he became interested in the Civil War, he tells them that he, as a young wire service newsman, walked into the Abraham Lincoln Book Shop in 1944, and, in a sense, never walked out. From that day forward, he was hooked. . . . Ralph Newman encouraged his interest . . ." Newman served as a mentor to Long and helped him find access to people in historical research and publishing. He did the research for *American Iliad*,written by Newman and Otto Eisenschiml. With Newman, he co-authored *The Civil War Digest.*

Talking about Long's research for Allan Nevins, Barbara Long noted that: "For volumes seven and eight of *Ordeal of the Union*, Pete would rough out long, raw chapters, and Nevins would hone them down and cast them in his own magnificent prose. But the framework, the foundation of the chapters is mostly Long, sometimes cut down too much, sometimes fully utilized."

Adding a personal touch to her account of the years working with Nevins, Barbara Long related that: "During some of [this] time, we stayed with Allan and Mary Nevins in their lovely home in Pasadena. Nevins, as you know, was a man of enormous vigor despite his age. At breakfast, he would announce, "Historians eat cereal for breakfast," and with that he would fill a big bowl for Pete. That Pete didn't really want the cereal didn't matter; he ate it dutifully . . . Allan always treated Pete like a son."

Barbara Long talked about her husband's struggle to get an academic appointment: "Knowing what I know now, I marvel at Pete's intrepidity. Imagine trying to get onto a campus without a degree of any kind! Such audacity!"[4] It started out as a discouraging search, but in the late 1960s some breaks came—visiting lectureships at both the University of

California (at Riverside and San Diego) and at the University of Illinois (Chicago Circle). His perseverance was rewarded. In 1969, he and Barbara moved to Wyoming where he became associate professor and ultimately professor of American Studies at the University of Wyoming at Laramie.

Barbara Long did a great deal of research and writing with her husband. Bell Wiley once told her that she probably knew as much as he did, as a result of the research she had done with Pete, about the war on the homefront—the "people aspects."[5] A talented artist, she has drawn maps for numerous Civil War books, including some of Frank Vandiver's. Vandiver calls her a "map maker par excellence," and the best he's ever encountered.[6]

In the newsletter's summary of the June program, Dave Richert wrote that: "John Y. Simon discussed Pete as a scholar, particularly his major role in two areas—as director of research for Catton's *Centennial History of the Civil War* and as editor of the 1952 [one-volume] edition of Grant's memoirs. He added that *The Civil War Day by Day* best expressed Pete as a scholar—'everything is correct in that work.'" Barbara Long remembers how pleased her husband was when he was chosen as the 1979 Nevins-Freeman honoree. "He was so grateful," she said, "to The Civil War Round Table and cherished the award."[7]

The time had come again for the change of officers. Glen Wiche turned over the presidential gavel to Merlin E. Sumner.

Marshall Krolick made this announcement in the September 1979 newsletter: ". . . By way of introduction, your new editor of the newsletter is Dave Richert. Rest assured, he is no raw recruit—for without question, he has 'seen the elephant.' We were fortunate to have Dave join us in September 1977 as assistant editor and the following year he became co-editor. In the latter position, he was responsible for both the lead story and the review of the previous meeting. To paraphrase Lee's description of George Meade, Dave Richert will make no mistake as your editor . . ."

Merlin Sumner, 1979-80 President, in 1981

The September newsletter carried the announcement of the death of the 1976 Nevins-Freeman recipient, T. Harry Williams. Dr. Williams, 70, who had recently retired as Boyd Professor of History at Louisiana State University, had died on July 6.

On Sunday, October 21, The Round Table went on a tour of the Milwaukee-Racine-Kenosha, Wisconsin area. In Milwaukee, they were joined by members of the Milwaukee Civil War Round Table for a tour of Civil War sites and exhibits in Milwaukee.

On April 11, 1980, Ralph G. Newman spoke on "The Lights Go On Again at Ford's Theater," about the reopening of Ford's Theater in 1968 and the history that preceded that reopening. Dave Richert wrote that: "Ralph explained that the restoration of Ford's Theater was not intended to recall a moment of fate, but to recreate those moments when Lincoln found respite from the cares of his office. It was to be a living memorial to the man and a tribute to Lincoln's love of the theater."

Merlin Sumner, 1979-1980 president, remembers some of the "peripheral circumstances" of that evening: "A week or so before the meeting, the Chicago Bar Association's president decided he needed the room in which The Round Table customarily met. I was faced with a horrible situation and had to get the newsletter revised to conform with a new location. After many telephone calls, we obtained space in the Adventurer's Club on Michigan Avenue and the newsletter went out announcing the revised location, all accomplished in a matter of a few days. Then, in order to avoid any possible troubles, I asked my wife Pat to station herself at the Chicago Bar Association building to direct people to the Adventurer's Club.

The event itself was something of a catastrophe because most of the attendees had to leave the room where they ate and go into another room to be packed, sardine-like, in order to hear Ralph. Worse, Ralph delivered his speech only a few feet from an object pendulumed from the ceiling, which afterwards people told me was the penis of a whale!"[8]

The Round Table lost another of its Nevins-Freeman honorees and the historical community lost one of its best scholars and writers on April 4, 1980. Bell I. Wiley died at the age of seventy-four.

1980 Nevins-Freeman Award Recipient Edwin C. Bearss

The thirtieth annual battlefield tour (May 14-18) traveled to the Shenandoah Valley. The tour covered Jackson's Campaign of 1862, New Market, and the 1862 Campaigns of Early and Sheridan. Among the speakers were Edwin C. Bearss and Robert Krick.

The 1980 Nevins-Freeman Award went to National Park Service Historian and dear friend of The Round Table Edwin C. Bearss. The June 13 dinner was held at Stouffer's Restaurant; the program once again was in the G.A.R. Rooms of the Chicago Public Library Cultural Center. "To everyone who has been on a battlefield tour with The Round Table," Dave Richert wrote , "the name Ed Bearss has a special meaning. As our chief guide, his encyclopedic knowledge of the battles and the participants, and his ability to communicate that knowledge, has greatly enhanced both understanding and enjoyment. His enthusiasm and total involvement with the subject at hand, in pouring rain and blistering sun, has served as an inspiration. . . . But Ed's abilities as a guide and companion on battlefield tours . . . is only one of his many accomplishments. He is also a prolific author, captivating speaker, and tireless promoter of Civil War scholarship . . ."

Bearss, whose interest in the Civil War began at the age of ten when his father began reading Civil War books to him, named the cattle on his family's Montana ranch for Civil War generals and battles. He served in the Marine Corps during World War II, where he gained a reputation for knowing a lot about the Civil War. But he didn't really feel he knew that much. "However," Richert related, "the twenty-eight months he spent in the hospital after he was wounded did give him time to do a great deal of reading. After getting out of the hospital, Ed attended college and then went to work for the Department of Defense in a very boring job. A visit to the Shiloh battlefield got him interested in being a Park historian." His first Park Service assignment was at Vicksburg. Since 1961 Round Table battlefield tours have been greatly enhanced by his expertise.

At the traditional June installation of officers, the president's gavel was passed from Merlin Sumner to Robert G. Walter. Margaret April became the first woman to be elected to the Board of Trustees. Mary Vinck became the first female committee chairperson. She was co-chairperson, with her husband William, of the Publicity Committee.

In October of 1980, The Round Table changed meeting places. The new site was the Como Inn on Milwaukee Avenue. (The September meeting had been held at an interim site, the Midland Hotel.)

The Round Table lost a past president and devoted member on January 6, 1981 when Ver Lynn Sprague died. "His was a rare sense of humor," Ralph Newman wrote in the newsletter, "and good fellowship. Among his delightful 'projects' was an attempt to have President Eisenhower pardon the unknown horse thief who stole Abraham Lincoln's horse just before he was discharged as a soldier in the Black Hawk War and the picketing of the Wisconsin Travel Bureau with pretty girls carrying signs reading, 'When Abraham Lincoln went to Wisconsin, his horse was stolen—vacation in Illinois. As a poet, he did not rival Keats or Shelley, but he made us feel light of heart . . . He was a delightful gentleman . . . and always regarded The Civil War Round Table as one of the most important and fulfilling parts of his life . . ."

Patricia Krelle Sumner remembers when she met Ver Lynn Sprague on the 1980 battlefield tour to the Shenandoah Valley. It was her first tour. "I didn't realize who he was," she recalls, "but I got very close to him during that battlefield tour. I later learned how sick he was, but I was unaware of this at

Robert G. Walter, 1980-81 President

the time. He was very thin. After the tour, I was told that he used to weigh 300 pounds.

"When there was a mountain or hill to be climbed, he wasn't able to do it. He'd say to me: 'You go up and come back down and tell me what they said.' Every time I went up, I'd pick a flower and tell him: 'You can put this in your lapel tonight and tell everyone you got it at the top of the mountain. They won't know that you weren't up there.'

"We started talking about Civil War humor and I said that, although I had read some hilarious examples of it, I had never seen a book on Civil War humor. He told me that he had always meant to write one. At that point, I said, "I think I will. Some day, I'm going to write a book about Civil War humor.' He reached over and squeezed my hand real hard and said: 'Please promise me that you will. That's something I wanted to do and I'm not going to be able to do it. But promise me that you will.' In less than a year, he was gone. Now I feel honor-bound. I told him I was going to do it—and some day, I will."[9]

On February 13, The Round Table heard former President Gerhard P. Clausius speak on a topic other than his hero Steven Augustus Hurlbut. "Doc," as he was affectionately known, spoke on a subject about which he felt strongly— Mary Todd Lincoln, one of the most unfairly maligned women in American history. The title of his address was "The Drama of Mary Todd Lincoln."

Another loss came on March 30 when Pete Long died at the age of sixty-two. Ralph Newman wrote about him in the newsletter: "Pete returned [to Chicago] for the last time on Monday, March 30 when he spoke to The Westerners and some members of The Civil War Round Table on "The Saints and the Union: Utah Territory during the Civil War." This was the title of his latest book which was published that day. His talk was superb, his spirits were high. He left the Chicago Press Club, where the meeting had been held, and walked with his niece a few blocks to the Allerton Hotel. After bidding his niece goodbye, he went to his room, called his beloved Barbara; told her what a grand day and evening he had had; told her that he loved her, and shortly after he completed the conversation, died of a heart attack.

"He was one of the most conscientious and honorable men I have ever known. He never failed to lend a helping hand when it was requested, and even if it was not asked. He was so generous to many who worked in the Civil War field that he could have properly been listed as co-author for many works on which he contributed impeccable research and editorial advice . . ."

The Civil War Round Table observed its 400th meeting on April 10, 1981 at the Como Inn. Dave Richert wrote in the

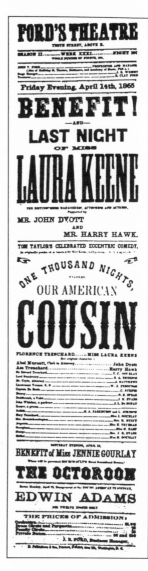

400th MEETING

PROGRAM APRIL 10, 1981
the COMO INN, Chicago
Presiding ROBERT G. WALTER President

ROUND TABLE HISTORY
RALPH G. NEWMAN

MEMORABLE MOMENTS
Recounted by Past Presidents

PRESENTATION OF SPECIAL MESSAGES

ROUND TABLE ARCHIVES

"SONGS OF THE SIXTIES"
Schimmelfennig Singers

April newsletter that: "The Master of Ceremonies will be our founder, Ralph G. Newman, who will provide us with a brief history of The Round Table and introduce past presidents, each of whom will speak for a few minutes about the high- (and low-) lights of his administration. In addition, Ward Smidl and the renowned Schimmelfennig Singers will perform 'Songs of the Sixties.' And, before and after the program, material from The Round Table archives will be on display."

An 8-1/2 -by 11-inch program which opened up into one large page which was equal to eight pages of that size was produced as a souvenir of the evening. Among other things, it listed all the battlefield tours and Honorary Life Members. It contained a brief history of The Round Table and listed each president, along with the major events of his administration. A handsomely produced item, it was designed by Jerry Warshaw and printed by Al Meyer—fondly known to The Round Table as the proprietors of "Gratis Arts" and "Gratis Printing" for all the work they did for the group, expecting no monetary compensation. Members of the 400th Meeting Committee were: Glen N. Wiche, Chairman; Brooks Davis; C. Robert Douglas; Ralph G. Newman; Marvin Sanderman; and Jerry Warshaw.

By this time, there were only four surviving founders: David Annan, Elmer Gertz, Percival G. Hart, and Ralph G. Newman. Many of the other earlier members were also gone by now. "To underscore that point," Dave Richert reported in the May newsletter, "the evening concluded with the playing of taps for the comrades no longer with us."

Vicksburg was the destination of the thirty-first annual battlefield tour (April 29-May 3). In addition to Vicksburg, sites visited included Port Gibson, Raymond, Jackson, and Champion Hill. The tours were getting a little more expensive by now: $445 for one-to-a-room and $480 for two-to-a-room. However, this still included plane fare along with food and lodging.

James I. (Bud) Robertson, Jr. received the 1981 Nevins-Freeman Award on June 5. The dinner was held at Stouffer's Restaurant and the program in the G.A.R. Rooms at the Cultural Center. Robertson, who served as executive director of the Civil War Centennial Commission, has been the author or editor of numerous books on the Civil War, including *The Stonewall Brigade* (1963) and *The Concise Illustrated History of the Civil War* (1961).

It was time for the usual change of officers. The president for the 1981-1982 term was Robert H. Franke.

An item in the June newsletter announced that: "An auction of the books from Ver Lynn Sprague's library will be held June 6 at 11:00 a.m. in front of the Book Shop at 18 East

1981 Nevins-Freeman Award Recipient James I. (Bud) Robertson, Jr.

Chestnut. Ver Lynn, a long-time member and past president who passed away January 6, left his collection to The Round Table which will receive all proceeds from the auction."

Lincoln and Civil War history was still retaining its popularity in the 1980s. An item in the September newsletter reported that Springfield, Illinois and the Lincoln home rated as the fourth most popular U.S. tourist attraction. (The three top-rated spots were New York City, Washington, D.C., and Disneyland.)

The Civil War Round Table experienced another "first" on April 9, 1982. The first woman to address a regular Round Table meeting, Pat Newman, wife of Ralph, spoke on "Julia Dent Grant." (As mentioned previously, Alice Cromie addressed a special "Ladies Night" meeting on February 14, 1967, before women were admitted to membership.)

Pat Newman, the first woman to address a regular meeting of The Round Table

Gettysburg was the site chosen for the thirty-second annual battlefield tour (May 5-9). It was announced in the tour newsletter that: "Our tour guides will be two eminently qualified gentlemen with whom many of you are already acquainted: Ed Bearss, chief historian for the National Park Service, author, lecturer, and an acknowledged expert on most areas of the Civil War; and Marshall Krolick, attorney, past president of The Civil War Round Table, lecturer, teacher, and acknowledged authority on the Civil War, particularly Gettysburg and the cavalry."

Dave Richert reported in the June 1982 newsletter that: "The highlight of the tour occurred on the third day when, following a reenactment of sorts of Pickett's charge (led by Bill Mallory and John Divine carrying Confederate flags), a moving ceremony was held at the site of the High Water Mark of the Confederate advance. There, by order of The Round Table Executive Committee, a new monument was dedicated—The Marshall Krolick Memorial Tower (formerly known as the National Tower). As most know, Gettysburg is Marshall's favorite battlefield, and he has often made mention of the Tower. Thus, it was thought fitting he have a monument there, and that it be the Tower. Although Dan Sickles may not have a monument at Gettysburg, Marshall Krolick now does.

"It is unknown whether the owners of the Tower will be changing their signs. However, it is reported that Marshall, in all modesty, will continue to call it 'that thing' or 'that monstrosity.' It should also be noted that Marshall received the Confederate Purple Heart this year—for backing into an electrified fence around a pasture."

Percival G. Hart, founding member and the speaker at the first meeting of The Civil War Round Table, died on May 25 in California. This left The Round Table with three surviving founders.

1982 Nevins-Freeman Award Recipient Frank E. Vandiver

The 1982 Nevins-Freeman Award went to another longtime friend of The Round Table: Frank E. Vandiver. The June 11 dinner was held at the Illinois Athletic Club; the program, as had become customary, took place at the Cultural Center. Dr. Vandiver, as has been noted earlier, holds the record as the youngest person to address The Round Table. Thirty-five years later, he was presented with the group's highest honor.

In a publication issued in 1984 on its Nevins-Freeman recipients, it was written that: "Frank Vandiver stopped attending regular school classrooms after the seventh grade. Educated privately, mainly by his father, he was admitted directly to the University of Texas graduate school in 1946, by special examination. . . . His career as a scholar has been spectacular. His many distinguished works include *Ploughshares Into Swords: Josiah Gorgas and Confederate Ordnance* (1952), . . . and *Mighty Stonewall* (1957) . . . . As an educator, he served as the chairman of the history department at Rice University; acting president and finally provost of Rice. He then became president of North Texas State University, and in 1981 became president of Texas A & M University . . ."[10] For his acceptance address, Dr. Vandiver presented a personal portrait of the two men for whom the award is named. Dr. Vandiver said that he was honored to be able to call both Allan Nevins and Douglas Southall Freeman his mentors.

Bob Franke turned over the presidential gavel to Marvin Sanderman for the 1982-1983 term. And, Patricia Krelle, the new treasurer, became the first woman officer of The Civil War Round Table.

Marvin Sanderman, 1982-83 President (right), with longtime member Nate Yellen

Founding Round Table member David H. Annan died on June 14 in Houston, Texas following heart surgery. He was ninety-five. This left The Round Table with two surviving founders (Elmer Gertz and Ralph G. Newman).

The Round Table sponsored a fall tour to Springfield, October 30-31. Among the places visited were Lincoln College [in Lincoln, Illinois], the Lincoln home, the Old State Capitol, and New Salem State Park.

Stephen B. Oates, professor of history at the University of Massachusetts at Amherst, addressed The Round Table on November 12. His topic was "John Brown: Catalyst for the Civil War." "Dr. Oates is a prolific writer and lecturer," Dave Richert wrote. "In addition to numerous articles and essays in various scholarly journals, he is the author of several books, including a quartet of biographies written about Americans profoundly affected by the moral paradox of slavery and race in a land based on the ideals of the Declaration of Independence: *To Purge This Land With Blood: A Biography of John Brown* (1970); *The Fires of Jubilee: Nat Turner's Fierce Rebellion* (1975); *With Malice Toward None: The Life of Abraham Lincoln* (1977); and . . . *Let the Trumpet Sound: The Life of Martin Luther King, Jr.* (1982).

On December 10, 1982, The Round Table began meeting at a new site: the Illinois Athletic Club on South Michigan Avenue. That evening, Perry D. Jamieson spoke on "Artillery Tactics of the Civil War Era." Harpers Ferry Park Historian Dennis Frye addressed the group on January 14, 1983 on "The Cow's Tails Mystery: The Siege and Capture of Harpers Ferry." Popular battlefield tour companion and guide John E. Divine, of Loudon County, Virginia, spoke on March 11 on "Cavalry Campaigns: A Prelude to Gettysburg."

The thirty-third annual battlefield tour traveled to Chattanooga and Chickamauga. Spots visited on the Chattanooga battlefield included Missionary Ridge, Orchard Knob, and Lookout Mountain. Among the sites explored on the Chickamauga battlefield were Snodgrass Hill, Lee and Gordon's Mill, and Crawfish Springs. Saturday night, the group enjoyed a cruise on a Tennessee River showboat. The tour was a memorable one for Mary Abroe—it was her first. "It was as a result of this battlefield tour," she said, "that I was drawn into active participation in The Round Table. Even though I had been a member since the previous fall, it was only after meeting and getting to know people on the tour that I realized what The Civil War Round Table was all about and knew, without a doubt, that it was something I wanted to be a part of."[11] Because of this indelible experience, this tour will always be Abroe's favorite one.

The 1983 tour was Larry Gibbs' third tour, but it was the

first time he'd been to Chattanooga or Chickamauga, and it was a special tour for him too. He talked about the knowledge he'd gained during the tour: "I think the battle of Chattanooga proved that the terrain of the battlefield was more important there than at any other battle in the Civil War. . . . The Union had a seemingly impossible task trying to take over Missionary Ridge, but they did it."[12] He pointed out how illuminating it can be to actually visit the battlefield sites. This experience can impart knowledge and understanding which cannot be gained by just reading about the battles in books.

Gettysburg National Military Park research historian Kathy Georg spoke on May 13 on "Actions at the Rose Farm on the Second Day at Gettysburg." Bill Sullivan remembers this talk as one of his favorites, "because it was so different. She had come up with some new interpretations based on her research. It was the first Round Table talk, I believe, that showed people what historians do for a living—and some of the people in the audience were less than aware of what historians do for a living. In her talk, she made a point of the famous Gettysburg photographs of fallen South Carolinians lying in the dirt, who had previously been identified as Michiganders. Part of her work was to determine whether these were in fact the black frock coats of pre-war South Carolinians or gray coats that had been dampened, giving them a darker cast. Someone asked me afterwards: 'What difference does it make?' I replied that if she could answer that question, it would probably tell us more about the condition of Lee's army at Gettysburg than Douglas Southall Freeman ever did.'"[13]

1983 Nevins-Freeman Award Recipient John Hope Franklin

Honorary Life member John Hope Franklin was chosen as the 1983 Nevins-Freeman Award winner. Dr. Franklin, James B. Duke Professor of History at Duke University, has been recognized as the nation's foremost authority on the Reconstruction era and African-American history. "In a teaching and writing career that has spanned five decades," Dave Richert observed in the June newsletter, "Dr. Franklin has produced a prodigious volume of work—nearly twenty books and some eighty articles. It is a measure of the quality of his work that he has been elected president of numerous professional organizations, such as the American Historical Association. Even more a measure of that quality is the many honors and awards he has received, and the fact that he has been given honorary degrees from sixty-six colleges and universities."

The Award presentation program was different this year. "Old traditions were joined," Richert wrote, on Saturday, June 11, "when The Round Table combined the presentation of its 1983 Nevins-Freeman Award with the first annual

Nevins-Freeman Assembly. The program consisted of a day-long seminar held at the Chicago Historical Society. During the morning session the over 100 people in attendance were privileged to hear Alan T. Nolan evaluate the Federal commanders; Dr. Wayne C. Temple point out many little-known, but important aspects of Abraham Lincoln; and Karen Osborne describe the career of 'Mother' Bickerdyke, the famous army nurse and hospital matron.

"These presentations were followed by an excellent catered luncheon and the presentation of the 1983 Award . . . to Dr. John Hope Franklin. In his acceptance remarks and his subsequent address on the career of George Washington Williams, the foremost black historian of the nineteenth century, Dr. Franklin amply demonstrated the qualities that have earned him a place alongside the gentlemen for whom our award is named.

"At the conclusion of Dr. Franklin's presentation, the program continued with a panel discussion on the issue of 'Civil Rights and the Civil War.' Participants on the panel were Dr. Franklin, Dr. Frank L. Klement, Dr. Duke Frederick, Dr. John Y. Simon, and our own Past President and founding member Elmer Gertz. The panel discussion was moderated by Past President Marshall D. Krolick. The remarks of the panelists generated a lively and controversial question and answer period."

Thus, the 1982-1983 term ended with a grand flourish. And the presidential gavel was passed from Marvin Sanderman to Donald E. Anderson.

Donald E. Anderson, 1983-84 President, at Burnside Bridge on the 1990 tour to Antietam

Chapter 14 ☆ *Maintaining Some Old Traditions, Beginning Some New Ones: From the Summer of 1983 to the Summer of 1987*

A NEW TRADITION WAS BORN IN JULY OF 1983. The Round Table had its first annual picnic. Something new was in store for September also. As the Illinois Athletic Club was closing its doors, a meeting site had to be found. On September 9, The Round Table began holding its monthly meetings at the Hotel Continental on North Michigan Avenue.

Although the setting was new, that evening was one of nostalgia. C. Robert Douglas, new assistant editor of the newsletter who began writing the meeting previews, noted that: "On February 16, 1943, Walter H. Hebert addressed the twentieth meeting of The Civil War Round Table on the life of General Joseph Hooker. On September 9, 1983, the 423rd meeting of The Round Table and the first of 1983-1984, he will repeat that address. . . . This will, in fact, be Mr. Hebert's third appearance before The Round Table. The publication of his book, *Fighting Joe Hooker* (1944) was the occasion of a gala dinner at our thirty-sixth meeting on October 18, 1944 . . ."

On October 23, The Civil War Round Table rededicated the grave marker of Civil War veteran Joseph Dana Webster at Rosehill Cemetery in Chicago. This project was conceived by former President Merlin Sumner. "Webster served as Grant's first chief of staff," Sumner related, "at Forts Henry and Donelson and Shiloh. He later became the military railroad superintendent at Memphis and Chattanooga and served as chief of staff for Sherman and Thomas. His gravesite in Rosehill Cemetery had been long neglected. A cross atop it had fallen off and I persuaded Rosehill's general manager to have it repaired. We obtained a mason's donation of his labor and a truck with a winch. We lifted the cross back to the top of the pedestal, had a pin inserted, and then epoxyed the thing. The cross is set firm for the next hundred years. We had some 200 reenactors, a fife and drum corps, newspaper reporters, and some distinguished Chicagoans meet at the cemetery to rededicate Webster's gravesite."[1]

Karen Osborne, who had spoken to the Nevins-Freeman

Merlin Sumner at the Joseph Dana Webster grave marker rededication on October 23, 1983

Assembly the previous June returned to address the December 9 meeting. She spoke about "Women in the Civil War."

At the February 17, 1984 meeting, The Round Table presented a reenactment of the "Senate Confrontation, November-December, 1860." Bob Douglas wrote in the newsletter that: "More than 120 years ago, the United States faced the prospect of the dismemberment of the Union, then only eighty-four years old. The election of Abraham Lincoln, a Northerner and a Republican, as well as an Anti-Slavery advocate, caused the Southern states to secede from the Union, and South Carolina would actually vote such action on December 20, 1860.

" In the nation's most deliberative body, the Senate of the United States, some of the most distinguished statesmen in our country's history debated the questions of secession, State's Rights, slavery, and sectionalism. At the 428th regular meeting of The Civil War Round Table on February 17, a distinguished panel of our members will recreate the mood of that critical period in a discussion of these issues. Ralph G. Newman, a founder of The Round Table, will serve as president pro tempore of the Senate. Marshall Krolick will express the views of the 'Radical Northerner' and Jim Vlazny will provide counterpoint with the views of the 'Radical Southerner.'

Honorary Life Member John Divine guided Round Tablers through Loudon County during the 1984 tour

Balancing the statements of these two members will be Gordon Whitney offering the opinions of the 'Moderate Northerner,' while Bill Sullivan expresses the position of the 'Moderate Southerner.'"

The Round Table had begun making cassette tapes from the older reel-to-reel tapes of earlier meeting addresses. Leslie W. McDonald, chairman of the Research Center Committee, was providing this service. The March newsletter informed members that twenty-nine tape cassettes were now available for $5 each. (Later, Hal Ardell would take over this project and reproduce many more of the older tapes, as well as taping each Round Table address and making the tapes available to members.)

The thirty-fourth annual battlefield tour traveled to Washington, D.C. and Northern Virginia (May 3-6). Stops included Fairfax Court House, Chantilly, Middleburg, Dranesville, Manassas Junction, and Blackburn's Ford. Also on the itinerary were tours of the Capitol building, the White House, Ford's Theater, and the Peterson House in Washington, D.C.

This was the first year that the group did not travel together in the same plane. Participants made their own transportation arrangements to and from the "Command Post" hotel at the tour site. The cost was now $285 per person for double occupancy and $345 for single accommodations. This included food, lodging, and everything else that had been part of the previous packages—with the exception of plane fare.

An announcement in the May 1984 newsletter informed members that the Nevins-Freeman Assembly would be held in September instead of June. However, the passing of the presidential gavel remained a June tradition. This year it passed from Don Anderson to J. Robert Ziegler.

Richard B. Harwell was chosen to be the recipient of the 1984 Nevins-Freeman Award. A biographical sketch prepared for the occasion states that: "The Civil War Round Table honors an old friend and a great historian. Librarian, bibliographer, and editor, Richard Barksdale Harwell is one of the finest interpreters of the cultural life of the Old South and is the foremost authority on the life and work of Margaret Mitchell. . . . He first appeared before us in January 1950, speaking on the "Songs of the Confederacy." His remarks became the sixth Round Table publication. (See Appendix L for a list of Round Table publications.)

"Rick Harwell has served many of our country's finest historical and academic institutions for over a half-century, including Emory University, the Huntington Library, Duke University, the Virginia State Library, the Boston Athenaeum, and the University of Georgia."[2] Mr. Harwell wrote a number of books; among them are *Confederate Belles-Lettres* (1941), *The Confederate Reader* (1957), and *The Union Reader* (1958). He won critical acclaim for his one-volume abridgements of Douglas Southall Freeman's Pulitzer Prize-winning biographies of George Washington and Robert E. Lee.[3]

The Nevins-Freeman Award was to be presented to Mr. Harwell on Saturday, September 15, 1984. However, due to illness, he was unable to attend. The all-day Assembly took place at the Cultural Center, with a break at noon for a luncheon in the Wedgewood Room of Marshall Field's department store. The morning's program consisted of short presentations on the theme: "20th Century Correspondents Cover the Civil War." John P. Hunter, Associate Editor of Madison, Wisconsin's *The Capitol Times*, discussed the life and writings of William B. Hesseltine. David L. Wilson, assistant editor of *The Papers of U.S. Grant*, reviewed the life and works of Lloyd Lewis. C. Robert Douglas talked about the life and works of Stanley Horn. Elmer Gertz's address dealt with the career and writings of Otto Eisenschiml. This portion of the program concluded with a presentation on the life and works of Bruce Catton by Ralph G. Newman.

1984 Nevins-Freeman Award Recipient Richard B. Harwell

The afternoon program featured a panel discussion, moderated by Ralph Newman. The topic was "Why Do Civil War Round Tables Exist? The Fascinating, Never-Ending Saga of 1861-1865."

October found the Round Table meeting at a new site: the Chicago Press Club in the Wrigley Building. That month, authors Jim and Alice Truelock, members of the Indianapolis Civil War Round Table, spoke on "Joshua L. Chamberlain." The following month, former President Merlin Sumner gave an address on "Grant's Staff: A Plus or a Minus?"

Another past president, Brooks Davis, began 1985 for The Round Table with a talk on January 11 on "The Grand Army of the Republic." He was followed, in February and March, by two Civil War scholars and authors. Herman Hattaway's topic on February 8 was "How the North Won"; Gary Gallagher's March 8 address was on "Stephen Dodson Ramseur: Lee's Gallant General." Both topics were also titles of books written by the speakers.[4]

The Round Table moved to yet another new meeting site on April 12: the Quality Inn at Halsted and Madison. That evening, Vice President William J. Sullivan gave an address on "The Trans-Mississippi in 1864: A Game of Pitch and Toss." (May would find the group temporarily back at the Chicago Press Club; they returned to the Quality Inn in June.)

The Round Table chose the 1864-1865 Campaign from Petersburg to Appomattox as the area for its thirty-fifth annual battlefield tour (May 1-5). Places visited, in addition to Petersburg and Appomattox Court House, included Fort Stedman, the Crater, City Point, Hatcher's Run, Five Forks, High Bridge, and Cold Harbor. An alternate tour on Friday afternoon went to Monticello and Michie Tavern. On Sunday afternoon, the Richmond Civil War Round Table hosted a cocktail party at the Confederate White House in Richmond.

This year, the tour had lost its familiar registrar. After serving for thirty-four tours, Margaret April had retired. 1985's tour registrar was Leslie W. MacDonald. In the battlefield tour newsletter each year, however, Margaret April is listed as Registrar Emerita (1951-1984), in gratitude for the fine job she had done for so many years.

Paul J. Beaver, professor of history at Lincoln College, addressed the June 14 meeting; his topic was "Lincoln's Political Rise in Illinois." At that meeting, several Honorary Life memberships were bestowed. Those so honored were: Robert Todd Lincoln Beckwith, great-grandson of Abraham Lincoln; Joseph P. Cullen, a National Park Service historian; 1984 Nevins-Freeman Award recipient Richard B. Harwell; and Civil War Round Table Past Presidents C. Robert Douglas, Marshall D. Krolick, and Jerry Warshaw. Also at that meeting, the president's gavel was passed from J. Robert Ziegler to Paul I. Kliger.

It was Nevins-Freeman time again, and the 1985 Award went to The Civil War Round Table's very special friend, Dr. John Y. Simon. Much has been said already about Dr. Simon. He had come a long way since his undergraduate years at Swarthmore College when he worked as a stock clerk at Ralph Newman's Abraham Lincoln Book Shop. After receiving his master's and doctoral degrees from Harvard University, he taught at Ohio State University before going to Southern

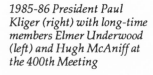

1985-86 President Paul Kliger (right) with long-time members Elmer Underwood (left) and Hugh McAniff at the 400th Meeting

Illinois University, where he is a professor of history.

Executive director of The Ulysses S. Grant Association and editor of *The Papers of Ulysses S. Grant*, Dr. Simon also edited The *Personal Memoirs of Julia Dent Grant* (1975). His other works include *Ulysses S. Grant Chronology* (1963) and *General Grant by Matthew Arnold with a Rejoinder by Mark Twain* (1966). For his acceptance address, Dr. Simon selected as his theme, "Editing the Papers of Ulysses S. Grant." He approached Grant's Civil War career and qualities as a military commander in terms of his correspondence, focusing on Grant's choice of words, his ability to communicate, and his administrative style. This year, The Round Table began holding the Nevins-Freeman Award Dinner at the regular meeting place.

1985 Nevins-Freeman Award Recipient John Y. Simon

The last descendant of Abraham Lincoln died on Christmas Eve, 1985. Robert Todd Lincoln Beckwith, great-grandson of the sixteenth president, was the son of Robert Todd and Mary Harlan Lincoln's daughter Jessie and Warren Beckwith. An Honorary Life member of The Civil War Round Table, Mr. Beckwith had participated in three special gatherings with Round Table members: the opening of the Robert Todd Lincoln Papers in Washington, D.C. in 1947; the final ceremonies of the Civil War Centennial in Springfield in 1965; and the final two days of the 1966 battlefield tour to Washington, D.C. At least three Round Table members were close friends of his: Ralph and Pat Newman and James Hickey.

"Our Ethnic Ancestors in the Civil War" was the title of The Round Table's meeting program on January 10, 1986. Five members presented summaries of the participation in the Civil War of various ethnic groups. Wayne Anderson analyzed the part played by the country's Scandinavian population; Marshall Krolick talked about Jewish participation; Bill Sullivan discussed the role of the Irish; Karl Sundstrom described the participation of those of German descent; and Jim Vlazny spoke about the contributions of African-Americans.

Mark E. Neely, Jr. returned to the Round Table podium on February 14 to speak about "Lincoln and Douglas: A Relationship to Consider." An item in that February newsletter announced that the Richmond National Battlefield Park would celebrate its fiftieth anniversary on March 2. The ceremonies were to recognize those individuals and organizations responsible for making the battlefield park a reality—especially the Battlefield Markers Association and the Richmond Battlefield Parks Corporation who, in the 1920s and 1930s, did so much work to get the battlefields properly located and marked and raised the funds to acquire the property. Spearheading these organizations, of course, were J. Ambler Johnston and his friend Douglas Southall Freeman.

The Civil War Round Table sponsored, on Saturday, March 15, 1986, an all-day Assembly on "Lieutenant General U.S. Grant: The Civil War Years." Held at the Holiday Inn in Hillside, Illinois, the chairman of the event was former President Merlin Sumner. "These eight Grant experts will be your guides through his Civil War years," a descriptive brochure advised. The experts and their topics were: John Y. Simon—"Grant as Commander"; Thomas Arliskas—"Grant at Belmont"; Wiley Sword—"Grant at Shiloh"; Marshall Krolick—"Grant's General Order No. 11"; Edwin C. Bearss—"Grant at Vicksburg"; Gordon Whitney—"Grant at Chattanooga"; Robert K. Krick—"Grant from the Rapidan to the James"; and Richard J. Sommers—"Grant at Petersburg." The Grant Assembly was a popular and critical success. Over 300 attended.

The April newsletter carried sad news of the deaths of two longtime members. The beloved Gerhard P. (Doc) Clausius, former President and twice a meeting speaker, died on March 7 at the age of seventy-nine. Brooks Davis remarked in his tribute in the newsletter that: "Members always looked forward to a humorous question of the speaker involving General Hurlbut at every meeting—indeed, Doc made history more interesting by his use of humor . . ."

Also gone was Don Russell, former newsletter editor, who died at the age of eighty-seven. A tribute to him by Ralph Newman appeared in the newsletter, in which he noted that: "While not a founding member of The Civil War Round Table, Don Russell was among our very early members, joining our group in the 1940s. He bridged the gap between the Old West and the Civil War. He was one of the organizers of The Westerners, which serves those dedicated to the history and legends of western history in the same manner that The Civil War Round Table brings together those who keep the memory of the Blue and the Gray alive. He worked for the *Chicago Daily News* in the great Carl Sandburg, Lloyd Lewis, and Henry Justin Smith days. As a copy editor, one of his jobs was to receive and prepare for publication the contributions of Carl Sandburg. Don's biography of Buffalo Bill is the definitive work on the subject.[5]

"Physically, he seemed to be the embodiment of a character out of his favorite period of history. Certainly Central Casting would have promptly selected him to portray an American living in the great plains west of the Mississippi. His slow drawl, his reserved sense of humor, and his vast fund of knowledge of our past caused all who met him to believe he was not an historian, but a character out of our past, come to meet with and enlighten us on the history of his era."

The 1862 Peninsula Campaign was the focus of the

thirty-sixth annual battlefield tour (May 1-4). It was stated in the tour newsletter that: "We will travel the length of the Peninsula from Fort Monroe to Richmond, examining all the major 1862 battle sites as well as other points of Civil War interest in the vicinity." Ed Bearss, as usual, was the chief tour guide. He was assisted by Bill Mallory, Chris Calkins, and Marshall Krolick.

The 125th anniversary commemorations of the Civil War were beginning and would continue over the next four years. An item in the May 1986 newsletter reports that: "To commemorate the 125th anniversary of the Civil War in Virginia, the Friends of Virginia Civil War Parks, Inc., is sponsoring commemorations at each of the five parks, beginning with Manassas, July 18-21, 1986, and ending with Appomattox in 1990."

James I. (Bud) Robertson, Jr., 1981 Nevins-Freeman Award recipient, returned on June 6 to speak on "General A.P. Hill: Symbol of the Confederacy." This was a historic evening for The Civil War Round Table. Eight-and-one-half years earlier, the opposition having been worn-down, the membership finally voted to admit women to the group. Tonight they would install the first woman president of The Civil War Round Table. Paul I. Kliger passed the presidential gavel to Patricia Krelle Sumner. Two other women served as officers for the 1986-1987 term: Leslie W. McDonald as secretary and Mary Munsell Abroe as assistant treasurer. Also, Jean Anderson was co-chairperson of the Battlefield Preservation Committee.

Patricia Krelle Sumner, 1986-87 President

1986 Nevins-Freeman Award Recipient Harold M. Hyman

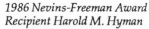

The 1986 Nevins-Freeman Award was presented to Harold M. Hyman on September 12. William P. Hobby Professor of History at Rice University in Houston, Texas, Dr. Hyman received his undergraduate degree at the University of California at Los Angeles and his masters and doctoral degrees at Columbia University. He taught at Earlham College, the University of California at Los Angeles, Arizona State University, and the University of Illinois before going to Rice. Among his published works are *The Era of the Oath: Northern Loyalty Tests During the Civil War and Reconstruction* (1954); *Stanton: The Life and Times of Lincoln's Secretary of War* (1962)—with the late Benjamin P. Thomas; and *Quiet Past and Stormy Present: War Powers in American History* (1986). After sharing some personal reminiscences of Allen Nevins and Douglas Southall Freeman, Dr. Hyman delivered his address on "Lincoln and Other 'Yuppie' Lawyers."

For the first time, an announcement about a particularly significant upcoming event appeared in the newsletter. The item in the October issue reported that: "A committee, under the chairmanship of past President Paul Kliger, has been formed to plan the fiftieth anniversary celebration of The Round Table, which will occur in 1990. The participation of members is welcome..." Thereafter, for the next few years, news of the work of the Fiftieth Anniversary Committee would be showing up in the newsletter.

Alan T. Nolan, Indianapolis, Indiana attorney and Civil War scholar and author, addressed the final meeting of 1986 on December 12. His topic was "A Historic View of Robert E. Lee." Mr. Nolan reviewed several times in the career of Robert E. Lee when he faced critical decisions and presented analyses of these decisions. He noted that, with the passing of time and less emphasis on sectional bias, Civil War scholars are better able to examine this period of American history objectively.

An item in the December 1986 newsletter reported news of both a preservation victory and the formation of an important organization: "The historic Grove Farm, south of Sharpsburg, where Lincoln met McClellan following the Battle of Antietam, has been saved. It will not become a shopping center. In August 1985, the Washington County commissioners rezoned a parcel of the Grove Farm from agricultural to business-general, thus opening the door for construction of a shopping center. Local preservationists, including members of the Harpers Ferry and Hagerstown Round Tables, organized the Save Historic Antietam Foundation (SHAF) to reverse the rezoning.

"Although 5000 people signed petitions asking the commissioners to rescind the rezoning, and despite letters from all over the country, the commissioners refused to budge, and SHAF filed a lawsuit. On October 2, 1986, Circuit Court Judge John Corderman ruled that the Washington County commissioners had violated the law by not following proper procedures when rezoning, and declared the business-general zoning null and void.

"Unfortunately, the victory did not come cheaply. The legal battle cost SHAF about $9000, and funds are urgently needed to pay this debt. You can send your tax-deductible contribution to the Save Historic Antietam Foundation.... You should note that, at its meeting October 25, The Civil War Round Table Executive Committee voted to contribute $500 to SHAF. The money comes from the Battlefield Preservation Fund, which is supported by the book raffle held at each meeting."

Also in the December issue was a photograph of the recently erected monument to General Stephen Augustus Hurlbut in Big Thunder Park in Belvidere, Illinois. An inscription on the monument reads: "Erected by the Belvidere High School Civil War Round Table. A portion of the funds was

*The monument to General
Stephen Augustus Hurlbut
in Big Thunder Park in
Belvidere, Illinois*

donated in memory of Dr. Gerhard P. Clausius."

January and February of 1987 found two former Round Table presidents return to the speaker's podium. On January 9, Marshall D. Krolick's topic was "Captain to Brigadier: The Promotions of Custer, Farnsworth, and Merritt." The "Father of The Civil War Round Table" Ralph G. Newman spoke on "Robert Todd Lincoln in the Civil War" on February 20.

There was news in the February newsletter of the beginnings of what became known as the "Third Battle of Manassas." A developer was seeking to build a gigantic commercial and residential complex on about 500 acres adjacent to the battlefield. This battle would continue for over two years.

An item in the April newsletter reported that: "The Battlefield Preservation Committee [of The Civil War Round Table] recently voted to donate $1500 to the Save Historic Antietam Foundation (SHAF) and another $1500 to the Campaign to Restore and Preserve the various Illinois-related monuments at Gettysburg. The money comes from the battlefield preservation fund, which is supported by a book raffle held at each meeting."

The thirty-seventh annual battlefield tour (April 30-May 3) headed for the Trans-Mississippi area. It was noted in the tour newsletter that: "This year, for only the second time in the history of The Civil War Round Table, the battlefield tour will be conducted entirely west of the Mississippi River. The battle sites to be visited in Missouri and Arkansas will bring forth a cast of characters mostly apart from the more familiar names of other areas of the Civil War which we have visited . . ." Battlegrounds visited included Carthage; Wilson's Creek; Pea Ridge; Newtonia; Prairie Grove; and Baxter Springs.

The campaigners at Pea Ridge in 1987

Richard McAdoo took over the job of registrar that year, and he served for two subsequent years. Dale Weitman was registrar for the 1990 tour.

Betty J. Otto, supervisor of "Volunteers in the Park" at the Antietam National Battlefield, addressed the May 8 meeting. Her topic was "Maryland Remembers the Civil War." In her twenty-third year with the National Park Service in 1987, she was in charge of 310 volunteers at the Antietam National Battlefield. These volunteers serve in such capacities as: natural and cultural resource management projects; Civil War soldier encampment programs; weapons demonstrations and military drills; and programs on the Sanitary Commission during the Civil War.

The May newsletter carried the announcement that: "Founding member Ralph G. Newman has been named the winner of the 1987 Barondess/Lincoln Award of the Civil War Round Table of New York. The award, given annually since 1962 in honor of the late Dr. Benjamin Barondess of New York, a Lincoln scholar and charter member of the New York Round Table is for 'contribution to the greater appreciation of the life and works of Abraham Lincoln.'"

Colonel Mark M. Boatner, III (Retired), author of *The Civil War Dictionary* (1959) and other works, addressed the June 5 meeting. Colonel Boatner, who taught military history for a number of years at West Point, spoke on "Reading, Writing, and Teaching Military History."

It was the month for The Civil War Round Table's annual "change of command." This year, the president's gavel was passed from Patricia Krelle Sumner to Daniel R. Weinberg.

In a recent interview, Pat Sumner was asked to comment on her year as the first woman elected to the presidency of The Civil War Round Table—which, for thirty-seven years had been an all-male bastion. Emphasizing that it was a very positive experience for her, she said that she felt supportiveness from most of the male members (and all of the female members), "though I really think some of those older members came to meetings out of curiosity. Men who had not been seen at a Round Table meeting in several years showed up during my tenure . . . One man came up to me and said 'Well, I voted against women. But I guess this is a sign of the times.' And I replied, 'Thank you, I think.' However, I believe that most of the men who had any reservations relaxed when they realized I was not turning The Round Table into a flower group, and ultimately accepted me."[6] Hers was not a "token" election. Sumner earned her elevation to the presidency, putting in every bit as much—maybe more—"grunt work" as any of the men who rose to the position. Since joining the group in early 1980, she had done her share of hard work—on various committees and during her term as treasurer (1982-1983). "I'm sure that the women presidents who come after me may be better presidents than I was," Sumner remarked, "but they won't have to work as hard as I did to get there."[7] The general consensus is that Sumner, in the performance of her presidency, set a fine example for all who follow her, no matter what their gender.

Chapter 15 ☆ *The Round Table Concludes its First Half-Century*

1987 Nevins-Freeman Award Recipient James T. Hickey

THE CIVIL WAR ROUND TABLE bestowed its 1987 Nevins-Freeman Award on Lincoln scholar and historical detective James T. Hickey. During World War II, Hickey served with the United States Army Air Force's 20th Division Photographic Squadron, which later photographed the atomic bomb attacks on the Japanese mainland. Upon his return, he continued his college studies, which had been interrupted by the war, and was graduated from Lincoln College. "After a decade of farming [in Elkhart, Illinois]," Bob Douglas wrote in the September 1987 newsletter, "he assisted our Honorary Life member, Raymond N. Dooley, then president of Lincoln College, in the reorganization of the college's Lincoln museum. While serving as the museum's curator, he taught the 'Life of Lincoln' course at the college.

In 1958, the Illinois State Historical Library in Springfield was reorganized, with the Lincoln collection established as a separate department and Jim as its curator. He served until his retirement in November 1985. In 1959, he was named historical consultant for the restoration of the Old State Capitol building in Springfield. He selected and arranged for the purchase of most of the 3000 items with which the restored building is now furnished. This work was followed by the restoration of the Lincoln-Herndon law office, . . . the Great Western Railway station (the site of Lincoln's farewell address to the citizens of Springfield on February 11, 1861), [and] . . . the governor's mansion in Springfield. . . . Currently, Jim serves his alma mater as chairman of the Heritage committee of the board of trustees and will soon assume the duties of chairman of the college's board of trustees. . . . Jim has established himself as a great historical detective through his discovery of Lincoln's bank and grocery ledgers dating back to the 1840s and 1850s . . ."

It was Jim Hickey who made the very exciting discovery of Robert Todd Lincoln's letter books and his "MTL Insanity File" containing material about his mother's 1875 competency trial. Mark E. Neely, Jr. and R. Gerald McMurtry wrote about this discovery in their 1986 book, *The Insanity File: The Case of Mary Todd Lincoln*. After relating that Robert Todd Lincoln Beckwith believed that his grandfather had destroyed his papers, they wrote that: "James T. Hickey, the indefatigable curator of the Lincoln collection at the Illinois State Historical Library, thought otherwise. Even as a boy, Hickey had discovered numerous Lincoln documents in Illinois courthouses long thought to have been exhausted in their supply of such valuable materials. A gentleman farmer like Beckwith, Hickey struck up a friendship with the last male descendant of Abraham Lincoln, who understandably avoided most other curators. Hickey was willing to wait and he was not discouraged by talk that Robert's papers no longer existed. Mr. Beckwith had no objection to letting him search the old family estate—Hildene—in Manchester, Vermont, but his sister Mary still lived there and wanted no such intrusions. She died in 1975 and Hickey subsequently made an anxious trip to Vermont."[1]

Hickey searched the house, checking the room which had served as Robert Lincoln's office and the attic first, to no avail. Neely and McMurtry continue the story by relating that: "Mr. Beckwith continued to insist that there were no papers, but Hickey could remember having read somewhere a statement by Robert indicating that he had removed all the papers from his other offices and residences to Hildene and burned most of them but that he 'kept his letter press books' containing onion-skin copies of his own correspondence.

"When he entered Robert's bedroom, Hickey's attention focused on a double-locked closet visible from Robert's bed. He opened it to find—amidst old coats, shoes, and ski equipment—shelving with forty letter books and a bundle of papers tied in a pink ribbon and marked "MTL Insanity File." Robert was a private man, but a meticulous recordkeeper. That he set up a file on his mother's case should come as no surprise. That he retained it for fifty years, on the other hand, seems completely out of character . . . Robert in the end proved willing to let history learn about the most controversial episode of his life.

"That bundle of papers, the Insanity File, made this book possible. The letters in the Insanity File filled the gap in the documentary record that had so troubled all writers on the subject from Barton's day to this. With its discovery it seemed possible at last to tell the whole story of the trial of Mary Todd Lincoln."[2]

In his introduction of James T. Hickey that evening, Ralph Newman called him "the unnamed co-author of many of the important books about Lincoln," because of the invaluable research and informational assistance he had so generously given to Lincoln scholars over the years. Mr. Hickey then gave an address on "Robert Todd Lincoln's Relationships with Authors and Artists." One hundred seventeen members and guests attended the Award dinner at the Quality Inn.

Two new people joined the newsletter staff this year: Barbara Hughett, to write the meeting summaries; and Daniel J. Josephs, to begin a new column, the "Battlefield Preservation Report." Bob Douglas continued writing the page-one article about the upcoming meeting. Dick Clark, the longtime employee of The Abraham Lincoln Book Shop (since 1952), continued to prepare "the New Books" list as he had done for many years. In the newsletter, Editor David Richert thanked Wayne Anderson who had been writing the meeting summaries for several years.

October's speaker was William Safire, *New York Times* columnist, author of several books on politics and language, and former special assistant and senior speechwriter for President Nixon. His most recently published work was *Freedom: A Novel of Abraham Lincoln and the Civil War* (1987). His topic on October 9 was "Lincoln's Excesses: Their Effect on Modern Presidents." The meeting was attended by 168 people.

On February 12, 1988—the 179th anniversary of the birth of Abraham Lincoln—the speaker was William Hanchett, author of a number of books and articles on the Civil War period, including *The Lincoln Murder Conspiracies* (1983). Dr. Hanchett's topic was "Abraham Lincoln—Man in the Middle." There was also a cake, and the 132 people in attendance sang "Happy Birthday" to Mr. Lincoln.

Harold Holzer and Mark E. Neely, Jr. spoke on March 11 on "The Confederate Image: Prints of The Lost Cause." This is also the title of a 1987 book written by the speakers as well as an exhibition, which traveled throughout the nation, of sixty original prints from the Confederacy.

The 1984 Nevins-Freeman Award recipient, Richard B. Harwell, died on March 3, at the age of seventy-three. In a brief eulogy delivered at the March meeting, Ralph Newman called Harwell "one of that group of gentle scholars that has enobled the Civil War field" and "a completely delightful gentleman."

Also in the March newsletter was the announcement of a new organization: "The Association for the Preservation of Civil War Sites, Inc. (APCWS) was formed . . . for the purpose of acquiring control, by donation or purchase, of land on Civil War battlefields and sites in the Virginia-Maryland-Pennsylvania theater that otherwise would be sacrificed to development. They will focus on locations not already protected in part by the National Park Service or other conservation agencies. Among the leaders of the Association are Gary Gallagher, Robert Krick, Brian Pohanka, and Merlin Sumner . . ."

Chancellorsville was the focus of the thirty-eighth annual battlefield tour. In addition to Chancellorsville, three other major battles were covered in depth: Fredericksburg, Chancellorsville, the Wilderness, and Spotsylvania. The group also went, among other sites, to Kelly's Ford and Brandy Station. Speakers included Edwin C. Bearss and Frank E. Vandiver.

Gerald F. Linderman spoke on May 13, 1988, on "Embattled Courage: The Experience of Combat in the Civil War." This is also the title of a 1987 book by Dr. Linderman.

The "Third Battle of Mannassas" was getting heated. This is from the May newsletter: "Last month's Battlefield Preservation Report discussed the attempt by a developer to put a large shopping mall adjacent to the Manassas Battlefield. Contributions to the Save the Battlefield Coalition were requested—here are some other things you can do to help . . ." Members were urged to write to the chairperson of the Board of Supervisors of Prince William County in Virginia, to write their senators and representatives, and to write to the editors of newspapers in the area near the battlefield.

The dates for The Civil War Round Table's Fiftieth Anniversary celebration were announced in the June newsletter: October 12, 13, and 14, 1990. Paul Kliger, chairman of the anniversary committee, said that he would welcome volunteers who would like to serve on the committee.

On June 10, Edward G. Longacre spoke on "Low Comedy and High Tragedy: The Union Army of the James, 1863-1865." The June "changing of the guard" took place as usual. This year, Daniel R. Weinberg passed the presidential gavel to William J. Sullivan.

Upon assuming office that evening, Bill Sullivan (who had first come to The Round Table in 1971, at the invitation of Marshall Krolick), in a brief speech, paraphrased a portion of the Gettysburg Address, in stating that: "One decade and six years ago Marshall Krolick brought unto this organization a new member, conceived in history and dedicated to the proposition that all Civil War battles were created interesting. The world will little note nor long remember what we say here, but they can never forget why we meet here . . ."[3]

William J. Sullivan, 1988-89 President

The 1988 Nevins-Freeman Award was conferred on Robert K. Krick, chief historian of the Fredericksburg and Spotsylvania National Military Park. Krick, who did his undergraduate work at Pacific Union College and received his master's degree from San Jose University, has been a National Park Service historian since 1967. His published works include *Maxcy Gregg: Political Extremist and Confederate*

General (1963) and three volumes in the Virginia Regimental Series.

The Nevins-Freeman Award Dinner was held on September 9. The title of Mr. Krick's acceptance address was "The Army of Northern Virginia in September 1862, Its Circumstances During that Critical Month, its Opportunities, and the Reasons It Should Not Have Been at Sharpsburg on September 15-18, 1862."

Beginning with the September 1988 issue, Barbara Hughett became the co-editor, with David Richert, of the newsletter and started writing the page-one article in the October newsletter. Dick Clark, after thirty-six years of work at the Abraham Lincoln Book Shop and, for nearly as many years, faithfully preparing the Book List for the newsletter, had retired. Bob Douglas began preparing the Book List in November.

Lance J. Herdegen and William J.K. Beaudot, of the Milwaukee Civil War Round Table, addressed the October 14 meeting on "The Charge on the Railroad Cut at Gettysburg." Their book on the same subject *(In the Bloody Railroad Cut At Gettysburg)* would be published in 1990.

1988 Nevins-Freeman Award Recipient Robert K. Krick

An item in the November newsletter reported that: "The 125th anniversary observation of the Gettysburg Address will be held in Gettysburg November 19. 'Abraham Lincoln' will be escorted by 3000 uniformed troops from the train station to the cemetary, where he will deliver the address. Chief Justice of the United States William H. Rehnquist will preside over the observation."

The year 1988 ended with Karen Osborne returning for the third time to The Round Table podium. Her topic on December 9 was "A Civil War Christmas."

Dan Josephs announced in December's Battlefield Preservation Report that: "On November 11, President Ronald Reagan signed 'The Technical Corrections Act of 1988' which included an amendment regarding Manassas National Battlefield Park. Under the terms of the legislation, approximately 600 acres will be added to the park . . . [T]his area includes Stuart's Hill, the site of Robert E. Lee's headquarters during the Second Battle of Manassas in 1862. *Preservation News* noted that purchase of this land will stop construction of the shopping mall planned for the site. The legislation also provides for a study of the relocation of Highways 29 and 34 which run through the park . . ." It seemed as if the preservationists had won the "Third Battle of Manassas."

Another preservation item appeared in that issue, noting that: "The Association for the Preservation of Civil War Sites needs to raise $50,000 by the end of the year. If they do, The Gilder Foundation of New York will give them an additional $50,000. APCWS's purpose is to acquire deeded interest in historic properties threatened with destruction across the Civil War's Eastern Theater. Only gifts of $250 or more will qualify for the matching grant." (The "Gilder Challenge" was met; the Foundation would offer another "challenge" for $35,000, which was also successful.)

James M. McPherson, author of the critically acclaimed *Battle Cry of Freedom: The Civil War Era* (1988), addressed The Round Table on February 10. One hundred-sixty-five members and guests heard Dr. McPherson speak on "Lincoln and Liberty." His *Battle Cry of Freedom* would win the Pulitzer Prize in history in a few months.

The theme for the thirty-ninth annual battlefield tour (May 4-7) was "The Atlanta Campaign and Andersonville." Sites visited included New Hope Church, Resaca, Kennesaw Mountain, Peachtree Creek, the Andersonville Prison camp, Pine Mountain, the Cyclorama, and the Atlanta Historical Society.

Talking about what impressed her during the trip to Andersonville, where so many young men died of disease, hunger, and mistreatment, Mary Abroe said that: "I think I was moved by a profound sense of being so personally insignificant. Here we were in 1989 with our cameras, trotting around there—and something so awful, so appalling happened there. I felt a deep sadness because of what those men had to go through. Yet, I also had a sense of how important that whole experience was and how we have to remember it. Their lives meant something—all those people who died. We need to remember what they did. Their lives do mean something."[4]

The 1985 Nevins-Freeman Award winner and Honorary Life member John Y. Simon addressed The Round Table on June 9. Dr. Simon spoke on "Edward D. Baker, Ball's Bluff, and the Politics of Command." At this meeting, William J. Sullivan passed the president's gavel to Richard McAdoo.

The Round Table had lost a number of its longtime members during the 1988-1989 term: Martin P. Dutch, Earl F. Bartholomew, Dr. Jan Tillisch, Don Jensen, Raymond Jankovich, Sr., and Maurice (Morrie) Fisher. There had been sad announcements from the podium on meeting nights. After thanking those who had assisted him during his tenure, Bill Sullivan had this to say: "Before I turn the mantle of leadership over to Dick McAdoo, I feel it only appropriate to think back. This has been a hard year on our organization. It seems that we have from this podium murmured name upon name of our dear friends. Thinking of those who have left us this year and other years, I feel it might be appropriate to quote perhaps Marshall Krolick's favorite figure—John Wayne—

Richard W. McAdoo, 1989-90 President, on the 1990 battlefield tour

when he, at the end of the film "Fort Apache," says to the surrounding crowd when reminded of those who were slain in the battle: 'They aren't dead; they are all still here. The names and faces change, but while the regiment lives, they live.' And none of our founders and members who have gone to their last posting are ever really not here. While The Civil War Round Table lives, they live."[5]

Renowned Lincoln scholar Mark E. Neely, Jr. was selected as the recipient of the 1989 Nevins-Freeman Award. Director of the Louis A. Warren Lincoln Library and Museum in Fort Wayne, Indiana and the editor of *Lincoln Lore*, Dr. Neely received his bachelor's and doctoral degrees from Yale University. Among the works of which he has been author or co-author are *The Abraham Lincoln Encyclopedia* (1982), *The Lincoln Image: Abraham Lincoln and the Popular Print* (1984), and *The Insanity File: The Case of Mary Todd Lincoln* (1986).

1989 Nevins-Freeman Award Recipient Mark E. Neely, Jr.

The Nevins-Freeman Award Dinner was held on September 8 at the Merchants and Manufacturers Club in Merchandise Mart Plaza. For his acceptance address, Dr. Neely explored the question, "Was the Civil War a Total War?" One hundred-three attended.

Beginning with the September 1989 issue, Barbara Hughett assumed the position of editor of the newsletter. Also joining the newsletter staff at this time was Mary Munsell Abroe, writing the Battlefield Preservation Report.

Abroe's first column focused on the fight to save a not-so-well-known Civil War site—Johnson's Island, Ohio, which had served as a prison camp for Confederate officers. "During the course of its operation [April 1862-September 1865], Abroe wrote, "8700 men were interned there; among them were Henry Kyd Douglas and Rooney Lee." She noted that the forts, intact despite 125 years of neglect were unique in that they constituted examples of earthworks *north* of the Ohio River. "At this point," she added, "280-acre Johnson's Island, the final resting place for 206 Confederate soldiers, is a relatively pristine scenic landscape." However, it was being threatened by developers. "In the final analysis," Abroe observed, "the nation has seen fit to remember the sacrifices of the Union soldiers who died at Andersonville by establishing the Andersonville National Historic Site. How, then, can it do any less for the Confederates who died at Johnson's Island—or for the present and future Americans who need to remember what happened there?"

Barbara Hughett on the 1990 battlefield tour

During the past couple of years, announcements had been appearing in the newsletter urging members to submit Round Table memorabilia to the Fiftieth Anniversary Committee. Archives Committee Co-chairman Jerry Warshaw was gathering these materials in preparation for the 1990 celebration and the publication of this history. The Anniversary Committee was having frequent meetings to plan the events to take place in October 1990.

The Round Table began 1990 with Bill Sullivan speaking on January 12 on "Heartland of Freedom: Chicago During the Civil War." For the February 9 meeting, the group was given a private viewing of a new exhibit at the Chicago Historical Society—"A House Divided: America in the Age of Lincoln."

The selection for the fortieth annual battlefield tour (May 2-6) was the Maryland Campaign of 1862, with a focus on Antietam. The Cliffside Inn in Harpers Ferry, West Virginia was the "Command Post" hotel and Thursday's tour schedule began in the historic village of Harpers Ferry. The group visited Charles Town that day, where John Brown was tried in 1859. Dennis Frye, historian of the Harpers Ferry National Historical Park, led all gathered down the execution route to the scaffold site where Brown was hung.

Friday's itinerary included the Kennedy Farm house, which served as the staging place for John Brown and his army of abolitionists prior to the raid on Harpers Ferry. ("It can be said . . . 'It all started here . . .' proclaims a card available at the farm house.) Antietam Furnace, the C & O Canal, South Mountain, and the Townsend War Correspondents Memorial were also included in Friday's schedule. A drenching rain that afternoon did not deter the indefatigable tour guide Ed Bearss, although more than a few campaigners elected to stay on the buses during the heaviest part of the storm.

Saturday was reserved for the main event of the tour: the Battle of Antietam. A thorough coverage of the battle was provided by the superb guides, Bearss and Frye. Stops included the Pry House (McClellan's headquarters during the battle), the North Woods, the Corn Field, the West Woods, Bloody Lane, and the Burnside Bridge. Campaigners enjoyed a picnic lunch on the lawn of the Piper Farm. (Happily, the weather cooperated with Saturday's plans.) Bill Sullivan, tour co-chairperson (with Mary Abroe), was the Fun Night master-of-ceremonies. Civil War music was provided by entertainer Jim Morgan. Bob Douglas, who was on that first tour in 1951, presented a nostalgic look at battlefield tours past. Ed Bearss was awarded the Confederate Purple Heart for so bravely holding out against the elements of nature the previous day. The final stops of the tour, on Sunday, were Blackford's Ford and the historic Grove Farm.

As usual, it was difficult for campaigners to leave. The people who share a battlefield tour experience become a "family" during those few days, living in a world of their

Charlie Falkenberg (right) on the 1974 battlefield tour with 1975-76 President Gerald Edelstein

own—sharing their interest in history and becoming part of their past. As has been noted earlier, strong bonds of friendship develop during the battlefield tours that frequently last a lifetime. Among the eighty-seven participants in 1990, were several people on their first tour. Susan Phillips was very impressed with the expertise of the tour guides and commented on how much knowledge there was to absorb in a short span of time. She also admitted that she was "hooked," and was looking forward to the next battlefield tour.[6] Roy Sanford called it "a life-changing experience."[7] Whether it was their first tour or, as in the case of Charlie Falkenberg, their twenty-seventh, the combination of scholarship, camaraderie, and of just "being there where it all happened" made this tour—as all others—a pleasurable and profoundly meaningful experience for all who participated.

What happens during these annual tours is a little difficult to put into words. Perhaps the following excerpts from an editorial written by Marshall Krolick, which first appeared in the April 1977 newsletter and which has been repeated several times thereafter, say it as well as it can be said: ". . . Those who have never been [on a battlefield tour] might ask why [people want to participate year after year] . . . The answer would probably be: 'It's The Battlefield Tour.' That begs the question, but to those who go, it's answer enough. What they're saying is really quite simple. It's not the places themselves that make them set aside the first weekend in May, it's the experience, maybe even the people and what they bring to each other.

"To analyze the experience, you must look at many things. Of course there is the scholarship and the chance to make three-dimensional what has previously only come to us

Ned Julian (left) and Will Plank

David R. Richert, 1990-91 President

from the printed page. The words of Ed Bearss, as he brings to life the drama of the battle; the lump in your throat when J. Ambler Johnston pulled Stonewall Jackson's watch from his pocket as we stood on the ground of Chancellorsville— these moments are 'The Battlefield Tour.'

"Then, too, there are the good times, the fun of comradeship with old friends. The sing-alongs as Miles Janusek pounded the piano; Pete Johnson throwing peanuts at the dancers on the showboat at Vicksburg; those same dancers turning their backs and lifting their skirts to prominently display Al Meyer's smile buttons; . . . Will Plank's car getting stuck in the mud at Manassas—these moments are 'The Battlefield Tour.'

"We cannot overlook the awards and those who have been lucky, or unlucky as the case may be, enough to win them. The look on the face of a true Daughter of the Confederacy as we thank her for opening her ante-bellum home by presenting her with a bust of Abraham Lincoln; . . . the Confederate Purple Heart meticulously created by John Margreiter and given without a straight face for sacrifice beyond the call of duty—these moments are 'The Battlefield Tour.'

"And, perhaps most important of all, for each of these moments there is a memory. Whether within your own mind or around the table wherever Round Table members gather, the stories are told and retold over and over. Each time the laugh wells up again, the wistful smile appears. Some of the old regulars are gone now, but each year as we get on that bus their spirit is already aboard, and so it will always be. The feeling they had is handed down to us and we in turn will pass it on. That too is 'The Battlefield Tour,' and thus the only question left is 'Where to next year?'"

From October through April (with the exception of February's special meeting at the Chicago Historical Society), The Round Table met at their usual site, the Quality Inn. Meetings in May and June were held at the Merchants and Manufacturers Club in Merchandise Mart Plaza. Jerry L. Rogers, the associate director for cultural resources for the National Park Service, ended the 1989-1990 term with an address on June 8. His subject was "The Invisible Consensus: A Proposal for the Protection of Battlefield Parks and Other Resources." This, of course, was a most appropriate topic for the members who were so recently back from the tour. The presidential gavel was passed this year from Richard McAdoo to David R. Richert.

For members of the Fiftieth Anniversary Committee, the summer would be filled with work completing the plans for the big celebration. A special event took place on June 23—a raffle, to help defray costs of the anniversary celebration. The

Ralph Newman, Win Stracke, Judge Abraham Lincoln Marovitz and Dan Weinberg at the rededication of Centennial Park on June 23, 1990

Abraham Lincoln Book Shop had moved in March to 357 West Chicago Avenue. That great old building on Chestnut Street is gone—Centennial Park is gone, to be replaced by a modern highrise. However, the Centennial Marker (the last replacement) remains intact.

Dan and Audrey Weinberg invited Round Table members and friends to come to the raffle, enjoy some refreshments and a program, and be on hand for the rededication of the Centennial Marker. As the original 1965 ceremony was to "lay to rest the Civil War Centennial," the rededication was to "lay to rest the 125th anniversary of the Civil War."

Several original Keith Rocco (a talented artist, specializing in Civil War scenes, who is also a Round Table member) prints and a number of books, donated by the Abraham Lincoln Book Shop and the Appomattox Book Shop, were raffled. It was an afternoon filled with nostalgia and good fellowship. The two surviving Round Table founders were present—Ralph Newman, who gave some brief remarks, and Elmer Gertz. Balladeer Win Stracke, recently returned to Chicago from Colorado, was there and led the group in singing his "The Greatest Little Park in the World (Centennial Park on Chestnut Street)."

The Civil War Round Table was just about ready for its "gala celebration," October 12, 13, and 14. Much work had been done and was still being done. Articles written by David Richert and Barbara Hughett, about The Round Table as it reached its half-century mark, appeared in national and statewide historical periodicals.[8] Mailings had gone out across the country. There were few remaining seats to be had for the anniversary celebration. People from all over the country had made reservations far in advance. (See Appendix M for the program for the Fiftieth Anniversary celebration.) The Civil War Round Table had indeed spent a half-century proving, very emphatically, that history can be fun.

Chapter 16 ☆ *Why People Care about the Civil War: A Look Forward to the Next Fifty Years of The Civil War Round Table*

F ASCINATION WITH THE AMERICAN CIVIL WAR is perhaps greater than it ever has been, as evidenced by a cover story in the August 15, 1988 issue of *U.S. News and World Reports* titled "Reliving the Civil War: Why America's Bloodiest Conflict Still Grips Us 125 Years Later"; the popularity of the 1989 movie *Glory;* the continual influx of books on various aspects of the war; the prevalence of reenactment groups; and the thriving of Civil War Round Tables. What makes the Civil War so compelling that the study of it seems to become more popular as time goes by? Why do thousands of people all over this country, as well as in other parts of the world, join Civil War Round Tables? Why are so many people concerned about preserving America's Civil War battlefields? What lies in the future for The Civil War Round Table and other Round Tables?

Hopefully, some of these questions have been partially answered in the text which preceded this chapter. But we will try to provide a further reply in this chapter, largely by letting some of the people who have been drawn to the study of what has been called "the middle period of American history" speak for themselves.

James M. McPherson has called the Civil War "the single most dramatic and crucial experience in American history." Dr. McPherson has pointed out that, from 1861-1865, "great issues were at stake, issues about which Americans were willing to fight and die, issues whose resolution profoundly transformed and redefined the United States. . . . In the process of preserving the Union of 1776 while purging it of slavery, the Civil War also transformed it. Before 1861, the words *United States* were a plural noun: 'The United States are a large country.' Since 1865 *United States* has been a singular noun. The North went to war to preserve the *Union;* it ended by creating a *nation.*"[1] That this war was the only one fought on this country's soil between brothers, of course, also makes it singularly intriguing.

Several members of The Civil War Round Table were

asked what first sparked their interest in the era they now study so avidly. For many of these people, the first seeds were sown in childhood; such was the case, noted earlier, with Round Table founders Ralph Newman and Elmer Gertz. Others—like Hal Ardell, Pat Sumner, and Dan Weinberg— had a general interest in history, but became "hooked" on the Civil War after reading books about it in adulthood.[2]

Jerry Slechta and Charles Wesselhoeft became interested in the Civil War as adults, also. For Slechta, it came during World War II. His wife bought him Douglas Southall Freeman's four- volume biography of Lee to take aboard ship with him. When he got out of the U.S. Navy, he searched out the Abraham Lincoln Book Shop, where he was immediately recruited for membership in The Civil War Round Table.[3] For Wesselhoeft, it was Carl Sandburg's *Abraham Lincoln: The War Years* that did the trick.[4]

Jerry Slechta, 1959-60 President, in 1981

The fascination began for some members upon learning in childhood that they had ancestors who had been part of the drama. For Brooks Davis, it started when he learned that his grandfather had served in the war and had been wounded. "After the conclusion of the war," Davis related, "he was at Fort Monroe when Jefferson Davis was brought in there. His was one of the three companies detailed to guard the former Confederate president. They discovered at that time that they were distant cousins. Jefferson Davis gave him a brass candlestick—which I still have—as a memento. Because of this and because of the kinship, I belong to both the Sons of Union Veterans and the Sons of Confederate Veterans."[5]

Ernest Griffin's grandfather served in Company B, 29th Infantry Regiment of the United States Colored Troops. Knowing this as a child, he developed an interest in the Civil War. But only after he had owned the Griffin Funeral Home on the south side of Chicago for fifteen years did he learn that, not only was it located on a portion of land that was once the site of Camp Douglas (the United States Army recruiting camp and prison for captured Confederate soldiers), but it was at this location that his grandfather had enlisted in the Union Army on January 5, 1864.[6]

In 1990, he commissioned the construction of a Heritage Memorial Wall on the grounds of his establishment to honor his grandfather and all those who fought "in that tragic period often called 'the brothers' war'"[7]—North and South. One side of the wall honors Union soldiers; the other side commemorates Confederate soldiers. The Wall was dedicated on May 26, 1990, in an impressive and moving ceremony that included addresses by Ralph G. Newman and Chicago Mayor Richard M. Daley and a performance by the Kennedy-King College Chorus.

*Ernest Griffin at the Heritage
Memorial Wall*

A couple other Round Table members discovered in childhood they were descended from people who played some significant part in the Civil War era. Luann Elvey learned that an ancestor of hers had been one of the carpenters who worked on the remodeling of the Lincolns' Springfield home in 1856. This sparked a lifelong interest in the study of both geneology and the life of Abraham Lincoln.[8] Roy Sanford discovered that his great-grandfather was a Union soldier who had been confined in both Salisbury Prison and the infamous Libby Prison in Richmond. He since has done considerable research on his great-grandfather's wartime activities. Sanford learned that nine members of the Northway family, including his great-grandfather, enlisted in the Cavalry of the 6th Ohio Volunteers. Three of them gave their lives in the war; his great-grandfather received a surgeon's discharge in 1865.[9]

Some members found that passionate interest in childhood during a visit to a battlefield or from the pages of a book, without having a family connection to the War. What "pulled the plug" for Frank Vandiver was a trip to Vicksburg when he was ten or eleven years old in the 1930s, and actually finding a rusty musket left by a fallen soldier on the battlefield.[10] Marshall Krolick was "hooked" on the Gettysburg battlefield during childhood visits to a relative who lived nearby.[11]

"I read a biography of Clara Barton," Mary Abroe

remembers, "when I was twelve years old. I loved reading biographies of famous women . . . There was a whole chapter in this book about Antietam because she was there—and was extremely important there. It talked about the night before the battle and mentioned a conversation she had with a little drummer boy who was killed the next day. It captured my imagination. There was one phrase about 'the dark quiet valley of Antietam' that night before the battle that grabbed me. And I never lost it. Admittedly, at that time what I had was a child's romanticized vision of what war was all about, but it grabbed me and kept me interested."[12] For the author of this book, it was reading a book on Abraham Lincoln, which I'd checked out from the library at the age of nine or ten. It was as if he reached out and touched me from the pages of the book, so compelling was his story. This prompted further reading on Lincoln and the Civil War period. When I walked into my first meeting of The Civil War Round Table, I knew I'd come home.

Mary Abroe on the 1990 battlefield tour

The Civil War Round Table has brought together a diverse group of people sharing a common interest in the Civil War and its era. For some, this interest is more general; for others, it is quite specific. Luann Elvey came to The Round Table, for example, with a very specific interest in the study of Abraham Lincoln and knew that some of the topics addressed there would center on Lincoln. "However, after I joined and started attending meetings regularly," Elvey observed, "I found myself enjoying talks that were not about Lincoln and, as a result, have really broadened my knowledge base about the age in which he lived."[13] This same story, changing only the names and subject matter, could be repeated over and over again for many people coming to the group with special focuses of study.

Sometimes the fun can be equally as important as the history. Marvin Sanderman, although he is a serious student of Civil War history, also concedes that Round Table activities, especially battlefield tours, can be a very pleasurable diversion. "Like hunting, fishing, or golfing," he remarked, "it's a way to get away from your phone and a busy schedule and amuse yourself with your friends."[14]

Older members occasionally claim that the group today isn't like it was in the "good old days." Reflecting on how The Round Table has changed over the years of his involvement (since 1961), Marshall Krolick felt it was "not better or worse, just different." One part of each meeting that had changed, he contended, was the question and answer session at the end of each talk. He said that: "Question and answer periods in the earlier days were not so much a seeking of information from the speaker as an opportunity to debate the speaker. People were in the audience who had made lifelong studies of particular aspects of the war.

"The stories told about Lloyd Miller, for instance, are absolutely true. If he disagreed with a speaker, he would let the president know that he wanted to say something. Invariably, he would be called upon first. He would get up to his full height and with his loud, booming voice, call out, 'Mr. Speaker, Bullshit!' That would set the tone for the question and answer period. Speakers would come to a meeting and actually shake during dinner because they were so nervous about the brutal question and answer session which would come at the conclusion of their talk. There often were people in the audience who knew more about the speaker's topic than the speaker did. Now, people are more polite. Although our members are knowledgeable, they are asking questions because they want to learn more; the speakers usually know more than they do."[15]

Bill Sullivan, who joined the group in 1971, however, feels that the membership is more scholarly now than when he first became a member. "The Round Table is getting more serious," he said. "More people are interested in a scholarly way. When I joined, it was probably fifty percent Civil War interest and fifty percent camaraderie. Now, it's more like seventy-five percent interest and scholarship and twenty-five percent camaraderie. Also, there's more involvement by a larger number of members, instead of only a few doing all the participating."[16]

Regardless of what changes may have occurred in the organization over the past fifty years, The Civil War Round Table has consistently served as a catalyst for Civil War interest. By providing a forum for scholars in the field, it encourages the flow of scholarly work. "The Civil War Round Table," John Y. Simon maintained, "has been a positive force in history. It has brought together professional historians and amateur historians. It started out as an organization of amateur historians— some on the edge of being professional— and gradually, it built up this kind of link which has been very constructive for both parties. . . . The enthusiasm for Civil War study has been nurtured by The Civil War Round Table, and all the Round Tables that have come after it . . . The Round Tables seem to be doing more now than ever before, especially in the area of battlefield preservation."[17]

What directions should The Civil War Round Table be taking in the future? One obvious answer is to do more towards battlefield preservation. Mary Abroe offered her opinion that: "I think we're [The Round Table] moving in a positive direction now in terms of battlefield preservation, but I think we have a long way to go. It's time to put our money where our mouths are. If this organization is, as stated in our newsletter, dedicated to the study of the Civil War and its era, I don't see how we can continue to study that era forever unless we hang onto the places where it all happened . . . There are several organizations which have sprung up recently and they are spearheading the movement to save the battlefields by building rational strategies for the future so that we can fight land developers and beat them at their own game, using modern technology and legislative techniques . . . I would like to see a more visible commitment on the part of our group. The Civil War Round Table needs to be in the vanguard of the battlefield preservation movement."

Speaking of the battlefields, she added: "People who say these places glorify war are myopic at best. Those battlefields, if anything, are the best examples of showing how terrible war is and what it does to people. I can sit in my living room and think about Bloody Lane and this feeling comes over me. . . . I wonder if I could ever endure what they had to endure. . . . They were just boys, most of them. . . . The battlefields are tangible reminders of what happened there and they point out the appalling nature of what war really is. . . . If we are going to have any kind of cultural memory, we need to have these physical places. They impress your past on you in a way that words and pictures never can . . ."[18]

"My concern," Merlin Sumner expressed, "is not so much with what The Civil War Round Table was as with what The Civil War Round Table will be. How many Civil War sites will there be left to visit fifty years from now if we don't work diligently on battlefield preservation?" "I keep thinking," he reflected, "about the Coliseum in Rome. At some point in time, somebody had to have taken a stand and said, 'Hey, let's not knock it down.' At some point, someone had to say, 'That's unthinkable!' Now the whole world believes it's unthinkable. We have to get to that same place with Civil War sites."[19]

As the preceding paragraphs have illustrated, the Civil War is still producing strong feelings of cause and commitment. That this war was waged over great and important issues has something to do with the undiminishing interest and powerful emotions it continues to engender.

Round Table members realize that we are part of our past, and that the past is indeed relevant to the present—and the future. "We need to be reminded, " Roy Sanford emphasized, "of what was required to keep the United States together. In studying the lives of the people who fought and died in that war, perhaps especially for those of us who had an ancestor serving in the conflict, we learn on a personal level what the Civil War meant to the common people. In achieving this understanding, we are inspired to preserve and value our heritage for what it is. As we remember why it's good to be an American, we renew our own ideals and spirituality."[20] Henry Steele Commager noted in his 1950 Introduction to *Blue and Gray* that: "We have fought five major wars in the last century or so, and three since Appomattox, but of them all it is the Civil War that has left the strongest impression on our minds, our imaginations, and our hearts."

The combination of scholarship and fellowship has been a winning one for The Civil War Round Table. The scholarship continues at a high level. The warm good fellowship between members is perhaps more evident than ever. Pat Sumner said that The Round Table "is the only organization I have ever belonged to or been aware of where the people care so much about the other people."[21] Many others would echo her statement.

Will The Civil War Round Table be around fifty years from now? "The names and faces will change," Bill Sullivan observed, "but I think The Civil War Round Table will continue for a long, long time. I really think that, fifty years from now, someone will be writing a history of the *second* fifty years of The Civil War Round Table."[22]

Notes

Chapter 1

1. Interview with Ralph G. Newman, June 20, 1989.
2. Ibid.
3. For a number of years, speakers were presented with plaques commemorating the occasion. Over the past several years, the gift for speakers has been a pewter mug bearing the inscription: "For Gallant Service, The Civil War Round Table, (speaker's name), (date of speaker's appearance)"

Chapter 2

1. Interview with Barbara Long Pleiter, December 30, 1989.
2. Interview with Frank Vandiver, September 10, 1989.
3. Interview with Ralph G. Newman, November 21, 1989.
4. Interview with Elmer Gertz, July 27, 1989.
5. Interview with Barbara Long Pleiter, December 30, 1989.
6. Interview with John Y. Simon, August 7, 1989.
7. Interview with Margaret April, July 18, 1989.
8. Neely, Mark E., Jr., in Newman, Ralph Geoffrey, *Preserving Lincoln for the Ages: Collectors, Collections, and Our Sixteenth President,* The Sixth Annual R. Gerald McMurtry Lecture, Delivered at Fort Wayne, Indiana, 1983. Fort Wayne: Louis A. Warren Lincoln Library and Museum, 1989, last page.
9. Mearns, David C. at meeting of the Lincoln Group of Washington, D.C. in the 1960s.
10. Interview with Elmer Gertz, July 27, 1989.
11. Ibid.
12. Carl Sandburg to Elmer Gertz in a message written in a book he inscribed for him. Interview with Elmer Gertz, July 27, 1989.
13. Newman, Ralph G. in the newsletter of The Civil War Round Table, December 1982, p. 4.
14. Eisenschiml, Otto. *Reviewers Reviewed.* Ann Arbor: The William L. Clements Library, 1940.
15. Interview with Elmer Gertz, July 27, 1989.
16. Newman, Ralph G. in *"O.E. At 80",* Chicago: published under the auspices of The Civil War Round Table, June 16, 1960.
17. Sandburg, Carl in ibid.
18. Elmer Gertz to Barbara Hughett, interview of July 27, 1989.
19. Betsey Davis to Barbara Hughett, interview of September 7, 1989.

20. John Y. Simon to Barbara Hughett, interview of August 7, 1989.
21. The last meeting in 1951 was on May 11, at which time the change of officers for the 1951-1952 term took place. (June would become the traditional changing-of-the guard time in 1953.) Thus, Seymour G. Frank, rather than Joseph L. Eisendrath, Jr., president for the 1950-1951 term, was Round Table president during the first battlefield tour (May 31-June 3, 1951).
22. Interview with Ralph G. Newman, November 21, 1989.
23. Dick Clark to Barbara Hughett, interview of August 30, 1989.
24. Ralph G. Newman to Barbara Hughett, interview of June 20, 1989.
25. Ibid.
26. Ibid.
27. Ibid.
28. Ibid.

Chapter 3

1. *The Civil War Round Table Year Book: 1940-1956,* Chicago: The Civil War Round Table, 1956, p. 6.
2. *Lincoln Herald,* Volume XLIV, Number 3-4, October-December, 1942, pp. 16 and 20-24.
3. Author unknown, *The Diary of a Public Man,* Chicago: The Abraham Lincoln Book Shop, 1945.
4. Elmer Gertz to Barbara Hughett, interview of July 27, 1989.
5. Interview with Ralph G. Newman, June 20, 1989.
6. Nicolay, John G. and John Hay, *Abraham Lincoln: A History,* 10 vols., New York: Century, 1890.
7. Interview with Ralph G. Newman, June 20, 1989.
8. Interview with Frank Vandiver, September 10, 1989.
9. Interview with Al Meyer, September 12, 1989.
10. Interview with Elmer Gertz, July 27, 1989.
11. Interview with Al Meyer, September 12, 1989.
12. Interview with Barbara Long Pleiter, December 30, 1989.
13. *The Civil War Round Table Year Book: 1940-1956,* Chicago: The Civil War Round Table, 1956, p. 7.
14. Ibid.
15. Ralph G. Newman to Barbara Hughett, interview of June 20, 1989.
16. *The Civil War Round Table Year Book: 1940-1956,* Chicago: The Civil War Round Table, 1956, p. 9.

Chapter 4

1. Gertz, Elmer, "The 100th Meeting of The Civil War Round Table" in the *Lincoln Herald,* Summer 1951, p. 29.
2. Ibid.
3. Percival G. Hart to Ralph G. Newman, letter of February 9, 1951.
4. Interview with C. Robert Douglas, August 12, 1989.

5. As noted, women were not admitted to Round Table meetings. At this special meeting in Harrogate, Tennessee, apparently the rules were relaxed to allow for the presence of the new Mrs. Pratt.

Chapter 5

1. Newman, Ralph G. in the newsletter of The Civil War Round Table, October 1978, p. 2.
2. After the death of Lincoln collector Oliver R. Barrett in 1950, his collection was offered to the state of Illinois for $220,000. Although the campaign to raise the funds by public subscription failed, a substantial sum was collected and spent on many choice Lincoln items when the "Immortal . . . Lincolniana Collected by the late Oliver J. Barrett . . ." was sold at auction at the Parke-Bernet Galleries on February 19-20, 1952. In addition to the items the state of Illinois purchased at the auction, Lincoln's letter to his stepbrother, John D. Johnston, which had been bought by Round Table member Foreman M. Lebold, was given to Illinois after Lebold's death.
3. Numerous interviews with Round Table members conducted by Barbara Hughett in 1989 and 1990.
4. Newman, Ralph G. in meeting notice of The Civil War Round Table for meeting of October 17, 1952.
5. Newman, Ralph Geoffrey, *Preserving Lincoln for the Ages: Collectors, Collections, and Our Sixteenth President*, The Sixth Annual R. Gerald McMurtry Lecture, Delivered at Fort Wayne, Indiana, 1983. Fort Wayne: Louis A. Warren Lincoln Library and Museum, 1989, p. 24.
6. Ibid.
7. Geldhof, A.E., in the *Lincoln Herald*, Fall, 1952 issue, regularly featured column on "The Civil War Round Tables," p. 28.
8. Ibid.
9. Gertz, Elmer in introducing Townsend the evening of October 17, 1952; taken from tape of address.
10. This and tapes of other addresses presented before The Civil War Round Table are available. Tape Librarian Hal Ardell has restored many tapes of older addresses and continues to tape the current talks. To order one, or to obtain a list of tapes available, contact the offices of The Civil War Round Table, 357 West Chicago Avenue, Chicago, Illinois 60610, (312) 944-3085.

Chapter 6

1. Geldhof, A.E., "The Civil War Round Table, Third Annual Battlefield Tour" in the *Lincoln Herald*, Summer 1953, p. 20.
2. Ibid.
3. Interview with Frank Vandiver, September 10, 1989.
4. Johnston, J. Ambler, *Echoes of 1861-1961.* Milwaukee, Wisconsin: Philip J. Hohlweck, 1971, p. 2.
5. Ralph G. Newman to Barbara Hughett, conversation of July 18, 1990.
6. Because the second battlefield tour in 1952 was held later than usual (June 19-22) and the 1953 tour took place at the normal early May period (May 7-10), Elmer Gertz was one

of two Round Table presidents to have two battlefield tours during his tenure. (Arnold Alexander, president in 1964-1965, was the only Round Table president, since battlefield tours began, to have no tour occur during his tenure. Due to Civil War Centennial activities, the 1965 tour was postponed until October. Because of this, Brooks Davis, 1965-1966 president, also had two tours take place during his term in office.)

Chapter 7

1. Sandburg, Carl in meeting notice of The Civil War Round Table for the Civil War Round Table of New York's observance of Frederick Hill Meserve's eighty-eighth birthday on November 1, 1953.
2. Interview with Ralph G. Newman, June 20, 1989.
3. Interview with C. Robert Douglas, August 12, 1989.
4. Interview with Margaret April, July 18, 1989.
5. Ibid.
6. In 1953, member O.H. Felton developed the Round Table insignia into a lapel pin, in yellow or white gold. The pin, with the same basic design, has been produced at various times throughout the ensuing years. Member Jerry Warshaw designed and produced the latest version in 1989, and it remains available to members.

Chapter 8

1. Hixson, Harold B., in introduction of Ambler Johnston at the January 17, 1957 meeting of The Civil War Round Table, as reprinted in Johnston, Ambler J., *Echoes of 1861-1861,* Milwaukee, Wisconsin: Philip J. Hohlweck, 1971, p. 2.
2. Johnston, Ambler J., in address to The Civil War Round Table, January 17, 1957, as reprinted in Johnston, Ambler J., *Echoes of 1861-1961,* Milwaukee, Wisconsin: Philip J. Hohlweck, 1971, p. 82.
3. Ambrose, Stephen, "The Civil War Round Tables," in *Wisconsin Magazine of History,* Summer, 1959, Vol. 42, No. 4, p. 257.
4. Ibid., p. 262.

Chapter 9

1. Interview with Margaret April, July 18, 1989.
2. " *O.E. At 80",* Chicago: published under the auspices of The Civil War Round Table, June 16, 1960.
3. Hart, Percival G. in the newsletter of The Civil War Round Table, November, 1960, p. 1.
4. Ibid.
5. Most book editors and historians agreed that this code was impractical and it was forgotten.
6. Ralph G. Newman to Barbara Hughett, letter of June 26, 1990.
7. Interview with Glen Wiche, July 1, 1989.
8. The newsletter of The Civil War Round Table, February, 1963, p. 2.

9. Johnston, J. Ambler, quoted by Gil Twiss in the newsletter of The Civil War Round Table, September, 1962.
10. Interview with Betsey Davis, September 7, 1989.
11. Ibid.
12. Interview with Brooks Davis, September 7, 1989.
13. Interview with Ralph G. Newman, June 20, 1989.
14. Ibid.

Chapter 10

1. Ralph G. Newman to Barbara Hughett, letter of June 26, 1990.
2. Interview with Betsey Davis, September 7, 1989.
3. Interview with Elmer Gertz, July 27, 1989.
4. Excerpt from former President Truman's message, reprinted in the newsletter of The Civil War Round Table, February, 1966.
5. Interview with Margaret April, July 18, 1989.
6. Interview with Betsey Davis, September 7, 1989.
7. Interview with Barbara Long Pleiter, December 30, 1989.
8. Interview with Margaret April, August 30, 1989.
9. Interview with Barbara Long Pleiter, December 30, 1989.
10. Twiss, Gil in the newsletter of The Civil War Round Table, April, 1966, p. 1.
11. Message of former President Dwight D. Eisenhower, reprinted in the newsletter of The Civil War Round Table, May, 1966, p. 3.
12. Interview with Marshall Krolick, September 21, 1989.
13. Twiss, Gil in special report on 1966 battlefield tour, which was distributed to Round Table members.
14. Interview with Frank Vandiver, September 10, 1989.

Chapter 11

1. Marshall Krolick to Round Table members, letter of May 24, 1967.
2. Report on 1968 battlefield tour in supplement to the newsletter of The Civil War Round Table, June, 1968.
3. Powers, Irene, "Ball Is Scholars' Annual Bit of Levity" in the *Chicago Tribune*, February 13, 1969.
4. Jerry Warshaw at 282nd regular meeting of The Civil War Round Table, June 6, 1969; obtained from author's copy of remarks.
5. Dr. Freeman won the Pulitzer Prize in 1933 for *Grover Cleveland: A Study in Courage* (1932) and in 1937 for *Hamilton Fish: An Inner History of the Grant Administration* (1936).
6. *New Yorker* magazine, May 13, 1961, pp. 36-37.
7. Interview with Marshall Krolick, March 16, 1989.
8. Catton, Bruce, quoted in the newsletter of The Civil War Round Table, December, 1971, p. 1.

Chapter 12

1. Whitney, Gordon in the newsletter of The Civil War Round Table, battlefield tour edition, April, 1972, p. 1.
2. Interview with Marshall Krolick, September 21, 1989.
3. Marshall Krolick to Barbara Hughett, telephone conversation of June 15, 1990.
4. Interview with Bill Sullivan, September 26, 1989.
5. Since the mid-1980s, the Nevins-Freeman Award has consisted of a two-volume set of books: Douglas Southall Freeman's *The Gateway To History* (1938) and Allan Nevins' *The South To Posterity* (1951). The books are inscribed and bound in full-grey and full-blue Morocco and encased in a blue cloth, fleece-lined slipcase.
6. Arnold Alexander to Round Table members, letter of November 15, 1974. (Unfortunately, all of the plans for the Civil War Research Center did not come to fruition. After Ralph G. Newman was no longer president of the board of directors of the Chicago Public Library, his successor and the mayors who succeeded Mayors Richard J. Daley and Michael A. Bilandic were not interested in the fulfillment of the plans for the Research Center.)
7. Bill Sullivan to Barbara Hughett, telephone conversation of July 9, 1990.
8. Interview with Bill Sullivan, September 26, 1989.
9. Bill Sullivan to Barbara Hughett, telephone conversation of July 9, 1990.
10. Interview with Bill Sullivan, September 26, 1989.
11. Ibid.
12. Interview with Dan Weinberg, August 2, 1989.
13. The 1977 Round Table roster lists 259 members. Of this number, 58 lived out of the Chicago area, thus disqualifying them to vote on this issue. Of the 201 eligible voters listed on the 1977 roster, 155 voted.
14. Interview with Marshall Krolick, September 21, 1989; interview with Marvin Sanderman, August 24, 1989.

Chapter 13

1. Interview with Margaret April, July 18, 1989.
2. *The Nevins-Freeman Award: The First Decade, 1974-1983*, Chicago: published under the auspices of The Civil War Round Table, 1984.
3. Craig, George, quoted in *The Civil War Round Table Digest*, Vol. I, No. 9, September, 1978, p. 1.
4. Long, Barbara in speech delivered before The Civil War Round Table on the evening her husband, E.B. (Pete) Long, was honored as the Nevins-Freeman winner, June 8, 1979.
5. Interview with Barbara Long Pleiter, December 30, 1989.
6. Interview with Frank Vandiver, September 10, 1989.
7. Interview with Barbara Long Pleiter, December 30, 1989.
8. Merlin Sumner to Barbara Hughett, letter of April 7, 1990.
9. Interview with Patricia Sumner, October 8, 1989.
10. *The Nevins-Freeman Award: The First Decade, 1974-1983*, Chicago: published under the auspices of The Civil War Round Table, 1984.
11. Mary Abroe to Barbara Hughett, telephone conversation of July 16, 1990.

12. Larry Gibbs to Barbara Hughett, telephone conversation of July 12, 1990.
13. Interview with Bill Sullivan, September 26, 1989.

Chapter 14

1. Merlin Sumner to Barbara Hughett, letter of April 7, 1990.
2. *The Nevins-Freeman Award: The First Decade, 1974-1983,* Chicago: published under the auspices of The Civil War Round Table, 1984.
3. Harwell, Richard B., *Lee,* New York: Charles Scribners' Sons, 1951 and *Washington,* New York: Charles Scribners' Sons, 1968.
4. Hattaway, Herman, *How The North Won,* Jackson, Mississippi: University Press of Mississippi, 1983; Gallagher, Gary W., *Stephen Dodson Ramseur: Lee's Gallant General,* Chapel Hill, North Carolina: University of North Carolina Press, 1985.
5. Russell, Don, *Lives and Legends of Buffalo Bill,* Norman, Oklahoma: University of Oklahoma Press, 1860.
6. Interview with Patricia Sumner, October 8, 1989.
7. Ibid.

Chapter 15

1. Neely, Mark E., Jr. and R. Gerald McMurtry, *The Insanity File: The Case of Mary Todd Lincoln,* Carbondale and Edwardsville: Southern Illinois University Press, 1986, pp. 131-132.
2. Ibid., pp. 132-133.
3. Bill Sullivan at 472nd regular meeting of The Civil War Round Table, June 10, 1988; obtained from author's copy of remarks.
4. Interview with Mary Abroe, September 9, 1989.
5. Bill Sullivan at 482nd regular meeting of The Civil War Round Table, June 9, 1989; obtained from author's copy of remarks.
6. Susan Phillips to Barbara Hughett, conversation of May 6, 1990.
7. Roy Sanford to Barbara Hughett, telephone conversation of July 20, 1990.
8. Richert, David, "Chicago To Celebrate 50th Round Table Anniversary" in *The Civil War News,* June, 1990, p. 22; Hughett, Barbara, "The Civil War Round Table Anniversary Celebration" in *Dispatch,* a publication of the Illinois State Historical Society, Series 12, Vol. 4, June/July, 1990, p. 6; Hughett, Barbara, "Chicago Round Table Turns 50!" in *Blue and Gray,* Vol. VII., Issue 6, August, 1990, pp. 29-30; Hughett, Barbara, "The Civil War Round Table Celebrates Its 50th Anniversary" in the *Lincoln Newsletter,* a publication of Lincoln College, Lincoln, Illinois, Vol. IX, Number 2, Summer 1990, p.4.

Chapter 16

1. McPherson, James M., "A War That Never Goes Away" in *American Heritage,* March 1990, p. 47.
2. Hal Ardell to Barbara Hughett, conversation of June 8, 1990; interview with Patricia Sumner, October 8, 1989; interview with Dan Weinberg, August 2, 1989.

3. Interview with Jerry Slechta, September 9, 1989.

4. Interview with Charles Wesselhoeft, December 15, 1989.

5. Interview with Brooks Davis, September 7, 1989.

6. Ernest Griffin to Barbara Hughett, telephone conversation of August 1, 1990, as well as previous conversations in 1989 and 1990.

7. Excerpt from inscription on bronze plaque on Heritage Memorial Wall, grounds of the Griffin Funeral Home, 3232 Martin Luther King Drive, Chicago, Illinois.

8. Luann Elvey to Barbara Hughett, conversation of June 16, 1988 and telephone conversation of July 20, 1990.

9. Roy Sanford to Barbara Hughett, conversations of May 5 and May 26, 1990 and telephone conversation of August 1, 1990.

10. Interview with Frank Vandiver, September 10, 1989.

11. Interview with Marshall Krolick, September 21, 1989.

12. Interview with Mary Abroe, September 29, 1989.

13. Luann Elvey to Barbara Hughett, telephone conversation of July 20, 1990.

14. Interview with Marvin Sanderman, August 24, 1989.

15. Interview with Marshall Krolick, September 21, 1989.

16. Interview with Bill Sullivan, September 26, 1989.

17. Interview with John Y. Simon, August 7, 1989.

18. Interview with Mary Abroe, September 9, 1989.

19. Interview with Merlin Sumner, October 8, 1989.

20. Roy Sanford to Barbara Hughett, telephone conversation of August 1, 1990.

21. Interview with Patricia Sumner, October 8, 1989.

22. Interview with Bill Sullivan, September 26, 1989.

Appendix A

Speakers and Topics at the Monthly Meetings of
The Civil War Round Table

Meeting		Speaker and Topic
	1940	
1	December	Percival G. Hart, "Stonewall Jackson's Valley Campaign"
	1941	
2	January	Elmer Gertz, "Wilbur F. Storey and the *Chicago Times* in the Civil War"
3	February	Robert L. Kincaid, "Cumberland Gap in the Civil War"
4	March	Otto Eisenschiml, "Civil War Battlefields I Have Visited"
5	April	John W. Curran, "America's Greatest Conspiracy: The Trial of the Lincoln Conspirators"
6	May	Newton C. Farr, "The Secession Movement and Some of Its Fathers"
7	October	Monroe F. Cockrell, "General Nathan Bedford Forrest"
8	November	Stanley F. Horn, "The Army of The Tennessee"
9	December	Ralph G. Newman, "General Benjamin F. Butler"
	1942	
10	January	Stewart W. McClelland, "Following the Trail of Jefferson Davis' Flight"
11	February	Norman Bruce Sigband, "General John A. McClernand and the Civil War"
12	March	Seymour J. Frank, "King Cotton and the Blockade"
13	April	A Symposium: "General George Brinton McClellan." Addresses by Otto Eisenschiml and Percival G. Hart. Maps by Joseph Parrish. Elmer Gertz, Moderator. Addenda by David H. Annan, Monroe F. Cockrell, Carl B. Davis, Newton C. Farr, and Ralph G. Newman
14	May	R. Gerald McMurtry, "Ben Hardin Helm, `Rebel' Brother-in-Law of Abraham Lincoln"
15	September	Garnett W. Eskew, "The Mississippi River in the Civil War"
16	October	Dedication of the Civil War Library of Lincoln Memorial University, Harrogate, Tennessee. Stanley F. Horn, Chairman; Harry Howard and Roy F. Basler
17	November	Harry E. Pratt, "The Personal Finances of Abraham Lincoln"
18	December	Carl B. Davis, "Some Medical Aspects of the Civil War"
	1943	
19	January	LeRoy H. Fischer, "Lincoln's Gadfly—Adam Gurowski"
20	February	Walter H. Hebert, "Fighting Joe Hooker"

21	March	Paul M. Angle, "B. H. Grierson: Cavalryman"
22	April	Ernest Samuels, "The Adams Family and the Southern Question"
23	May	Walter S. Holden, "Abraham Lincoln, Man of Inner Conflict"
24	June	Don Russell, "Illinois Monuments on Civil War Battlefields"
25	September	Franklin J. Meine, "Frontier Humor in Early Illinois"
26	October	Jay Monaghan, "Alaskan Slavery and the Civil War"
27	November	Robert S. Henry, "Nathan Bedford Forrest"
28	December	Louis A. Warren, "Herndon's Contribution to Lincoln Mythology"

1944

29	January	Chester L. Fordney, "The United States Marine Corps in the Civil War"
30	February	Informal Discussion: *Lincoln the Lover* articles in the *Atlantic Monthly* and *The Diary of a Public Man*. Participants: Seymour J. Frank, Elmer Gertz, John M. Hamer, Ralph G. Newman, and Carl Sandburg
31	March	William E. Beringer, "How to be Rich Though a Historian, or Cosmic Forces in AmericanHistory, or Lincoln and Other Presidential Candidates"
32	April	Herbert E. Kahler, "Civil War Battlefields—Their Preservation and Treatment"
33	May	James G. Randall, "Generals, Secretaries, and Some Senators"
34	June	M. L. Houser, "Lincoln, Stanton and the Maryland Triumvirate"
35	September	Elmer Gertz, "Some Aspects of Civil War Journalism"
36	October	A Gala Dinner celebrating the publication of important books by Round Table members: Walter H. Hebert, *Fighting Joe Hooker* and Robert S. Henry, *"First with the Most" Forrest*. Otto Eisenschiml, Chairman; Avery Craven, Walter H. Hebert, Stanley F. Horn, Robert S. Henry
37	December	Lester O. Schriver, "Was Lincoln a Seer, Saint, or Mere Politician?"

1945

38	January	Marshall Winfield, "Robert E. Lee"
39	February	Lloyd D. Miller, "The Battle of Franklin"
40	March	Symposium: "Jefferson Davis." Otto Eisenschiml, Monroe F. Cockrell, Seymour J. Frank, Carl B. Davis, and Elmer Gertz
41	April	Robert L. Huttner, "The Slavery Epoch and Slave Trade in American History"
42	May	John M. Hamer, "Abraham Lincoln, Hoosier"
43	June	Otto Eisenschiml, "The Story of Shiloh"
44	September	U. S. Lesh, "A Knight of the Golden Circle"
45	October	Robert L. Kincaid, "Kentucky in the Civil War"
46	November	Preview of American battle scenes and Civil War books donated by the Commandery of the State of Illinois, Military Order of the Loyal Legion of the United States to the Chicago Historical Society
47	November	Seymour J. Frank, "A Civil War Illusion—Northern Prosperity"
48	December	Wesley Carty, "That Traitor—Breckenridge"

1946

49	January	Avery O. Craven, "The Many-Caused Civil War"
50	March	Parker C. Webb, "Chickamauga—A Study in Original Sources"
51	March	Herbert A. Kellar, "Repercussions of the Civil War upon Rockbridge County, Virginia"
52	April	Newton C. Farr, "Reconstruction After the Civil War"
53	May	John P. Long, "Spy and Counter-Spy in the American Civil War"
54	June	Robert B. Browne, "Escape of John Hunt Morgan from the Columbus Penitentiary"
55	September	Otto Eisenschiml and E. B. Long, "What Kind of Man was Edwin M. Stanton?"
56	November	Presentation of David H. Annan Library of the Civil War to the Chicago Historical Society and Gettysburg Address Memorial: Wright Howes, Paul M. Angle, and William Herzog
57	December	G. T. DesJardins, "Fabius Maximus Comes to Georgia—The Atlanta Campaign of Joseph E. Johnston"

1947

58	January	Joseph L. Eisendrath, Jr., "Lincolniana in the Official Records"
59	February	Reinhard H. Luthin, "Fields for Research in Lincolniana"
60	March	Harry G. Hershenson, "Military Government"
61	April	Stanley F. Horn, "The Cruise of the Confederate Cruiser *Shenandoah*"
62	May	Charles S. Schwartz, "The Development and Use of Weapons in the Civil War"
63	June	Donald W. Riddle, "Lincoln Runs for Congress"
64	July	Opening of the Lincoln Papers in the Library of Congress, Washington, D.C. Special meeting at the home of Walter Trohan
65	September	Benjamin P. Thomas, "Portrait for Posterity—Lincoln and His Biographers"
66	October	Robert L. Huttner, "Some British Observers of the American Civil War"
67	November	Roy P. Basler, "The Job of Editing Lincoln's Writings"
68	December	Frank E. Vandiver, "Josiah Gorgas"

1948

69	January	"The Battle of Gettysburg": a discussion of the Columbia Broadcasting System radio program, *CBS is There*, October 21, 1947, recorded for the Civil War Round Table
70	February	Frank J. Welcher, "The Atlanta Campaign"
71	March	Andrew Nelson Lytle, "The Failure of Southern Leadership; The Quality of the Southern Failure"
72	April	Don Russell, "Lincoln Raises an Army: The (Dis)organization of the Union Army"
73	May	Don Armstrong, "The Applicability of Lessons of the Civil War to the Atomic Age"
74	June	Guests of Dr. Charles W. Olsen at the South Shore Country Club. Informal discussion on "John Brown." Participants: Donald W. Riddle, Robert L. Hunter, Elmer Gertz, and others

75	September	Otto Eisenschiml and E. B. Long, "The Ifs of the Civil War"
76	October	David C. Mearns, "The Robert T. Lincoln Papers"
77	November	Robert B. Browne, "The Confederate Cavalry"
78	December	Bell Irvin Wiley, "On the Trail of Billy Yank"

1949

79	January	Marshall Wingfield, "'Old Straight'—Lieutenant General Alexander P. Stewart, C.S.A."
80	February	Charles S. McCombs, "The Recapture of Galveston by the Confederates: An Amphibious Operation"
81	March	John N. Ware, "Streight's Raid"
82	April	R. Gerald McMurtry, "John L. Worden, the Commander of the *Monitor*, and his Contacts with Abraham Lincoln"
83	May	John G. Graef, "Gettysburg and General George Gordon Meade"
84	June	Donald W. Riddle and Robert L. Huttner, "John Brown: A Panel Discussion of a Controversial Figure"
85	August	Visit to the Railroad Fair of 1949 and to its pageant, *Wheels-A-Rolling*. Robert S. Henry, "The Railroads of the Confederacy"
86	September	Monroe F. Cockrell, "The Siege of Vicksburg by Land and Water"
87	October	Stanley F. Horn, "Biography by Anecdote: *The Robert E. Lee Reader*"
88	November	Frank Klement, "Middle West Copperheadism in the Civil War"
89	December	Otto Eisenschiml, "How Should History Be Written"

1950

90	January	Richard Barksdale Harwell, "Confederate Carrousel: Southern Songs of the Sixties"
91	February	Louis A. Warren, "The Lincoln Political Puzzle of 1864"
92	March	George S. Dalgety, "The Presidents and the Civil War"
93	April	Allan Nevins, "Could the Civil War Have Been Avoided, and If So, How?"
94	May	Clarence E. McCartney, "Grant and His Captains"
95	September	Benjamin P. Thomas, "Freedom's Firebrand—Theodore Weld"
96	October	Colonel Robert R. McCormick, "The Fight for the Border States"
97	November	Harrison Platt, "Editing the Civil War"
98	December	William B. Hesseltine, "Davis vs. Lee: Post-War Careers of the Confederate Leaders"

1951

99	January	Harry E. Pratt, "Peace in 'Our One Common Country'—The Hampton Roads Conference"
100	February	Robert S. Henry, "Rehearsal in Mexico: Trial by Battle of Civil War Leaders"
101	March	Lloyd D. Miller, "The Spring Hill Affair"
102	April	Boyd B. Stutler, "John Brown and Abraham Lincoln"
103	May	Robert L. Kincaid, "General Oliver Otis Howard, Soldier in Peace and War"
104	June 1-3	Informal meeting in the Lincoln Room, Lincoln Memorial University. Speaker: William H. Townsend. Comments: Allan Nevins

105	September	Seymour J. Frank, "We'll Hang Jeff Davis From a Sour Apple Tree"
106	October	Holman Hamilton, "Old Rough and Ready and the Civil War"
107	November	Jim Dan Hill, "The Red River Campaign"
108	December	Ralph Korngold, "The Nature of Secession"

1952

109	January	Elmer Gertz, "Charles A. Dana: The Eyes of the Government at the Front"
110	February	Raymond Dooley, "Abraham Lincoln, Logan County, Lincoln, Illinois"
111	March	Herbert O. Brayer, "The Fall of Fort Fillmore"
112	April	E. B. (Pete) Long, "Ulysses S. Grant—The Man Behind the Memoirs"
113	May	Lloyd D. Miller, "The Union Left Flank, July 2, 1863"
114	June	Otto Eisenschiml, "Gettysburg: The Most Inexcusable Battle" (Part of the Second Annual Battlefield Tour)
115	September	W. Norman Fitzgerald, Jr., "The Mobile Campaign"
116	October	William H. Townsend, "Cassius Marcellus Clay: The Lion of Whitehall"
117	November	Benjamin P. Thomas, "The President Reads His Mail"
118	December	Colton Storm, "The William Tecumseh Sherman Maps"

1953

119	January	Harry G. Hershenson, "Thaddeus Stevens: Thorn in Lincoln's Side"
120	February	Donald W. Riddle, "Congressman Lincoln"
121	March	O. H. Felton, "Harpers Ferry"
122	April	Bruce Catton, "Sheridan and Warren in the Battle of Five Forks"
123	May	V. C. (Pat) Jones, "What Mosby Added to the Civil War" (Part of the Third Annuual Battlefield Tour)
124	June	Bernard A. Weisberger, "Reporters for the Union"
125	September	George Edgar Turner, "Victory Rode the Rails"
126	October	Robert L. Kincaid, "Joshua Fry Speed, Lincoln's Confederate Agent in Kentucky"
127	November	W. T. Duganne, "Mallory's Men"
128	December	Joseph P. Renald, "Another Look at Wirz"

1954

129	January	Robert B. Browne, "Brice's Crossroads: A Study in Military Leadership"
130	February	A symposium, "Has the Lincoln Theme Been Exhausted—A Reappraisal." Ralph G. Newman, Moderator. Participants: Joseph L. Eisendrath, Jr., Seymour J. Frank, Elmer Gertz, Ralph Korngold, William Herzog, and E. B. (Pete) Long
131	March	T. Harry Williams, "The Pattern of an Historian"
132	April	James D. Horan, "Confederate Agent"
133	May	Willard L. King, "Around the Circuit with Davis and Lincoln"
134	September	Robert S. Holzman, "Stormy Ben Butler"
135	October	Hartnett T. Kane, "Spies of the Blue and Gray;" Louis M. Starr, "The Civil War's Newsmen in Action"
136	November	Harold M. Hyman, "The Loyalty Oath in the Civil War"

137	December	Monroe F. Cockrell, O. H. Felton, Lloyd D. Miller, M. Kenneth McIntyre, "Stonewall Jackson in 1862"

1955

138	January	Daniel O'Flaherty, "Undefeated Rebel, General Jo Shelby"
139	February	Bruce Catton, "Lincoln the Amateur Soldier"
140	March	Clyde C. Walton, Jr., "The Civil War and the Indians"
141	April	R. Gerald McMurtry, "Zollicoffer and the Battle of Mill Springs"
142	May	T. Harry Williams, "Beauregard the Man"
143	June	Otto Eisenschiml, "An Unorthodox View of the Civil War" Celebration of the 75th Birthday of Dr. Eisenschiml
144	September	Don Russell, "Buffalo Bill in the Civil War"
145	October	Benjamin P. Thomas, "A Candid View of Grant"
146	November	Robert B. Browne and Don Russell, "George Armstrong Custer"

1956

147	January	Kenneth P. Williams, "Buell's March on Chattanooga"
148	February	Charles H. Coleman, "Thomas Lincoln: Father of the President"
149	March	Avery O. Craven, "The Civil War; One HundredYears After"
150	April	William B. Hesseltine, "The Prison at Andersonville"
151	May	Colonel Allen P. Julian, "The Atlanta Campaign"
152	June	Guilbert L. Piper, "Civil War Fire Arms andAmmunition"
153	September	Gilbert E. Govan, "Confederate Miscellany"
154	October	Colonel Allen P. Julian, "Savannah Campaign"
155	November	D. C. (Pat) Jones, "Guerrilla Warfare in the Eastern Theatre"
156	December	Bish Thompson, "How to Enjoy a War"

1957

157	January	J. Ambler Johnston, "Lee and Freeman"
158	February	E. B. (Pete) Long, "Lincoln and Ft. Sumter"
159	March	Robert B. Browne, "Some Minor Actors in the Great Drama"
160	April	Special Meeting at Lincoln National Life Foundation, Ft. Wayne, Indiana. Bruce Catton,"Lincoln as Commander-in-Chief"
161	May	Speech as part of Shenandoah Valley Battlefield Tour
162	May	Speech as part of Shenandoah Valley Battlefield Tour
163	June	Richard B. Harwell, "Modern Aspects of Confederate Literature"
164	September	Governor William G. Stratton, "U.S. Grant"
165	November	Harnett T. Kane, "The Gallant Mrs. Stonewall"
166	December	Elmer Gertz, "General James Harrison Wilson"

1958

167	January	Frederick Tilberg, "Command Decisions at Gettysburg, July 2 and 3, 1863"
168	February	R. Gerald McMurtry, "Lincoln's Address at Gettsyburg"
169	March	Ray A. Billington, "Frontier Origins of the Civil War"
170	April	Bell I. Wiley, "The Confederate Congress"
171	May	Otto Eisenschiml, "Why the Civil War?"
172	June	Edward E. Barthell, Jr., "Some Civil War Apochrypha"
173	September	Colonel J. Gay Seabourne, "The Great Cavalry Battle at Brandy

		Station"
174	October	Joint Meeting of Civil War Round Tables and the Illinois State Historical Society at the Lincoln- Douglas Debate Centennial, Galesburg, Illinois
175	November	Avery O. Craven, "Did Lincoln's Election Justify Secession?"
176	December	Avird Fairbanks, "Lincoln Sculptures"

1959

177	January	Hubert H. Hawkins, "John Hunt Morgan and His Raid Across the Ohio"
178	February	William B. Hesseltine, "Lincoln's Plan of Reconstruction"
179	March	Edwin C. Bearss, "Crisis in Movement: The Battle of Champion Hill"
180	April	Clyde C. Walton, "Recent Writings on the Civil War"
181	May	Major General U.S. Grant 3rd, U.S.A. (Retired) and Karl S. Betts, "A Centennial for All Americans"
182	June	Oliver J. Keller, "Major General John F. Reynolds"
183	September	Allan Nevins, "The Darkest Hour of the War in the Northwest"
184	October	Ladies' Day. Civil War Tour of Chicago
185	November	Stephen Ambrose, "Old Brains: The Civil War Career of Henry Wager Halleck"
186	December	Norman A. Graebner, "Lincoln and the National Interest"

1960

187	January	Alan T. Nolan, "Brawner Farm—The Baptism of the Iron Brigade"
188	February	Robert Lee Kincaid, "Memorable Moments Along the Lincoln Trail"
189	March	James I. Robertson, Jr., "Jackson's Stone Wall—The Stonewall Brigade"
190	April	Symposium on Battlefields of Virginia to be Visited on the Tenth Annual Battlefield Tour. Ralph G. Newman, Moderator. Panelists: Otto Eisenschiml, E. B. (Pete) Long, and John Patrick Hunter
191	May	T. Harry Williams, "The Generalship of North and South"
192	June	Ladies Night. Paul M. Angle, "The Civil War Collections of the Chicago Historical Society"
193	September	Colonel Allen P. Julian, U.S.A. , "Glory, or Good Management"
194	October	Robert J. Womack, "The Civil War in Tennessee"
195	November	Percival G. Hart, "The Campaign of Chancellorsville"
196	December	Ladies Night. Charles L. Dufour, "The Night the War Was Lost"

1961

197	January	Joseph P. Cullen, "The Peninsular Campaign of 1862"
198	February	Glenn H. Seymour, "Stephen A. Douglas"
199	March	Richard N. Current, "The Continuing Civil War, 1865-1877"
200	April	Frank E. Vandiver, "The Confederacy and the New South"
201	May	Robert D. Meade, "Judah P. Benjamin, Confederate Statesman"
202	June	Ladies Night. Panel Discussion: "If the South Had Won the Civil War." Leaders: Clyde C. Walton, Ralph G. Newman
203	September	Otto Eisenschiml, "Ethics and the Civil War Historian"
204	October	Harold M. Hyman, "Lincoln's Mars: The Lincoln-Stanton Relationship"

| 205 | November | Ladies Night. "Civil War Songs" at JAZZ, Limited |
| 206 | December | Panel Discussion: "Civil War Medicine -Surgery" Chairman: A. V. Berquist. Panelists: Harry Hertz, Harry Haver, Otto Eisenschiml |

1962

207	January	Grady McWhiney, "Braxton Bragg: Misplaced General"
208	February	Landry Genosky, "Some New Lights on the Lincoln-Pickett Relationship"
209	March	William M. Landers, "Rediscovering a Lost Hero—General Rosencrans"
210	April	Richard Dyer Mudd, "The Assassination of Abraham Lincoln and the Trial and Imprisonment of Dr. Samuel A. Mudd"
211	May	Everett Lewy, "The Battle of Chickamauga"
212	June	Donald L. Smith, "The Twenty-Fourth Michigan, a Regiment of the Iron Brigade"
213	September	Ladies Night. Bell I. Wiley, "Kingdom Coming," Commemoration of the Emancipation Proclamation's Centennial
214	October	James I. Robertson, Jr., "Billy Yanks from Iowa: An Example of Midwestern Gallantry"
215	November	"Songs of the Civil War," at JAZZ, Limited
216	December	Panel Discussion: "Legal Aspects of the Civil War." Arnold Alexander, Moderator. Panelists: Reuben Flacks, Phillip B. Kurland, John V. McCormick

1963

217	January	Edward F. Coffman, "The Civil War Career of Captain Thomas H. Hines"
218	February	David C. Mearns, "The Gettysburg Address: The Mysteries of the Manuscripts"
219	March	Colonel Allen P. Julian, "Battle Creek Gap: The Historians and the Principles of War"
220	April	Robert W. Waitt, Jr., "Sin and the Civil War, or the Kinsey Report of the War"
221	May	James V. Murphin, "Antietam: The Enigma and the Significance"
222	June	Charles V. Dufour, "Henry Holtze: Rebel Propagandist"
223	September	Bruce Catton, "Politics and the Army of the Potomac"
224	October	Gilbert E. Govan, "The President and the General"
225	November	Shelby Foote, "Grant's Seven Failures Above Vicksburg"
226	December	Ladies Night. Songs and Music by Win Stracke, Ginni Clemens, Ray Tate; Monologues by Beverly Younger

1964

227	January	Edward F. Coffman, "The Civil War Career of Captain Thomas H. Hines"
228	February	State Senator Paul Simon, "Lincoln the Legislator"
229	March	Clyde C. Walton, "Battles by the Book: Training of the Civil War Soldier"
230	April	T. Harry Williams, "The Civil War in Louisiana"

231	May	Harold M. Hyman, "Lincoln's Wartime Education"
232	June	Grady McWhiney, "Confederate Defeat"
233	September	Leroy H. Fischer, "Another View of Adam Gurowski"
234	October	John Hope Franklin, "The Military Occupation of the South, 1865-1866"
235	November	Lloyd D. Miller, "The Battle of Franklin"
236	December	Stanley F. Horn, "The Battle of Nashville"

1965

237	January	Edwin C. Bearss, "The Ironclad Gunboat *Cairo*"
238	February	Ladies Night. Autographing Party with Alice Hamilton Cromie, author of *A Tour Guide to the Civil War*, at the Abraham Lincoln Book Shop, 3:30 p.m.; Film, *Red Badge of Courage* at the Chicago Historical Society, 9:00 p.m.
239	March	Major General Jim Dan Hill (Retired), "Command Structure in the Union and Confederate Navies"
240	April	Victor Searcher, "Lincoln's Last Journey." DePaul University Reception for members in appreciation of the gift to the University Library of the Otto Eisenschiml Collection
241	May	Glenn Tucker, "Chickamauga"
242	June	T. Harry Williams, "The Valley Campaign of 1864"
243	September	Clement M. Silvestro, "None But Patriots; The Union Leagues in the Civil War"
244	October	Kevin McCann, "James Shields: General and Senator from Illinois"
245	November	Colonel Wilbur S. Nye, "Milroy is Gobbled Up"
246	December	Ladies Night. General Mark W. Clark, "America's Wars." 25th Anniversary of the Civil War Round Table

1966

247	January	D. Alexander Brown, "Grierson's Raid"
248	February	J. Ambler Johnston, "Grant and Lee—Clairvoyants"
249	March	E. B. (Pete) Long, "A Reappraisal of the Mississippi Valley Campaigns"
250	April	Sir Denis Brogan, "The War as a War"
251	May	Robert W. Johannsen, "Stephen A. Douglas and the South"
252	June	Frank E. Vandiver, "Toward the Second Centennial"
253	September	S. I. Neiman, "Judah P. Benjamin"
254	October	Ralph G. Newman, "Benjamin Franklin Butler: Politician, 1/c; Hero, j.g."
255	November	Colonel Allen P. Julian, "Gallant John Hood"
256	December	Frank L. Klement, "Vallandigham and the Civil War"

1967

257	January	George J. Fleming, "Political Generals"
258	February	Ladies Night. Alice Hamilton Cromie, "Serendipity and the Civil War;" also Joan Bennett in *Jane* at the Ivanhoe Theatre
259	March	Colonel Harold B. Simpson (Retired), "Jefferson Davis and the United States Camel Corps"
260	April	Fred G. Benton, Jr., "The Battle and Siege of Port Hudson"; Cocktail Party Introducing *The Papers of Ulysses S. Grant*, Volume 1, 1837-1861

261	May	Henry E. Simmons, "Northern Censorship of the Press: Necessary or Needless?"
262	June	J. Robert Smith, "General Mike Lawler"
263	September	Elmer Gertz, "The Assassinations of Presidents Lincoln and Kennedy as Seen by Jack Ruby's Lawyer"
264	October	Mark M. Krug, "Abraham Lincoln and Lyman Trumbull—Moderate Republicans"
265	November	Ladies Night. Ralph G. Newman, "Readin', Writin' and Round Tables;" Puppet Show: Excerpts from *The Sound of Music* and *Paint Your Wagon*
266	December	Philip R. Davis, "Justice in the Confederacy"

1968

267	January	Glenn H. Seymour, "Illinois in the 1850s"
268	February	Lloyd Ostendorf, "The Faces of Lincoln"
269	March	Shelby Foote, "Grant Comes to Washington"
270	April	Rodney C. Loehr, "Civil War Blitzkrieg: Cavalry Operations of J. H. Wilson Around Selma
271	May	LeRoy H. Fischer, "The Civil War in Today's Perspective"
272	June	T. Harry Williams, "A Yank at Oxford, or Teaching the Civil War to the English"
273	September	Lloyd D. Miller, "The Union Left—The Second Day at Gettysburg"
274	October	Virgil Carrington Jones, "How Not to Start a War—Union Naval Errors"
275	November	Francis F. Wilshin, "The Recapture of a Battlefield: First Bull Run in Light of Newly Discovered Evidence"
276	December	Francis A. Lord, "Weapons and Their Effect on Tactics"

1969

277	January	Don Russell, "Custer's First Charge—Custer in the Civil War"
278	February	Ladies Night. Grand Review Ball. E. J. Kupjack, "History in Miniature"
279	March	Brooks Davis, "The Battle of Perryville"
280	April	Warren W. Hassler, Jr., "A New Look at McClellan"
281	May	William K. Alderfer, "Illinois' Wartime Capitol"
282	June	Charles L. (Pie) Dufour, "The Blue and the Gray in Mexico"
283	September	John T. Hubbell, "James Birdseye McPherson"
284	October	Bell I. Wiley, "Mary Boykin Chestnut's Diary from Dixie"
285	November	E. B. (Pete) Long, "The Lost Six Months of Armies in Virginia"
286	December	Okon E. Uya, "Robert Smalls of South Carolina"

1970

287	January	Archer Jones, "Military Leadership, North and South"
288	February	Gala Ladies Night with Philip D. Jordan, Preston Bradley, and Bruce Catton. Preston Bradley, "If Lincoln Were Here"
289	March	Thomas L. Connelly, "Lee and the War in the West"
290	April	John Y. Simon, "Grant at Belmont—Victory or Blunder?"
291	May	Jerry Warshaw, "Civil War Film Night"

292	June	A. P. (Al) Andrews, "Major General Earl Van Dorn—Saint or Sinner?"
293	September	Albert Castel, "Lee and His Critics: The Western School"
294	October	Edwin C. Bearss, "Grant's Assaults on Vicksburg, May 19-22, 1863"
295	November	Joseph A. Daley, "The Battle at Pilgrim's Point—A Combat Won Against Publishers"
296	December	John Patrick Hunter, "Haskell of Gettysburg: The Iron Brigade's Finest"

1971

297	January	Hobart C. Cawood, "The Battle of Cold Harbor"
298	February	Harry H. Anderson, "The Sioux Campaign During the Civil War Years"
299	March	Frank G. Rankin, "Morgan's Raid"
300	April	Ladies' Night. Colonel Allen P. Julian, "Margaret Mitchell and *Gone With The Wind;*" Ralph G. Newman, "The Civil War Round Table—We Point With Pride"
301	May	Harry M. Caudill, "The Guerrilla War in Kentucky"
302	June	Joseph L. Eisendrath, "The Lincoln Myths"
303	September	Grady McWhiney, "Jefferson Davis and His Generals"
304	October	Jerry L. Schober, "Mary Ann Pitman, Rebel Soldier, United States Citizen and Patriot;" Special Ladies' Night Meeting, World Premiere of the play, *Assassination, 1865,* by Stuart Vaughan at the Goodman Theatre, Chicago, Friday, October 20, 8:00 p.m.
305	November	Charles Wesselhoeft, "Civil War Railroads"
306	December	E. B. (Pete) Long, "War Beyond the River: The Trans-Mississippi and the Influence of the War on the West"

1972

307	January	James I. Robertson, Jr., "The Stonewall Brigade"
308	February	Jay Luvaas, "Civil War Tactics: The Dream and the Reality"
309	March	Alan T. Nolan, "The Iron Brigade—And the Reasons Why"
310	April	T. Harry Williams, "Grant as President." Joint meeting with the Ulysses S. Grant Association, the Illinois Special Events Commission, and the Friends of the Chicago Public Library commemorating the 150th birthday of Grant (1822-1985)
311	May	Damon Wells, Jr., "Stephen A. Douglas and the South." Autograph and Cocktail Party to meet Wells, author of *Stephen A. Douglas: The Last Years, 1857-1861*
312	June	Robert H. Fowler, "New Discoveries About the Civil War"
313	September	Lowell H. Harrison, "General John C. Breckenridge, C.S.A."
314	October	Dan J. Lapinski, "The Battle of Island No. 10"
315	November	Dick Peterson, "Our Terrible Tragedy: The Great American Civil War"
316	December	Richard M. McMurry, "John Bell Hood"

1973

317	January	Victor Hicken, "The Civil War Fighting Man: Comparisons with the Past and Present"
318	February	Philip L. Schutt, "General John Alexander McClernand"

319	March	Ladies Night. Bell I. Wiley, "Women of the Lost Cause"
320	April	Dana M. Wegner, "Commodore William D. `Dirty Bill' Porter"
321	May	Edward C. Johnson, "Embalming Surgeons of the Civil War"
322	June	George B. Hartzog, Jr., "An Endangered Species: Our Civil War National Parks"
323	September	Frank E. Vandiver, "Jefferson Davis"
324	October	Gerhard P. Clausius, "Lincoln's Friend Steve Hurlbut, Hero of Hatchie River"
325	November	Frank L. Klement, "The Copperhead Movement"
326	December	Philip J. Hohlweck, "Berdan's Sharpshooters"

1974

327	January	Stephen Z. Starr, "Border Ruffians, Jaywalkers, and Guerrillas: The Kansas-Missouri Border,1864-1865"
328	February	Ladies Night. Featuring Dick Blake's, A Look at Lincoln and the Schimmelfennig Singers
329	March	Marshall D. Krolick, "Lee and Longstreet at Gettysburg"
330	April	Robert Womack, "The Battle of Stone's River"
331	May	Albert P. Scheller, "The Red River Campaign"
332	June	Ladies Night. Nevins-Freeman Award Dinner honoring Bruce Catton. Tributes by E.B. (Pete) Long, Ralph Newman, and Samuel S. Vaughn
333	September	Edwin C. Bearss, "Fort Donelson"
334	October	Harold M. Hyman, "The Andrew Johnson Impeachment: From Appomattox Through Watergate"
335	November	Wilbur Kurtz, Jr., "Lincoln, Sherman, and Lloyd Lewis"
336	December	Shelby Foote, "Writing Civil War History"

1975

337	January	William C. (Jack) Davis, "The Battle of New Market"
338	February	Gordon Whitney, "The Battle of Nashville"
339	March	Frank G. Rankin, "The Orphan Brigade"
340	April	Harold B. Simpson, "Hood's Texas Brigade: Lee's Grenadier Guard"
341	May	Ralph G. Newman, "Abraham Lincoln's Incredible Funeral"
342	June	Nevins-Freeman Award Dinner honoring Ralph G. Newman. Tributes by John Hope Franklin, John Y. Simon, and Carl Haverlin
343	September	Wiley Sword, "Shiloh: Myth Versus Historical Record"
344	October	Alfred C. Raphelson, "General Alexander Schimmelfennig"
345	November	George M. Frederickson, "Lincoln on Racial Equality"
346	December	Harry W. Pfanz, "The First Day at Gettysburg"

1976

347	January	William J. Sullivan, "The Civil War on the Plains"
348	February	James T. Hickey, "Lincolniana in Illinois"
349	March	Roger G. Holloway, "Great Britain and the American Civil War"
350	April	Symposium: "Where Goes the Civil War?"
351	May	Albert P. Scheller, "Illinois Officers and Units in Mississippi"
352	June	Nevins-Freeman Award Dinner honoring T. Harry Williams, "Why I Am Fascinated with the Civil War, or The Confessions of an Addict"

353	September	Joseph P. Cullen, "The Battle of Cold Harbor"
354	October	William W. Hassler, "The Haunting Mystery of A.P. Hill"
355	November	Brooks Davis, "The Mississippi Marine Brigade"
356	December	Robert Orr Baker, "The Battle of Brice's Crossroads"

1977

357	January	James I. Robertson, Jr., "Lee and Jackson: The Confederacy's Premier Team"
358	February	Mark E. Neely, Jr., "'To Distinguish Myself'—Lincoln and the Mexican War"
359	March	William E. Parrish, "The Bohemian Brigade: The Eastern Press Covers the War in Missouri in 1861"
360	April	Elden E. Billings, "Sherman: A Critical Character Sketch"
361	May	Richard J. Sommers, "Siege of Petersburg"
362	June	Nevins-Freeman Award Dinner honoring Lloyd D. Miller. Film Review of Past Battlefield Tours Narrated by the Honoree
363	September	Lowell Reidenbaugh, "Stonewall Jackson's Valley Campaign"
364	October	John Patrick Hunter, "The Capture and Captivity of Jefferson Davis"
365	November	E. B. (Pete) Long, "A Broader Approach to Civil War History"
366	December	Lewis H. Croce, "Lincoln and the Federal Bureaucracy"

1978

367	January	Sherman Lavigna, "Benjamin Franklin Butler: Beast or Benefactor?"
368	February	Thomas Buckley, "The Civil War and the Modernization of the Navy"
369	March	James I. (Bud) Robertson, "Civil War Chaplains"
370	April	Marshall D. Krolick, "The Battle of Brandy Station"
371	May	Kenneth Carley, "The Sioux Uprising of 1862"
372	June	Nevins-Freeman Award Dinner honoring Bell I. Wiley. "Reminiscenses of the Civil War Historian"
373	September	Merlin E. Sumner, "The 67th Ohio Volunteer Infantry Regiment"
374	October	Harold M. Hyman, "Has the Lincoln Murder Conspiracy Theme Been Exhausted?"
375	November	Gordon Whitney, "General Jefferson C. Davis"
376	December	Brooks Davis, "The Perryville Campaign"

1979

377	January	Grady McWhiney, "Confederate Generals—Their Strengths and Weaknesses"
378	February	Mark E. Neely, Jr., "Lincoln's Image: Photos, Prints, and Cartoons of the 1860s"
379	March	Herman Hattaway, "Stephen D. Lee"
380	April	William Frassanito, "Antietam: The Photographic Legacy of America's Bloodiest Day"
381	May	Chris Calkins, "The Appomattox Campaign"
382	June	Nevins-Freeman Award Dinner honoring E. B. (Pete) Long. Tributes by Ralph G. Newman, John Y. Simon, and Barbara Long
383	September	William Mallory, "Actions North of the James River, September 29 and 30, 1864"

384	October	Robert Krick, "E. P. Alexander, Peerless and Insightful Cannoneer"
385	November	Daniel P. Jordan, "Richmond, First City of the Confederacy"
386	December	Henry Pomerantz, "Aldie, Middleburg, and Upperville"

1980

387	January	John Y. Simon, "Grant as Historian: The Memoirs Revisited"
388	February	James Lee McDonough, "The Final Day at Stones River"
389	March	John G. Barrett, "From Glory to Disrepute: Sherman in the Carolinas"
390	April	Ralph G. Newman, "The Lights Go On Again At Ford's Theatre"
391	May	Walter L. Brown, "Albert Pike's Confederate Service"
392	June	Nevins-Freeman Award Dinner honoring Edwin C. Bearss. "My Interest in the Civil War"
393	September	C. Craig Caba, "On U.S. Military Uniforms Used Early in the War"
394	October	John Schildt, "Roads to Gettysburg"
395	November	Gordon E. Dammann, "Civil War Medical Instruments and Equipment Illustrated"
396	December	Robert G. Hartje, "General Van Dorn"

1981

397	January	Howard C. Westwood, "The Joint Committee on the Conduct of the War"
398	February	Gerhard P. Clausius, "The Drama of Mary Todd Lincoln"
399	March	Marshall D. Krolick, "Stuart's Cavalry in the Gettysburg Campaign"
400	April	Ralph G. Newman, "Round Table History;" Memorable Moments Recounted by Past Presidents; "Songs of the Sixties" by the Schimmelfennig Singers
401	May	Archie P. McDonald, "Jed Hotchkiss, Jackson's Topographer"
402	June	Nevins-Freeman Award Dinner honoring James I. (Bud) Robertson, Jr., "Anecdotes Regarding My Interest in the Civil War"
403	September	Albert Castel, "The Not-So-Fine Art of Lying: Some Civil War Generals and Their Reports"
404	October	Kenneth Hafendorfer, "The Battle of Perryville"
405	November	Lowell Reidenbaugh, "Jackson at White Oak Swamp"
406	December	Edward Longacre, "Cavalry Raids: A Critical Comparison"

1982

407	January	William C. Davis, "The Siege of Charleston, 1861-1865"
408	February	David Lilley, "Ezra Ayers Carman—The Unheralded Historian of Antietam"
409	March	Gordon Whitney, "The Mystery of Spring Hill"
410	April	Pat Newman, "Julia Dent Grant"
411	May	Zenos Hawkinson, "Mr. Lincoln's War and the Immigrant Imagination"
412	June	Nevins-Freeman Award Dinner honoring Frank E. Vandiver, "Personal Portraits of Allan Nevins and Douglas Southall Freeman"
413	September	Ralph G. Tanner, "The Shenandoah Valley Campaign of 1862"
414	October	Richard W. Hatcher, "The Wilson's Creek Campaign"
415	November	Stephen Oates, "John Brown: Catalyst for the Civil War"

416	December	Perry D. Jamieson, "Artillery Tactics of the Civil War Era"

1983

417	January	Dennis Frye, "The Cows' Tails Mystery: The Siege and Capture of Harpers Ferry"
418	February	C. Robert Douglas, "General George H. Thomas: Time and History Will Do Me Justice"
419	March	John E. Divine, "Cavalry Campaigns: A Prelude to Gettysburg"
420	April	Robert W. Johannsen, "Stephen A. Douglas and the Spirit of the Age"
421	May	Kathe Georg, "Actions at the Rose Farm on the Second Day at Gettysburg"
422	June	First Annual Nevins-Freeman Assembly. Award Luncheon honoring John Hope Franklin. Wayne C. Temple, "Some Things You Never Knew About Abe Lincoln"; Alan T. Nolan, "An Evaluation of Federal Army Commanders"; Karen Osborne, "The Saga of Mother Bickerdyke." Panel Discussion: "Civil Rights and the Civil War": Moderator: Marshall D. Krolick. Participants: John Hope Franklin, Duke Frederick, Elmer Gertz, Frank L.Klement, and John Y. Simon
423	September	Walter H. Herbert, "Fighting Joe Hooker"
424	October	Robert K. Krick, "The Battle of Cedar Mountain"
425	November	William M. Anderson, "Colonel Lawler and the Lawless 18th Illinois"
426	December	Karen Osborne, "Women in the Civil War"

1984

427	January	Myron (Mike) Cohen, "The Signal Corps and the Military Telegraph in the Civil War"
428	February	Recreation of the Senate Confrontation, November-December, 1860; Ralph G. Newman, president pro tempore of the Senate. Participants: Marshall Krolick, James Vlazny, William J. Sullivan, Gordon Whitney
429	March	Colonel Roy K. Flint, "Eight Minutes to Live: Defeat of the Federal Assault at Cold Harbor, 3 June 1864"
430	April	Richard M. McMurry, "John Bell Hood"
431	May	Walter N. Trennery, "John Pope: His Political Problems and His Pratfall at Second Bull Run"
432	June	Dan Jordan, "A Ride With the Gray Ghost: The Life and Adventurous Times of Colonel John S. Mosby, C.S.A."
433	September	Second Annual Nevins-Freeman Assembly. Award presentation to Richard B. Harwell. Symposium: "20th Century Correspondents Cover the Civil War"; Panel Discussion: "Why Do Civil War Round Tables Exist?" Moderator: Ralph G. Newman. Panelists: Bill Thomas, Merlin Sumner, Charles Shields, Philip Holhweck, John Hunter, and James Vlazny
434	October	Jim and Alice Truelock, "Joshua L. Chamberlain"
435	November	Merlin Sumner, "Grant's Staff: A Plus or a Minus?"
436	December	David D. Finney, "The Death of Stonewall Jackson"

1985

437	January	Brooks Davis, "The Grand Army of the Republic"

438	February	Herman Hattaway, "How the North Won"
439	March	Gary W. Gallagher, "Stephen Dodson Ramseur: Lee's Gallant General"
440	April	William J. Sullivan, "The Trans-Mississippi in 1864: A Game of Pitch and Toss"
441	May	Jeffry D. Wert, "'Old Jube' and 'Little Phil': Generalship in the Shenandoah Valley Campaign"
442	June	Paul J. Beaver, "Lincoln's Political Rise in Central Illinois"
443	September	Nevins-Freeman Award Dinner honoring John Y. Simon, "Editing the Papers of U. S. Grant"
444	October	Kent Brown, "Alonzo Cushing and His Battery at Gettysburg"
445	November	Donald C. Pfanz, "Negligence on the Right: The 11th Corps at Chancellorsville"
446	December	Christopher M. Calkins, "The Ragged and Starved Confederates: An Examination of the Condition of Lee's Army, 1864-65"

1986

447	January	Wayne Anderson, Marshall Krolick, William J. Sullivan, Karl Sundstrom, and James Vlazny, "Our Ethnic Ancestors in the Civil War"
448	February	Mark E. Neely, Jr., "Lincoln and Douglas: A Relationship to Consider"
449	March	Third Annual Assembly, "Lieutenant General U.S. Grant—the Civil War Years." Participants: John Y. Simon, Tom Arliskas, Wiley Sword, Marshall Krolick, Ed Bearss, Gordon Whitney, Robert Krick, and Richard Sommers.
450	April	Edgar Archer, "An Important Medical Aspect of the Civil War—Orthopedic Surgery"
451	May	Gordon Whitney, "The President Will Now Make a Few Remarks"
452	June	James I. Robertson, Jr., "General A.P. Hill: Symbol of the Confederacy"
453	September	Nevins-Freeman Award Dinner honoring Harold M. Hyman, "Lincoln and Other Yuppie Lawyers"
454	October	Richard F. Selcer, "Two Gentlemen From Virginia: The Lee and Pickett Connection"
455	November	A. Wilson Green, "The Bloody Angle of Spotsylvania: May 12, 1864"
456	December	Alan T. Nolan, "A Historic View of Robert E. Lee"

1987

457	January	Marshall D. Krolick, "Captain to Brigadier: The Promotions of Custer, Farnsworth and Merritt"
458	February	Ralph G. Newman, "Robert Todd Lincoln in the Civil War"
459	March	Howard McManus, "The Battle of Cloyd's Mountain"
460	April	Mike Chesson, "The Richmond Bread Riot"
461	May	Betty J. Otto, "Maryland Remembers the Civil War"
462	June	Colonel Mark Boatner, "Reading, Writing, and Teaching Military History"
463	September	Nevins-Freeman Award Dinner honoring James T. Hickey, "Robert Todd Lincoln's Relationships with Authors and Artists"
464	October	William Safire, "Lincoln's Excesses: Their Effect on Modern

Presidents"
| 465 | November | James Ramage, "John Hunt Morgan: Folk Hero of the Confederacy" |
| 466 | December | Gordon E. Dammann, "In Defense of the Civil War Surgeon" |

1988
467	January	James C. Vlazny, "Robert Barnwell Rhett: Father of Secession"
468	February	William Hanchett, "Abraham Lincoln: Man in the Middle"
469	March	Harold Holzer and Mark E. Neely, Jr., "The Confederate Image: Prints of the Lost Cause"
470	April	Michael Snyder, "The Battle of Seven Pines"
471	May	Gerald F. Linderman, "The Experience of Combat in the American Civil War"
472	June	Edward G. Longacre, "The Army of the James"
473	September	Nevins-Freeman Award Dinner, honoring Robert K. Krick, "The Army of Northern Virginia in September, 1862, Its Circumstances During that Pivotal Month, Its Opportunities, and the Reasons It Should Not Have Been at Sharpsburg on September 15-18, 1862"
474	October	Lance J. Herdegen and William J. K. Beaudot, "The Charge on the Railroad Cut at Gettysburg"
475	November	Gordon Whitney, "Sherman and His Lieutenants"
476	December	Karen Osborne, "A Civil War Christmas"

1989
477	January	Bruce Bazelon, "Gettysburg—After the Fight"
478	February	James M. McPherson, "Lincoln and Liberty"
479	March	Jerry L. Russell, "The Battle of Pea Ridge"
480	April	Charles Wesselhoeft, "The Army of the Tennessee Under Grant"
481	May	Brigadier General Edwin H. Simmons, "Fort Fisher: Amphibious Finale to the Civil War"
482	June	John Y. Simon, "Edward D. Baker, Ball's Bluff, and the Politics of Command"
483	September	Nevins-Freeman Award Dinner, honoring Mark E.Neely, Jr., "Was the Civil War a Total War?"
484	October	Gary W. Gallagher, "Edward Porter Alexander: Fighting for the Confederacy"
485	November	Herbert Schiller, "The Bermuda Hundred Campaign"
486	December	Armin G. Weng, "The Gods of War and the Prince of Peace"

1990
487	January	William J. Sullivan, "Heartland of Freedom: Chicago During the Civil War"
488	February	Special Meeting at the Chicago Historical Society. Private viewing of "A House Divided: America in the Age of Lincoln"
489	March	Michael Andrus, "General Edward (Allegheny) Johnson"
490	April	Richard M. McMurry, "Confederate Journalism"
491	May	William E. Parrish, "Confederate Governors"
492	June	Jerry L. Rogers, "The Invincible Consensus: A Proposal For the Protection of Battlefield Parks and Other Resources"

Appendix B

Presidents of The Civil War Round Table

1945-46	Monroe F. Cockrell		1968-69	Jerry Warshaw
1946-47	Newton C. Farr		1969-70	Clyde Walton
1947-48	Harry Hershenson		1970-71	Dan J. Lapinski
1948-49	Lloyd D. Miller		1971-72	Marshall D. Krolick
1949-50	Alfred Whital Stern		1972-73	Charles V. Falkenberg, Jr.
1950-51	Joseph L. Eisendrath, Jr.		1973-74	Gordon Whitney
1951-52	Seymour J. Frank		1974-75	Ward C. Smidl
1952-53	Elmer Gertz		1975-76	Gerald M. Edelstein
1953-54	M. Kenneth McIntyre		1976-77	Terry Carr
1954-55	Ralph G. Newman		1977-78	Myron Cohn
1955-56	E. B. (Pete) Long		1978-79	Glen N. Wiche
1956-57	Harold B. Hixson		1979-80	Merlin E. Sumner
1957-58	Marshall W. Rissman		1980-81	Robert G. Walter
1958-59	Lorenz G. Schumm		1981-82	Robert H. Franke
1959-60	Jerry M. Slechta		1982-83	Marvin Sanderman
1960-61	C. Robert Douglas		1983-84	Donald E. Anderson
1961-62	Gerhard P. Clausius		1984-85	J. Robert Ziegler
1962-63	Warren A. Reeder		1985-86	Paul Kliger
1963-64	H. George Donovan		1986-87	Patricia K. Sumner
1964-65	Arnold Alexander		1987-88	Daniel R. Weinberg
1965-66	Brooks Davis		1988-89	William J. Sullivan
1966-67	Michael S. Lerner		1989-90	Richard McAdoo
1967-68	Ver Lynn Sprague		1990-91	David R. Richert

Appendix C

Battlefield Tours

1951　Nashville, Franklin, Chickamauga, and Cumberland Gap
1952　Antietam, Gettysburg, and Harpers Ferry
1953　Peninsular Campaign, Richmond, and Williamsburg
1954　Shiloh and Vicksburg
1955　Frederickburg, Chancellorsville, The Wilderness, and Spotsylvania
1956　Chattanooga and Atlanta Campaign
1957　Shenandoah Valley
1958　Fort Donelson, Nashville, Franklin, and Stone's River
1959　Charleston and Savannah
1960　Richmond and Manassas
1961　Vicksburg
1962　Gettysburg, Antietam, and Harpers Ferry
1963　Richmond
1964　New Orleans
1965　Chattanooga and Cumberland Gap
1966　Washington, D.C.
1967　Missouri and Arkansas
1968　Fredericksburg
1969　Shiloh and Northern Mississippi

1970　Charleston and Savannah
1971　Shenandoah Valley
1972　Vicksburg
1973　Gettysburg
1974　Chattanooga and Chickamauga
1975　Richmond and Petersburg
1976　Manassas and Antietam
1977　Middle Tennessee
1978　Fredericksburg
1979　Shiloh and Northern Mississippi
1980　Shenandoah Valley
1981　Vicksburg
1982　Gettysburg
1983　Chattanooga and Chickamauga
1984　Washington, D.C. and Northern Virginia
1985　Petersburg and Appomattox
1986　1862 Peninsular Campaign
1987　Trans-Mississippi
1988　Chancellorsville
1989　Atlanta Campaign
1990　1862 Maryland Campaign, with a focus on Antietam
1991　Shiloh

Appendix D

Honorary Life Members

Arnold Alexander*
Paul M. Angle*
David H. Annan*
Margaret H. April
Henry B. Bass*
Edwin C. Bearss
Robert Todd Lincoln
    Beckwith*
Elden E. Billings
Bruce Catton*
Richard E. Clark
Gerhard Clausius*
Miner T. Coburn*
Monroe F. Cockrell*
Avery Craven*
Joseph P. Cullen
Brooks Davis
John Divine
Raymond N. Dooley
Charles A. Dornbusch
C. Robert Douglas
Paul H. Douglas*
Joseph L. Eisendrath, Jr.
Otto Eisenschiml*
Fred C. Evers*
Newton C. Farr*
Maurice Fisher*
John Hope Franklin
Douglas Southall Freeman*

Abe E. Geldhof*
Elmer Gertz
Vernon Hanson*
Percival G. Hart*
Richard B. Harwell*
Carl Haverlin*
Walter H. Hebert
Robert S. Henry*
Harry G. Hershenson*
William B. Hesseltine*
James T. Hickey
Harold B. Hixson*
Stanley F. Horn*
Harold M. Hyman
Alexander J. Isaacs*
Craig R. Johnson*
J. Ambler Johnston*
Allen P. Julian*
Stanley J. Kearney*
Henry W. Kennedy*
Otto Kerner*
Robert L. Kincaid*
Robert K. Krick
Marshall D. Krolick
E.B. (Pete) Long*
William Mallory
Roscoe C. Mathis*
Hugh P. McAniff
David C. Mearns*

Frederick Hill Meserve*
Al Meyer
Lloyd D. Miller*
Mark E. Neely, Jr.
Allan Nevins*
Ralph G. Newman
C. Norton Owen*
Harry E. Pratt*
Barbara Long Pleiter
James G. Randall*
James I. Robertson, Jr.
Don Russell*
Carl Sandburg*
John Y. Simon
Paul Simon
Jerome N. Slechta
Ray D. Smith*
Win Stracke
Merlin E. Sumner
Frederick Tilberg*
William H. Townsend*
Gilbert G. Twiss*
Elmer R. Underwood*
Frank E. Vandiver
Jerry Warshaw
Bell I. Wiley*
Francis F. Wilshin
Mrs. T. Harry Williams
T. Harry Williams*

*Deceased

Appendix E

Baffartt Award Winners

1955   John R. Peacock
1956   William L. Tierney
1957   William H. Milton
1958   Jerry Slechta
1959   James L. Capel
1960   Harold B. Hixson
1961   Robert Larkin
1962   Wilson A. Smith
1963   Miles A. Janousek
1964   T. H. Will
1965   Gil Twiss
1966   Bobbette and Donald Burhans
1967   Paul C. Behanna

Appendix F

Fellowship Award Recipients

1965   David Edward Meerse, University of Illinois, $3000
           Mary F. Berry, University of Michigan, $500

1966-67   Richard William Iobst, University of North Carolina, $3000

1967-68   Stuart L. Bernath, University of California, $3000

1968-69   Thomas D. Schoonover, University of Minnesota, $3000

1969-70   Okon E. Uya, University of Wisconsin, $3000

Appendix G

"The Biggest Little Park in the World (Centennial Park on Chestnut Street)"

Words and Music by Win Stracke

Dedicated to the veterans of the Centennial (the Civil War Round Table) who, while they spilled no blood in commemorating the events of a hundred years ago, did manage to spill and dribble liberal quantities of scotch, bourbon, beer, champagne, and other potables in pursuing their valiant efforts.

Win Stracke
October 6, 1965

(Verse)

1. Tivoli Park is in Old Copenhagen, the
  Bois de Boulogne's in the heart of Paree
  Golden Gate Park is in gay San Francisco, in
  London there's Hyde Park to see. *But*
  we have a park close to downtown Chicago, with
  flowers well-tended and lawn kept so neat;
  others may boast of their size and attractions, but
  by God, our park is petite, Oh,

(Chorus)

  Centennial Park on Chestnut Street, the
  biggest little park in the world,
  Centennial Park on Chestnut Street, may its
  flag that waves so proudly never be furled. As the
  years roll by, it will grow in repute, even
  schnausers and poodles raise a leg in salute to
  Centennial Park on Chestnut Street, the
  Biggest Little Park in the World.

(Verse)

2. Central Park is famous for muggings, and
  Lincoln Park has its share of rape;
  Brookfield is plagued by the illegal feeding of
  elephant, dolphin, and ape. *But*
  Bughouse Square once echoed to Wobblys, with
  deviate blossoms it's now in full-bloom, but the
  park that I sing of has no sin at all, for there
  simply is not enough room. Oh,

(Repeat Chorus)

Appendix H

"Part of Me"

(Composed for and first sung at the Twenty-fifth Anniversary of The Civil War Round Table, Tuesday, December 14, 1965, by Win Stracke.)

Verses

1. Part of me was cowering on the bank at Pittsburg Landing.[1]
  Part of me fought fiercely, knowing Claiborne[2] was commanding.
  Part of me, with Thomas, stormed up Missionary Ridge.[3]
  Part of me died recklessly at Burnside's Bloody Bridge.[4]

(Chorus)

   I've got the same set of guts, and the same blood in my veins,
   The same heart beats per minute, by and large the same brains.
   Can I live and die with honor as the Blue and Gray of yore?
   Can I strive for Peace as bravely as they fought in Civil War?

2. Part of me laid waste to Georgia while in Sherman's band.
  Part of me raised Hell in Tennessee in Hood's[5] command.
  Part of me wrought havoc over Alabama's[6] keel.
  Part of me in Kearsarge[7] brought the Rebel ship to heel.

(Repeat Chorus)

3. Part of me turned in for sick call when the battle started.
  Part of me rushed in the breach that day the front line parted.
  Part of me skedaddled at the Battle of Bull Run.
  Part of me led Pickett's charge in Gettysburg's hot sun.

(Repeat Chorus)

4. Part of me got plunder in Spoons Butler's occupation.[8]
  Part of me paid substitutes instead of serve the nation.
  Part of me died in Camp Douglas[9] from Chicago's cold.
  Part of me went into Libby[10] young and came out old.

(Repeat Chorus)

5. Part of me was Irish, charging up Marye's dread height.[11]
  Part of me was German "und mit Sigel" came to fight.[12]
  Part of me invoked the name of God for Northern aid.
  Part of me felt righteous when old Stonewall[13] knelt and prayed.

(Repeat Chorus)

6.   Part of me fought with mud along the wintry Rappahannock.14
          Part of me skulked in the hills when Stuart15 spread his   panic.
          Part of me hung innocents from lamp posts on Broadway.16
          Part of me heard liberty had come on New Year's Day.17

(Repeat Chorus)

7.   Part of me from Forrest's hate lives in Fort Pillow's shame.[18]
          Part of me fought "gallantly" when Crater's chance once came.[19]
          Part of me were soldiers at half-pay, without a gun.[20]
          Part of me on Steedman's left broke ranks, began to run.[21]

(Repeat Chorus)

8.   Some of us still think that making war's a wondrous game.
          Some of us think Lee, despite his protest, felt the same.
          But some of us think in our grasp is life so sweet to spend,
          That someday they will call a war and none will attend.

(Repeat Chorus)

9.   Some of us are dying in the jungles of Viet Nam
          Some of us once more are whispering: "Why not use the Bomb?";
          But all of me, with all my heart and mind, must answer "No!"
          War's no answer, War has had it, Cruel war must go.

(Repeat Chorus)

Glossary:

1. Union forces at Battle of Shiloh, April 6, 1862.
2. Patrick R. Cleburne, Confederate general.
3. General George H. Thomas and Union forces, November 25, 1863.
4. Battle of Antietam, September 15-17, 1862.
5. Confederate General John B. Hood at Battles of Franklin and Nashville, November 30-December 15, 1864.
6. Confederate raider, built in Liverpool.
7. Union warship which sank the Alabama, June 19, 1864.
8. General Benjamin F. Butler, who commanded Union forces occupying New Orleans. His nickname "Spoons" derived from his appropriation of silverware.
9. Camp holding Confederate prisoners.
10. Camp holding Union prisoners.
11. Irish Brigade at Fredericksburg, December 13, 1862.
12. General Franz Sigel, German-born Unionist who lead Germans throughout the war.
13. Stonewall Jackson, an elder of the Presbyterian Church.
14. The Union "mud march" after the Battle of Fredericksburg.
15. James Ewell Brown "JEB" Stuart, brilliant Confederate cavalry officer.
16. Draft riots in New York City, July 1863.
17. Emancipation Proclamation, effective January 1, 1863.
18. "Massacre" of Union Negro soldiers, April 12, 1864.
19. Negro division at the Battle of the Crater, July 30, 1864.
20. Use of Negro troops.
21. Battle of Nashville, December 15, 1864.

Appendix I

Confederate Purple Heart Winners

1973	Dan Lapinski	Presented pig to Marshall Krolick
1974	Jack Kaluf	Bumped from return flight
1975	Shirley Pacey	Turned ankle
1976	Will Leonard	Railroad bridge near-mishap
1977	Jackie Cohn	Broken toilet seat
1978	Denny Donnelan	Garbage bag raincoat
1979	Brooks Davis	Injured chasing burglar
1980	Marvin Sanderman	Trip to McDowell
1981	Bill Sullivan	Rocking chair collapse
1982	Marshall Krolick	Electric fence encounter
1983	Charles Falkenberg	Slide down hill
1984	Pat Sumner	Lost bus picture
1985	Joan Carlson	Erupting toilet
1986	Joan Carlson	Disintegrating toilet
1987	Don Anderson	Travel problems
1988	Hugh McAniff	Fell down
1989	Gordon Dammann	Fell in creek
1990	Edwin C. Bearss	Lecturing in the rain

Appendix J
"Ballad of General Hurlbut"

by Ver Lynn Sprague

(Ver Lynn Sprague led the singing of this ballad at the 324th regular meeting of
The Civil War Round Table, October 19, 1973.)

Let's all sing of Stephen Hurlbut
Filled the Rebels' hearts with fear—
How he held the line at Shiloh
Famous son of Belvidere

Other leaders looked for shelter,
Gave their orders from the rear.
But where fighting was the fiercest—
Stood the Son of Belvidere

Stood there in the awful orchard,
Til at last the day was saved.
Credit goes to Stephen Hurlbut,
As the bravest of the brave.

Chorus—Let's all sing, etc.

When at last the war was over
And the victory dearly won,
He returned to peace-time problems,
Hurlbut's work had just begun.

The Grand Army of the Republic
Sought a man to take command.
They selected Stephen Hurlbut—
As the greatest in the land.

Then they sent him off to Congress,
And he labored there until
He convinced his fellow members
And they passed the pension bill.

Chorus—Let's all sing, etc.

Some have said he filled his pockets
But we note with some relief—
That they never, never proved that
Stephen Hurlbut was a thief.

So we'll tell how Stephen Hurlbut
Filled those Rebel hearts with fear,
How he held the line at Shiloh
Famous Son of Belvidere.

And tonight we have a speaker
Gerhard Clausius is here
He will talk of Stephen Hurlbut
Fellow Son of Belvidere.

"A Ballad To A Straddle Trench"

by Ver Lynn Sprague

(Composed for a battlefield tour Fun Night in the mid-1960s)

For a hundred years of study,
We've pursued the battles bloody
And the men who fought the war which split the nation.
But as might have been expected—
One thing's always been neglected.
It's the matter of sanitation.

Oh, it's easy to dismiss it
When paying friends a visit,
And the room that's been provided's one you know
But when bullets are a-humming
And you're far away from plumbing
It's a different problem when you have to go.

Now a man is well-equipped
And we've got the problem whipped
When it's only one of public urination.
But a soldier has a fit
When he needs a place to sit
And he's miles from any human habitation.

So I want to call attention
To the army's great invention.
And for those who've not beheld one with their eyes,
Call it "sink" or say "latrine,"
It's the "straddle trench" I mean.
And it looks just like the simple name implies.

We don't know who first designed it
Or the thinking that's behind it.
But one thing in my memory of it rankles.
It is hard, seems to me,
To maintain your dignity
With your trousers drooping down around your ankles.

And if you get the duty
To go dig this thing of Beauty,
Here is something you should always keep in mind.
While it's shady in the brush,
Users sometimes have to rush.
Keep it handy, please, and not too hard to find.

And you never have to seek
To discover the technique
That would guard you, in its use, from making blunders.
For they knew a man could stumble
And the sides would often crumble,
So they taught you how to do it "by the numbers."

And when you've done the deed,
There's one other thing you need
That the quartermaster never thinks to issue.
For a bunch of leaves is keen—
And can wipe an orifice clean,
But it cannot take the place of modern tissue.

To perform this vital caper,
You should bring a piece of paper.
It's a practice no good soldier will impeach,
For I'd say a man has no luck
With a whole fat Sears and Roebuck
If it's lying in the bushes out of reach.

And we may as well be frank—
This is not a place where rank
Can do very much to help you, no it's not.
It may seem an imposition
But there's just one good position.
Even corps commanding generals have to squat.

It's appropriate that Sickels
Might be squatting in the thistles.
It could happen, say to Polk or Rosecrans.
But it's awfully hard for me
To imagine General Lee
With flanks exposed because he dropped his pants.

And I always have supposed
That the reason he posed
With his left side toward the camera and the light,
Sitting stiffly as he rode,
Was—his personal commode
Was swinging from his saddle on the right.

Now I must close the story—
Of the honor and the glory.
These are thoughts to give a veteran's heart a wrench.
We who know the battle's hell
Will never forget the smell
Of the one and only army straddle trench.

Appendix K

Nevins-Freeman Award Recipients

1974	Bruce Catton
1975	Ralph G. Newman
1976	T. Harry Williams
1977	Lloyd D. Miller
1978	Bell I. Wiley
1979	E. B. (Pete) Long
1980	Edwin C. Bearss
1981	James I. Robertson, Jr.
1982	Frank E. Vandiver
1983	John Hope Franklin
1984	Richard B. Harwell
1985	John Y. Simon
1986	Harold M. Hyman
1987	James T. Hickey
1988	Robert K. Krick
1989	Mark E. Neely, Jr.
1990	Marshall D. Krolick

Appendix L

Publications of The Civil War Round Table

1. *Ben Hardin Helm, "Rebel Brother-in-Law of Abraham Lincoln-with a Biographical Sketch of His Wife and an Account of the Todd Family of Kentucky,* by R. Gerald McMurtry, 1943, 72 pages. 225 copies were printed, each signed by the author.

2. *The Story of Shiloh,* by Otto Eisenschiml, 1946, 89 pages. Printed in a limited edition.

3. *Kentucky in the Civil War,* by Robert L. Kincaid, 1947, 12 pages. (Reprinted from the *Lincoln Herald)*

4. *Lincoln Raises an Army,* by Don Russell, 1948, 12 pages. (Reprinted from the *Lincoln Herald)* Edition limited to 500 copies.

5. *The Presidents and the Civil War,* by George S. Dalgety, 1950, 68 pages. Edition limited to 300 copies.

6. *Confederate Carrousel: Southern Songs of the Sixties,* by Richard Barksdale Harwell, 1950, 20 pages. (Reprinted from *The Emory University Quarterly)*

7. *The Conspiracy to Implicate the Confederate Leaders in Lincoln's Assassination,* by Seymour J. Frank, 1954, 28 pages. (Reprinted from *The Mississippi Valley Historical Review)*

(Source: The Year Book of The Civil War Round Table, 1956)

Appendix M

50th Anniversary Program

DINNER, October 12, 1990

Presentation of the Colors   4th U.S. Army Band and Round Table Color Guard

Invocation   Hon. Abraham Lincoln Marovitz

   Dinner

Cutting of The CWRT Birthday Cake   Margaret April

Introduction of Special Guests and Past Presidents   David Richert

Presentation of the 1990 Nevins-Freeman Award to Marshall Krolick   David Richert

Round Table Reminiscences   Marshall Krolick

Significance of The Round Table   John Y. Simon

The Camp Followers   Betsey Ross Davis

Recognition of Founder Elmer Gertz   John Brooks Davis

Presentation of Gift to Ralph G. Newman   C. Robert Douglas and John Duff

Remarks by Founder Ralph G. Newman

SYMPOSIUM: "Decisive Leadership in the Civil War", October 13, 1990

"A Contrast in Leadership—Abraham Lincoln and Jefferson Davis" *James I. (Bud) Robertson, Jr.*

"Jackson and Banks in the Valley"   *Robert K. Krick*

"Early and Sheridan in the Valley"   *Gary W. Gallagher*

   Lunch

"Battlefield Preservation"   *Jerry L. Russell*

"Lincoln and His Cabinet—The Emancipation Proclamation"   *Mark E. Neely, Jr.*

"Sherman and Hood at Atlanta"   *Edwin C. Bearss*

   Saturday Evening Dinner

Introduction of the Speaker   *Paul I. Kliger*

"The Civil War: The Struggle for a Unified Nation and the Legacy for the Future"
   James McPherson

Civil War Tour of Chicago, October 14, 1990

Index

Photographic Credits

Frontispiece—Wm. Franklin McMahon; page 7—Paul Kliger; pages 9 and 11—Round Table archives; page 12 (top)—Collection of Elmer Gertz; page 12 (bottom)—Round Table archives; page 13 (top)—Round Table archives; page 13 (bottom) and page 14—Collection of Elmer Gertz; page 15 and page 18 (top)—Round Table archives; page 18 (bottom)—Collection of Thomas F. Schwartz; page 20—Round Table archives; page 22—W. Franklin McMahon; page 24—Collection of Jerry Slechta; page 29—Round Table archives; page 31—Jerry Warshaw; page 32—Collection of Elmer Gertz; page 38—Gil Twiss; page 39—Round Table archives; pages 42 and 43—Collection of Jerry Slechta; pages 44, 45 and 46—Round Table archives; page 49—Collection of Jerry Slechta; pages 53, 54 and 55—Round Table archives; page 56—Collection of Jerry Slechta; page 59—*Commerce Magazine*, June 1964; page 62 (left)—Collection of Brooks Davis; page 62 (right)—Round Table archives; page 65—Paul Kliger; page 67—Round Table archives; page 69—Paul Kliger; page 70—Collection of Jerry Slechta; pages 71, 73 and 74—Jerry Warshaw; pages 75 and 76—Collection of Brooks Davis; page 78—Round Table archives; pages 81, 82 and 83—Jerry Warshaw; page 89 (top)—Collection of Jerry Warshaw; page 89 (bottom)—Round Table archives; page 91—Paul Kliger; page 93—Jerry Warshaw; page 99—Collection of Brooks Davis; page 101 (top)—Collection of Marshall Krolick; page 101 (bottom) and page 102 (left)—Round Table archives; page 102 (right)—Collection of Marshall Krolick; page 103—Wm. Franklin McMahon; page 105—Jerry Warshaw; page 106—Round Table archives; page 107—Paul Kliger; pages 108 and 111—Collection of Marshall Krolick; page 112 (top)—Round Table archives; page 112 (bottom) and page 116—Paul Kliger; page 117 (top)—Round Table archives; page 117 (center and bottom)—Paul Kliger; page 120—Round Table archives; pages 122, 124, 127 and 128 (bottom)—Paul Kliger; page 131—Collection of Don Anderson; page 133—Collection of Merlin Sumner; page 134—Donna Cook Richert; page 135—Round Table archives; page 136—Collection of Paul Kliger; page 141—Round Table archives; page 142—Hal Ardell; page 150—Barbara Hughett; page 153—Jerry Warshaw; page 154 (top)—Round Table archives; page 154 (bottom)—Donna Cook Richert; page 155—Barbara Hughett; page 157—Paul Kliger; page 158—Collection of Ernest Griffin; page 159—Marvin Sanderman

COLOPHON

The Civil War Round Table: Fifty Years of Scholarship and Fellowship was designed and typeset by Muriel Underwood on a Macintosh desktop system. It is set in Palatino and printed, from a laser printout, on 60 lb. Booktext Natural (acid-free). It is bound in Holliston Roxite bookcloth. The book jacket was designed by Donna Cook (Richert) on a Macintosh desktop system and is printed on 80 lb. enamel. Printing and binding was by Bookcrafters, Chelsea, Michigan.

This edition was limited to 800 copies.

DATE DUE

YOUNG MERLIN

YOUNG MERLIN

ROBERT D. SAN SOUCI
illustrated by
DANIEL HORNE

A Doubleday Book for Young Readers

A DOUBLEDAY BOOK FOR YOUNG READERS
PUBLISHED BY DELACORTE PRESS
Bantam Doubleday Dell Publishing Group, Inc.
1540 Broadway, New York, New York 10036
DOUBLEDAY
and the portrayal of an anchor with a dolphin
are trademarks of Bantam Doubleday Dell Publishing Group, Inc.

Design by Diane Stevenson/SNAP•HAUS GRAPHICS

Library of Congress Cataloging-in-Publication Data
San Souci, Robert D.
Young Merlin.
Summary: Presents the life of Merlin the magician
from his miraculous birth through the age of seventeen,
before he met King Arthur.
1. Merlin (Legendary character)   [1. Merlin (Legendary
character)   2. Folklore—
England]   I. Horne, Daniel, ill.   II. Title.
PZ8.1.S227Yo 1990 398.2′1′0942   88-30916
ISBN 0-385-24800-8
ISBN 0-385-24801-6 (lib. bdg.)
RL: 3.7

For Michael and Virginia San Souci,
Mark, Michelle, Nicholas, and Robert George
–R.S.S.

◆

To my wife, Joy
–D.H.

There are many stories of Merlin the Magician's birth, childhood, and youth. This is one. . . .

he handsome young man arrived in the village of Carmarthen one misty evening, having come on foot from the distant wood. His green eyes were flecked with gold, and he always had a gold coin in his hand when he needed it.

Not long thereafter, the prettiest young woman in the village fell deeply in love with him, and he took her to be his wife. When she told him they were going to be blessed with a child, he seemed neither pleased nor displeased. But his wife was troubled to find him often staring across the meadows to the distant woods, or standing with his head cocked to one side, as if he were listening to sounds only he could hear.

Just before the child was born, the stranger disappeared into the mists of evening, as mysteriously as he had come. While his wife grieved after him, the villagers whispered that the one who had vanished had surely been an elf or demon. They were sure that his wife was wasting away under some wicked enchantment.

In time, the local priest heard the rumor, and came to sprinkle the woman with holy water, and gave her into the keeping of the good nuns at the nearby convent. This was done for the sake of her soul, and for the soul of her unborn child.

"Holy water or none," the villagers told one another, "no mortal baby will come of *that* union."

But when the child was born, he seemed human enough—though he had a shock of coal-black hair, large ears, and eyes that sometimes seemed to flash with light.

He was named Merlin, and he was a fey little boy, who laughed a great deal but never cried.

The sisters taught him to read and write, and he was a clever child, wise beyond his years—but often disobedient. He would not sit still in chapel—"It makes me itch," he said—and hid when he was called to prayer. His small size made it easy for him to slip away and find a secret hiding place.

But while his mischief vexed the nuns, his strange talents made them fearful. He could see things that were hidden from view, read the future for other people (but not his own fate), and look into the past. Sometimes he said that he could see spirits that haunted lonely roads or woodland shadows.

He loved his mother deeply. He loved to curl up in her lap while she sat by a window or on a garden bench, her eyes filled with secret dreams and her head turned a little to one side, as though she were listening to distant music only she could hear.

At such times, she would tell him that his father was a spirit of air and darkness, a visitor from a shadowy fairyland who appeared to her as a handsome stranger with gold-flecked eyes. She would stroke his unruly black hair, and he would fall asleep, dreaming magical dreams.

When she caught a fever, and the sisters sorrowfully told Merlin his mother was dying, the boy stayed day and night by her side, ready to battle the angel of death. One night, however, he fell asleep and dreamed that death had come into the room. But he had come as a knight in golden armor, and Merlin's mother had risen from her bed and run happily to take his outstretched hand.

The next morning, when he awoke, Mother Hild, the abbess, hugged him and whispered, "You're an orphan now, my child— though a child of God is never truly alone."

Her words gave small comfort to the weeping boy.

Mother Hild told him the sisters would raise him as a ward of the Church. But Merlin soon made her regret this kindness. As he grew older, he tested the nuns' patience by stealing food from the kitchen, asking questions the sisters could not answer, continually being found where he shouldn't be, and never coming when called to run an errand. Mother Hild would grab him by the ear and try to shake some goodness into him, but the boy would slip away with a merry laugh that disturbed the holy silence of the convent.

"Surely there is some elf blood in him," the priest told the sisters. "But he never uses his gifts for wickedness, so we must not call them evil."

The villagers were not so kind. "Devil's child!" they would yell when Merlin went to fetch bread or milk for the sisters. Sometimes the cruelest would throw stones at the boy—only to be routed when the stones turned around in mid-flight and pelted the throwers.

But while this saved the boy some bruises, it did nothing to make him more popular with the villagers.

Often he would hide in the nearby woods. There he would eat nuts and berries and make up wildwood songs that charmed the deer and rabbits to his side. He tamed a huge stag with five-branched horns and a white forefoot and rode him through the forest glades.

Or he would return to the neighboring village, where he heard the folk talk about Vortigern, the King of Britain. He was a wicked man, they said, who had killed the rightful King and had driven the ruler's two sons across the sea to France.

"The princes will soon return," people muttered. "Even now the King is building a great tower to defend himself."

Such news interested Merlin. But when he asked the grown folk about the slain King and far-off princes, they chased him away, saying, "These matters don't concern children. Run off and play."

The village children called him an elf child, because of the stories that his father had come from fairyland. Since he was small for his age, the local bullies would pick fights all the time. But Merlin was tough and had such a temper that he always gave a good accounting of himself in a fight.

One day, when he was playing ball with several of the youngest children, who loved him in spite of their parents' disapproval, the miller's son began to call him names. Though the other boy far outweighed him, Merlin quickly bloodied the bigger boy's nose. Then the bully shouted, "You don't fight fair, you elf child. Your father wasn't human. You've bewitched me!"

Merlin raised his arm to strike again, but his hand was caught in a leather-gloved fist. Looking up, he found that the fist belonged to a mounted knight, whose other hand held the reins of his horse. Several more knights on horseback watched. Their helmets and breastplates were dusty, and their horses' flanks were sweaty, as though they had ridden a great distance.

"Say again what you said about this boy," Merlin's captor ordered the miller's son.

"He's an orphan, the devil's own child," said the boy, wiping his bloody nose. "His mother was human, but his father was a demon."

"You liar!" yelled Merlin, trying to break free. The miller's son stepped back, until he was sure Merlin couldn't twist loose.

"It's true enough," said other villagers, who were standing around gawking.

"King Vortigern ordered us to search the realm until we found a child who had a human mother but no human father," said the soldier. "He must be the one we seek."

He hauled Merlin up and sat the child in front of him on his horse. Then the knights galloped away toward the west.

"Where are you taking me?" Merlin cried.

"To the King," said the soldier, and he refused to answer any other questions the boy put to him.

everal times on their long journey, Merlin tried to escape. But each time he was caught and beaten for his efforts.

Once Merlin asked a farmer sitting beside the road for some water, but the man refused him. Then the boy laughed.

"Why are you laughing?" asked the soldier seated behind him.

"Because that greedy man, who refuses to give away a drop of water, is sitting over a buried treasure."

"How do you know this?"

"Pictures pass before my mind of things that are or will be," said Merlin.

The soldier snorted, clearly not believing a word.

Farther on, they saw a peddler sitting in the shade of a tree. He was eating a loaf of bread and mending an old pair of shoes. When the boy begged a few crumbs, the man ignored him.

Merlin laughed again.

"Why are you laughing?" asked the knight.

"Because the fellow thinks he's going to wear those shoes, but they'll be stolen before he puts them on."

"Faugh!" said the soldier. "A child can't have such powers!"

Next they met a funeral procession. "If you're able to see things," the knight challenged Merlin, "tell me how this man died."

"By falling, by hanging, and by drowning," said the boy.

"How can a man die three deaths?" the soldier sneered.

But an old woman in the procession said, "Indeed, the boy is right. Poor William fell from a rock into a tree, and hung upside down by his heels with his head underwater, and so he drowned."

The soldier was silent, but Merlin knew the man now believed what he said.

t last, they came to Vortigern. The King stood under an awning in front of his fine tent at the foot of a hill, which overlooked the surrounding plain. At its crown, hod carriers, stonemasons, joiners, and other laborers were raising a huge fortress-tower.

Beside the King, arguing among themselves, were three old men with long gray beards and brown robes.

Merlin was dragged before the King. When he protested this rough treatment, the knight, who held him by the tunic, boxed his ears. The boy decided it was better to keep still.

The soldier quickly explained that Merlin was the child they had been sent to find. At this, Vortigern smiled in a way that made Merlin think of a fox just come upon an unguarded henhouse.

"You have been chosen for a great honor, boy," said the King. He pointed toward the half-built fortress at the top of the hill. "Three times I've raised my tower up, and three times it has come crashing down. But my wizards have found the answer."

He beckoned to the old men, who stopped arguing and drew close. The one with the longest beard said, "We have studied the stars carefully. They have told us what Vortigern must do."

The second wizard continued, "Find a boy who had no human father, slay him, and sprinkle his blood on the cornerstone."

The third said, "Then the spirits of this place will let the King's tower stand for a thousand years."

Angrily Merlin shouted, "That is not true! My blood won't help!"

"Quiet!" ordered the King.

"My lord," said the soldier who held Merlin captive, "listen to the lad. He sees what others cannot."

Vortigern looked doubtful, but he said, "Tell me what makes my tower tumble down, and I may spare your life."

So Merlin said, "There are two dragons in a cave beneath your tower. One is white as milk; the other is red as fire. They fight all the time, and their struggle shakes the hill and knocks your tower down."

The wizards called Merlin a liar, but Vortigern silenced them. Then he ordered his laborers to dig into the side of the hill.

They soon broke through into a secret cave, releasing two dragons—red and white, just as Merlin had said—which burst half-blinded into the daylight, hissing and coiling around each other. They scorched each other's scales with blasts of fire.

Merlin and the others ran for cover as the tail of the white dragon flattened Vortigern's tent.

The creatures raged back and forth across the plain, fighting with fang, claw, tail, and flame, until the white one burned the red one to ashes. Then the victor rose into the air and flew slowly away to the west.

After that, Vortigern's tower went up quickly—and remained standing. The King kept Merlin at his court as chief counselor, though the other wizards grumbled about having a child set over them.

But shortly after Vortigern's tower was completed, word came that the sons of the true King—the princes Aurelius and Uther—had come across the sea from France. They were leading a great army against Vortigern.

Vortigern summoned Merlin to his throne room, where he sat surrounded by his nobles and knights.

"Who will win?" the King asked the boy.

"The princes," Merlin answered honestly. "They are like the white dragon. You will die by fire, just as the red dragon did."

"Treason!" screamed Vortigern. "Guards! Seize the traitor and lock him in the deepest dungeon."

But Merlin escaped them as easily as he had once run away

from Mother Hild when she'd caught him stealing bread and honey from the convent kitchen.

He hid behind a curtain until the hue and cry had quieted down. At evening, he slipped out the gates and hurried toward the distant hills that circled the plain. He spent the night in a cave.

In the morning, he awoke to discover the army of the princes camped on the plain below Vortigern's tower. Even as he watched, Vortigern sent his soldiers out to battle. But the King's men surrendered and cast their lot with the princes. Then they laid siege to the tower, setting it afire. Just as Merlin had seen, Vortigern perished in the flames, and his fortress was reduced to ashes.

or a time, Merlin lived happily in the woods, growing into a young man. He learned to unlock the healing magic of plants. He read signs and wonders in cloud shapes or flights of birds or the stars. And he discovered how to change his shape, so that he could take on the form of any man or beast.

Eventually, word of his magic reached the new King, Aurelius, and his brother, Uther, who was general of his army. They decided to invite Merlin to their court, and so they sent a messenger to the magic spring, deep in the forest, where Merlin was most often found.

But Merlin, who loved to joke, turned himself into a huge stag with five-branched horns and a white forefoot. When the King's messenger arrived, he found only the beast drinking at the spring beneath a spreading oak. So he returned empty-handed.

Aurelius sent another messenger, who found an ugly old woman in rags, dipping water out of the spring and pouring it on the roots of a sweet-apple tree. The hag only laughed when asked about Merlin, and so the messenger went away.

Finally Uther went himself and found himself standing across the spring from a ferocious wild man, beside a flowering white thorn. The monster was eighteen feet tall, covered with black, bristly hair, and clad in a wolfskin. He had ears as large as fans, burning eyes as big as an ox's, and a mouth as broad as a dragon's, filled with sharp teeth.

The creature roared and pranced and shook its oaken club at Uther, but the man drew his sword and stood his ground.

Suddenly the wild man began to laugh. Then he called out, "You're a brave one!" Before Uther's eyes, the monster turned into a handsome young man dressed in fine clothes.

"Are you Merlin, who is called the Magician?" asked Uther.

"Indeed," said Merlin, smiling and bowing.

So it was that Merlin entered the service of King Aurelius.

These were dangerous times. Aurelius was a good man and a just King, who ruled wisely and well, but his kingdom was torn apart as first one and then another rebel lord challenged his right to the crown.

Merlin offered wise advice to the King and his brother and helped them with his magic arts. Sometimes, when the King was sorely worried, the young magician would amuse Aurelius and Uther by turning himself into a mischievous dwarf or a beautiful woman or a greyhound or a stag. He became like a third brother to the others; they became the family he had never known.

When reports came that the rebels had combined their armies on Salisbury Plain, Merlin rode beside Aurelius and Uther to meet the enemy. All three knew that the outcome of the struggle would decide the fate of Britain.

The evening before the final battle, Aurelius and Uther came to Merlin's tent, where he sat gazing into the flames in a bronze bowl.

"Will we win tomorrow?" asked Aurelius.

"Yes," said Merlin. But both brothers could see that he was deeply troubled.

"Will my brother and I be safe?" asked Uther.

There were tears in Merlin's eyes as he said, "One of you will die."

After a silence, Aurelius asked, "Which?"

"That I cannot tell you," Merlin said, though he had seen clearly enough who would fall.

he fighting the next day was fierce. Merlin took the form of the giant wild man and spread terror among the enemy. By day's end, the rebels retreated, with the King's army in pursuit.

But Merlin found Aurelius where he knew he would, fallen beneath his battle flag with the picture of a fire-spitting dragon. Tenderly he carried his friend's body back to camp.

At Merlin's urging, Uther was proclaimed King by all the soldiers. And the new King's first command to Merlin was "Raise a fitting monument to my brother here, upon this battlefield. Build him a tomb that will last forever."

Then Merlin had a vision of a circle of standing stones, called the Dance of Giants, on a mountain in Ireland.

Summoning all his magic, he floated the massive bluestones through the night sky and drew them down into a towering circle, just as they had stood in distant Ireland.

At that instant, a huge star of dazzling brightness appeared over the circle of stones. It grew until it became a ball of fire, which took the shape of a dragon. From its mouth blazed rays that extended east and west, as far as the eye could see. Everyone stared and murmured and wondered.

"What does it mean?" asked Uther.

"Take heart," said Merlin, his hand upon his friend's shoulder. "The fiery dragon is you. The rays foretell that you will have a son whose fame will reach to the ends of the earth."

Uther named the circle of standing stones Aurelius's Rest and buried his brother at the center. In the years that followed, however, local folk called it Stonehenge.

And Uther's son was King Arthur, whom Merlin also served, and whose famous legend lives on until today.